ST. PAUL'S

VOYAGE AND SHIPWRECK

THE VOYAGE AND SHIPWRECK OF ST. PAUL

WITH DISSERTATIONS ON THE LIFE AND WRITINGS OF ST. LUKE, AND THE SHIPS AND NAVIGATION OF THE ANCIENTS

By JAMES SMITH, Esq.

OF JORDANHILL, F.R.S. ETC.

FOURTH EDITION, REVISED AND CORRECTED BY

WALTER E. SMITH

With a Preface

BY THE

LORD BISHOP OF CARLISLE

AND A MEMOIR OF THE AUTHOR

Wipf and Stock Publishers

EUGENE, OREGON

Wipf and Stock Publishers
199 West 8th Avenue, Suite 3
Eugene, Oregon 97401

The Voyage and Shipwreck of St. Paul
Fourth Edition, Revised and Corrected
By Smith, James
ISBN: 1-57910-722-2
Publication date: August, 2001
Previously published by Longmans, Green and Co., 1880.

PREFACE.

THE question may well occur to many readers of this volume, Why should a solid standard work, such as 'Smith's Voyage and Shipwreck of St. Paul,' need a new preface to its fourth edition?

And the further question may be asked, Why should such preface, if needed, be furnished by the present writer?

To answer these questions it is necessary to insert a few words of personal explanation.

It so happened that in the course of last year I was desirous of purchasing a copy of this book. To my surprise I discovered not only that it was out of print, but that it was impossible (so at least my bookseller reported to me) to obtain a second-hand copy in London. This discovery induced me to communicate with the publishers. I complained that the work was permitted to be out of print; and I did this, not so much in consequence of my own trifling disappointment in being unable to procure a copy for a friend, as because I thought it a misfortune that so remarkable a book should slip out of sight, and gradually become comparatively unknown. My own admiration of the book is so great, that the prospect of its possible disappearance from the living literature of English-speaking people distressed me exceedingly.

The publishers treated my complaint with great courtesy, and, after due consideration, consented to produce a new edition, subject to a promise on my part that I would write an introduction or preface.

This, then, is the explanation of the existence of the present preface, and of the fact that the composition of it has been committed to and undertaken by myself. It was with much unwillingness that I assented to the proposal; it seemed to imply that words of mine were needed to commend a book which needs no commendation from me or from anyone else; but I did assent, because I knew that the publishers were much better judges than I could be of what was expedient, and because I was willing to do anything and everything to renew the book's lease of life.

A work which has gone through three large editions may perhaps be regarded as one which has found many readers. But if the number of readers is to be taken as any measure of the sterling value of a book, I should be disposed to say that Mr. Smith's great work has not been read so extensively as might have been expected, and as it ought to have been. Two reasons may perhaps be assigned for any neglect which it may have experienced.

In the first place, it is a book which requires careful study; it is a book to work at and not merely to read; it commends itself, not to the large body of book-readers, but only to those who may be termed students, and amongst these chiefly to the students of the New Testament. In the second place, the investigations and demonstrations made by Mr. Smith have been popularised and presented in more simple and condensed forms. No writer upon the 'Acts of the Apostles,' since the first publication of Mr. Smith's book, could possibly fail to make use of it, to give its results, and to acknowledge his obligations;[1] and a large portion of the readers of this second-hand information are presumably satisfied with what they have got, and do not care to go to the original fountain. But this is not as it should be. I remember once mentioning to the late Dr. Whewell the curious fact that I had sought a copy of Mr. Smith's book in the Cambridge University Library, and had not found one; to which he replied, 'Serves you right; everyone ought to buy that book.' If I remember rightly, Dr. Whewell went on to say that, in his opinion, no finer piece of demonstrative writing had appeared since the time of Paley. I quite agree with Dr. Whewell's estimate of the work: it is a book to be bought, and to be studied; a book that a man may be pleased to see upon his

[1] This remark applies not only to English, but to German, French, and American writers. For example, Lechter, who comments on the Acts of the Apostles in Lange's *Bibelwerk*, writes, 'The nautical and topographical incidents of this voyage have been illustrated, in a manner worthy of all praise, by a learned Englishman, James Smith, of Jordanhill, &c.'

Ernest Renan says, 'Pour la partie technique de la navigation, voir James Smith, *The Voyage and Shipwreck of St. Paul,*' and gives references.

And Hackett, in his excellent American Commentary, writes, 'I have availed myself freely of the illustrations of this valuable treatise in the commentary on this chapter and the next. No work has appeared for a long time that has thrown so much light upon any equal portion of the Scriptures.'

library shelves, and which he may read over and over again with intellectual delight.

In truth Mr. Smith possessed a rare combination of qualities fitting him to produce such a work as the 'Voyage and Shipwreck of St. Paul.' Imprimis, he was a yachtsman, and so was thoroughly acquainted with nautical matters, and in particular he knew well the whole scene of St. Paul's adventures. Then, again, he was not a mere yachtsman, but had a good amount of reading, both classical and in the department of general literature, which he was able to bring to bear with great force. Still further his head had all the clearness of perception which is necessary to the conduct of exact investigations. He had evidently a keen intellectual eye. But above all he applied himself to his task with the high purpose of elucidating a book which was precious to his soul. He perceived that an important chapter of biblical evidence was to be found in the history of St. Paul's voyage. He delighted in the work of verifying St. Luke's narrative, and causing to be seen the historian's accuracy and honesty in recording details capable of being put to the proof, because he discerned the reflected advantage which would accrue to the Christian argument in favour of the veracity of St. Luke's gospel, where no such proof was forthcoming. The following passage from the preface to the 'Dissertation on the Gospels,' which grew out of the present work, may be worth quoting in this place. 'Having in my former work,' he writes, 'shown by proofs independent of all others that the writings of St. Luke were those of a contemporary author, personally engaged in some of the most eventful scenes which he has recorded, I can, as Dr. Chalmers somewhere says, "take him from the bar and place him in the witness box." Now, nothing but the perfect truthfulness of his narrative could account for its agreement with facts which could only have been known to him from personal observation. The knowledge of these facts is only due to recent discoveries and the accurate researches of modern science. Had St. Luke's writings been discovered for the first time amongst the papyri of Herculaneum, these proofs of their authenticity must have been held conclusive by every one accustomed to investigate the truth or falsehood of sea-voyages of doubtful authenticity. But if it can be shown that the Acts of the Apostles are genuine and authentic, so must also be the Gospel, for not only is it mentioned in that work, but it is obviously by the same hand.' The feeling of the evidential importance of his investigations, indicated in this passage, fired, as I cannot doubt, Mr. Smith's zeal and earnestness, while happily there is no indication, so far as I am aware, that it ever warped his judgment.

I have before me, through the kindness of Mr. Smith's family, a volume of notices, from the pages of the public press, and also in the form of private letters, of the work in its earlier editions. It would be easy to quote from both sources abundance of expressions of opinion, confirmatory of that which I have endeavoured in these few prefatory pages to say concerning the value of Mr. Smith's work; but I will content myself with a single extract from a letter of the late Dean Alford, which, as coming from one who had devoted a large portion of his life to biblical study, seems to have a special value. 'I may venture to congratulate you,' writes Dean Alford, 'on the fact that your name will now, in all ages and countries, be handed down as having done substantial service in settling once for all a point in dispute deeply interesting for its own sake, and for the authenticity and credibility of the sacred narrative. When we commentators are deservedly forgotten, you will be known in enviable connection with the great Apostle's course of perils.'

I should have thought that it would have been conceded that, to use Dean Alford's words, the point of dispute between Malta and Meleda had been 'settled once for all' by Mr. Smith's book. The republication of Dr. Falconer's volume within the last few years, however, indicates that belief in Meleda is not yet entirely extinct. It is not my purpose, nor am I competent, to enter upon the controversy, but I will venture to say as much as this, namely, that the conviction in favour of Malta, arising in my own mind from Mr. Smith's minute and complete investigation, more nearly approaches to absolute certainty than in the case of almost any other point in ancient history which has been matter of controversy. Under Mr. Smith's guidance every sentence of the narrative falls into its proper place. There is positively no residuum of unexplained difficulty; some slight exceptions to this remark, which existed at the time of the first publication, have disappeared since.[1]

In the present, as in the last edition, published during the author's lifetime, the discussion of the voyage and shipwreck is prefaced by a 'Dissertation on the Life and Writings of St. Luke.' This dissertation takes the place of a much less elaborate essay, entitled 'Notices of the Life and Writings of St. Luke,' which was prefixed to the first edition. The investigation of the history of St. Paul's voyage and shipwreck gave rise not only to this dissertation, but also to a much more elaborate work, entitled 'A dissertation on the origin and connection of the Gospels,' to which reference has already been made. Concerning these dissertations I think it desirable to make two remarks. In the first place, they may be, and in one sense they ought to be, regarded as entirely distinct from the discussion of the voyage and shipwreck of St. Paul. In them the author is no longer the yachtsman, but only the scholar and the critic. He has no special qualification be-

[1] This last edition of Dr. Falconer's work contains large additions by the Editor, Thomas Falconer, Esq. In fact, the added matter exceeds the original in quantity. I presume that all which can be said in opposition to Mr. Smith's argument will be found in this volume.

yond many other investigators; and if his conclusions do not carry conviction, they are at least in this respect in the goodly company of the conclusions of many other acute students who have examined the same difficult subject. The security of the results of the discussion of the voyage and shipwreck must not therefore be considered as in any way jeopardised by companionship with conclusions obtained in a field of investigation of a very different kind. But, in the second place, while desiring to point out the difference between the two fields of inquiry to which Mr. Smith devoted his mind, and to guard against the danger of one being too much connected in the mind of the reader with the other, I am bound to express my own strong opinion of the value of Mr. Smith's discussion of the Synoptic Gospels, their mutual relations, and the origin of their materials. I cannot say that he carries me with him on every point; but I think that some of his conclusions are irrefragable, that his criticisms exhibit uncommon discernment, and that he has contributed much towards the solution of a problem which is confessedly difficult, and I venture to believe in all its fulness not soluble. I confess that I have often been surprised to find that Mr. Smith's labours have not influenced the argument concerning the Synoptic Gospels more extensively than they seem to have done.

The question of the composition of the Gospels, however, is not immediately before us. The present volume, as elucidating a remarkable passage in St. Paul's life, and indirectly giving evidence of the truthfulness and skill of St. Luke as a historian, is Mr. Smith's real monument. It is one for which readers of the Holy Scriptures may be thankful, and of which his family may be proud. The word family reminds me to say that I am answerable only for these introductory remarks, and that the work of editing has been entrusted to the competent hands of one of the author's grandchildren.

I shall perhaps be pardoned if I conclude this preface with a little piece of personal narrative, curiously illustrative of St. Paul's voyage.

Leaving Alexandria by P. & O. steamer in the month of January 1879, I made a remark to the captain upon the smiling character of the weather. 'The south wind blew softly,' the sky was blue, the sea like glass. 'Yes,' replied the captain, 'very pleasant *as long as it lasts.*' It did not last very long; and when we sighted Crete Euraquilo was blowing rather stiffly. I talked to the captain about St. Paul's voyage, the Island of Clauda, and other points. As we neared Crete the sea became somewhat rolling and rough. It was getting dark, and I went below. While reading I perceived that we were suddenly in smooth water. Going upon deck I found the captain, who, pointing to the starboard side of the ship, said, 'There is that island.' We were in the position of St. Paul, when 'running under a certain island which is called Clauda, they had much work to come by the boat.' Had our machinery broken down, or the ship become disabled, we should have drifted towards Malta, as did the ship which carried St. Paul.

It remains only to add that the present edition is a corrected reprint of the last published by the author; such alterations and additions as have been made are specified in the note appended to this preface by the Editor.

HARVEY CARLISLE.

ROSE CASTLE, 1880.

NOTE BY THE EDITOR.

It is hoped that this Edition will be found more correct than those which preceded it, as much care has been expended in correcting small errors, whether of the press or of the pen, especially in the quotations. In the few cases where any *substantial* correction or addition seemed needful, short notes have been introduced enclosed in square brackets [ ]. Accents have throughout been added to the Greek.

The Greek text of the narrative of the Acts printed at the foot of the page has been brought into harmony with the best results of modern criticism. This has been effected through the great kindness of Dr. Westcott and Dr. Hort, who have allowed me the free use of their text of the Greek Testament, which has been so long expected, and which will, I believe, be published very shortly. I have carefully followed their readings, except in four passages (ch. xxvii. 37 and 40, and ch. xxviii. 1 and 13), where I have retained the readings of Tregelles, which are in all these cases given as alternatives in the margin by Westcott and Hort. I have also in a few cases altered the accompanying English version, generally to make it tally with new Greek readings. It seemed unnecessary to adhere scrupulously to the Authorised Version (as the Author did in most cases), since every reader, if he wishes for that, has it at hand.

The Author perhaps failed fully to appreciate the weight of authority which exists against his view, with respect to the application of the term Adria. As the point is one of vital importance to our reading of the whole history, and as it is upon the usage of this name that the latest defender of the Meleda hypothesis [1] mainly rests his case,

[1] See *Dissertation on St. Paul's Voyage from Cæsarea to Puteoli, and on the Apostle's Shipwreck on the Island Melite.* By William Falconer, M.D., F.R.S. Third edition, with additional notes by Thomas Falconer, Esq. (one of the Judges of County Courts).

I have ventured to add an Appendix (No. VI.) in which I have attempted to discuss impartially the whole question. I have also replaced the note from Bochart which constitutes Appendix No. V. It appeared in the first and second editions, but was omitted in the third.

I must express deep gratitude to the Bishop of Carlisle for his kindness in writing the Preface, and also to A. H. Smith, who has undertaken the laborious and most useful task of constructing an index.

W. E. S.

CONTENTS.

NARRATIVE OF THE VOYAGE.

DISSERTATIONS.

APPENDIX.

LIST OF ILLUSTRATIONS.

VIEWS.

Ancient ship anchored by the stern in St. Paul's Bay in a gale from E.N.E. Background, Salmonetta Island on the left, under two sea-fowl, a place where two seas meet (τόπον διθάλασσον, Acts xxvii. 41), to which the ship must be driven. This illustration represents the situation of the ship at the moment described in verse 40, when the crew are cutting away the anchors (τὰς ἀγκύρας περιελόντες), loosing the bands of the rudders (ἀνέντες τὰς ζευκτηρίας τῶν πηδαλίων), and hoisting the artemon (ἐπάραντες τὸν ἀρτέμονα).

I am indebted to the talented marine painter, Mr. Smartley, of St. Heliers, for having combined artistical effect with the most rigid adherence to the authorities I furnished him with; and as it is my object in every case to put my reader in possession of the evidence upon which my conclusions are founded, I shall here enumerate them.

In the first place, I showed him on the chart the situation in which the ship must have been anchored, and the direction of the wind. He has represented the sea as it must have been running at the time, certainly without exaggeration; the dark clouds indicate the coming rain; whilst a gleam of the morning sun illuminates the sail (artemon) which the crew are hoisting, the gilded cheniscus (χρύσεος χηνίσκος), and the

'Carchesium late splendens.'

The background is from a view taken upon the spot: by enlarging the background in this edition, the place where two seas meet is more fully given. The ship is taken from the following authorities:—

1st. The ship of Theseus from Herculaneum; see figure at p. 135.

2nd. The ship on the tomb at Pompeii, figured at p. 206.

3rd. The African wheat ship, from a coin of Commodus, figured at p. 201.

4th. The shrouds which support the mast, with the blocks for setting them up, are taken from a coin figured in Montfaucon, iv. pl. 143.

5th. The undergirding was represented from the directions of the father of the artist, the only naval officer I have met with who had actually seen a ship undergirded.

For the reasons for anchoring the ship by the stern, which this view is meant to illustrate, see pp. 136 and 208.

I have to express my thanks to Mr. Adlard, the engraver, for the pains he took to render the whole scene accurately.

CHARTS.

Constructed on Mercator's projection, in order to give the true bearings. To the west of longitude 24°, it is taken from the English Admiralty chart by Admiral Smyth. To the east of that longitude it is taken from the French Admiralty chart, as being the latest.

From the French Admiralty chart of the eastern part of the Mediterranean, from recent surveys. The dotted line to the east of Fair Havens marks the traverses which a ship, approaching it from the east, with a north-west wind, would have to make. From that to the point where the compass lines intersect each other, the dotted line represents the course of a ship leaving Fair Havens for the

WOODCUTS.

The diagrams at pp. 230 and 233 represent the supposed position of the Oars in Triremes and Quinqueremes.

The sketch of Port Phenice, now Lutro, on p. 90, is taken from one of the French Admiralty charts, of the date of 1738, in the Knights' Library at Malta.

That of Lutro, p. 261, was drawn by the Rev. George Brown.

MEMOIR OF JAMES SMITH.

[The following memoir is mainly compiled from the obituary notice of Mr. Smith contained in the 'Proceedings of the Royal Society,' and also from an article in the new edition of Chambers's 'Biographical Dictionary of Eminent Scotsmen,' Blackie and Son, London and Glasgow, 1870. Both these accounts were written by his son, Archibald Smith.]

JAMES SMITH, of Jordanhill, Renfrewshire, was born in Glasgow, on August 15, 1782. He was the eldest son of Archibald Smith, an eminent West India merchant in that city, and of Isobel Euing, who died in 1855 in her 101st year. He was educated at the Grammar School and University of Glasgow.

In 1809 he married Mary Wilson, who died in 1847. She was a granddaughter of Dr. Alexander Wilson, the first Professor of Astronomy in the University of Glasgow, a man of the most versatile genius, who is remembered as the originator of the now received theory as to the origin of sun-spots.

Mr. Smith never took any active part in business, but was for many years a sleeping partner in the West India house of Leitch and Smith in Glasgow. He served for some years in the Renfrewshire Militia, then a permanently embodied force. In the prevailing dread of a French invasion, he was for nearly a year quartered with his regiment in the south of England. He threw himself into the profession of a soldier with the same ardour that distinguished him in every pursuit that pleased him, and he retained through life a strong interest in military matters.

In 1812 Mr. Smith retired from the militia, and took up his abode in the remaining wing of the old castle of

Rosneath. The greater part of the stately residence of the Duke of Argyll had been burned down ten years before, and the present castle was being built. In this charming residence, in one of the most beautiful spots on the west of Scotland, he spent some of the happiest years of his life, indulging in that passion for yachting which, with him, was lifelong, and for the exercise of which Rosneath afforded unequalled facilities. His first cruise in a yacht of his own was in the year 1806; his last in the year 1866. He was one of the earliest members of the Royal Yacht Club, now the Royal Yacht Squadron, and was one of the earliest commodores of the Royal Northern Yacht Club.

In 1821 his father died, and he shortly afterwards removed to Jordanhill, where he principally resided during the rest of his life, and where he died.

Most of Mr. Smith's scientific and literary researches were connected with his love of yachting. His earliest paper in any scientific publication was a notice in the 'Transactions of the Royal Society of Edinburgh' (March 17, 1833) of an undescribed vitrified fort in the Burnt Isles in the Kyles of Bute, discovered by him on accidentally landing from his yacht.

He was an ardent cultivator of geographical science, and an enthusiastic book collector, especially in the department of early voyages of discovery. He was keenly interested in the Arctic voyages which excited so much attention at that time, and was intimate with several of the distinguished officers engaged in them, especially with the late Captain Douglas Clavering, R.N., and with Sir Edward Sabine, R.A., late President of the Royal Society. It may be interesting to mention that it was by a Dutch map, cut from a volume in Mr. Smith's library, that Captain Clavering steered to the coast of Greenland and found Gael Hamke's inlet in the exact situation there laid down. In memory of this he gave the two capes at its entrance the names of Cape James and Cape Mary, and to the island at its head the name of Jordanhill. Moreover it is on a MS. copy of Captain Clavering's original chart, which Mr. Smith made for his own use, that the geography of East Greenland from lat. 72° to 76° depends, the original having been unfortunately lost.

Later in life he devoted himself principally to the science of geology, and especially to that part of it for which the possession of a yacht offered peculiar facilities—the comparison of the shells in the most recent geological deposits with those existing in the present seas. This comparison, originally suggested to him by Sir Charles Lyell, was begun about the year 1834, and was continued with unflagging zeal for many years. The results of his researches were remarkable, and form an era in the history of post-tertiary geology. The deposits which he examined are those of finely laminated clay, with marine remains, which occur in many places on the west of Scotland at various elevations, up to several hundred feet. By far the greater part of the shells in these deposits still inhabit the British seas, but many are no longer to be found. The missing shells are generally of an Arctic type, and most of them have been found in the Arctic Seas. From this fact he drew the conclusion, announced by him to the Geological Society in 1839, of the existence before the present geological epoch of a period of greater cold, now known as the glacial period. This opinion, which was then contrary to the general opinion of geologists, is now universally accepted.

The delicate health of some members of his family caused Mr. Smith to reside successively at Gibraltar, Lisbon, and Malta. At each of these places he carried out geological researches, the results of which have been preserved in valuable papers.

His residence at Malta during the winter of 1844–1845 was the occasion of the remarkable series of investigations by which he is best known in literature and theology. The 'Voyage and Shipwreck of St. Paul' was published in 1848, and was received from the first with the warmest appreciation.

The minute study of the writings of St. Luke to which Mr. Smith was led in the course of these investigations, suggested to him an original theory of the connection of the three Synoptic Gospels, which was unfolded in the introductory 'Dissertation on the Life and Writings of St. Luke.' This theory was illustrated with much care and ingenuity by a comparison of the whole of the passages common to two or all of the three evangelists in a separate 'Dissertation on the Origin and Connection of the Gospels,' published by Blackwood in 1853. But the theory will be found most clearly stated and most fully developed, although not drawn out in the greatest detail, in the 'Dissertation on St. Luke,' as rewritten for the third edition of the 'Voyage and Shipwreck of St. Paul,' in consequence of the discovery of the Curetonian Syriac, and of the Codex Sinaiticus, and here reprinted with slight corrections. The question of the connection of the Gospels was constantly in his thoughts during the last years of his life, and he was engaged in the collection of materials for a more extended dissertation when he was interrupted by his last illness.

He was in politics a Liberal-Conservative, and a supporter of Sir Robert Peel. He unsuccessfully contested the burgh of Greenock at the general election in 1837, but made no further attempt to enter Parliament. He was warmly attached to the Church of Scotland, and took a lively interest in the questions discussed in her courts. He sat in the General Assembly in 1866 as a ruling elder for Renfrew, having been first returned for that burgh in 1806. He was a fellow of many scientific societies: of the Royal Society, the Geological Society, the Royal Geographical Society, and the Royal Society of Edinburgh. In Glasgow he was President of the Geological Society and of the Archæological Society, and also of the Andersonian University (now Anderson's College). He was unwearied in his exertions for the benefit of this institution, and founded and greatly contributed to the improvement of its valuable museum.

Throughout life he was remarkable for his lively interest in almost every form of intellectual activity. He read with facility most of the Romance and Teutonic languages. He was a practical as well as a theoretical architect, and was a zealous student of family and historical antiquities. His knowledge of archæology was considerable, especially in regard to nautical matters, on which subject his 'Dissertation on the Ships of the Ancients' is an accepted authority. He had a keen appreciation of the beauties of painting and sculpture, and was well read in all branches of English literature. In fiction his favourite authors were Sir Walter Scott and Miss Austen, whose works he read again and again, and constantly quoted. Reading was his unfailing resource and inexhaustible pleasure. He would often begin in the early morning, in winter long before it was light, and read with little intermission until bed-time, unless, indeed, he found a worthy antagonist at chess or other games to beguile him from his books. In such case the games were pursued with the same unflagging ardour.

Mr. Smith was a close observer in matters that interested him, and an acute and candid critic. He was a charming companion, full of playful humour, with a breadth of sympathy which caused him to number among his friends able men of all ranks, tastes, and opinions. He was distinguished by his warm affections, his bright, cheerful disposition, his unfailing fairness and toleration for opinions differing most widely from his own, and his readiness to be helpful to all. Even to the end he retained an almost youthful freshness and vivacity of feeling and expression.

He enjoyed vigorous health up to the spring of 1866, when a slight stroke of paralysis enfeebled his body without affecting his mind. A further attack towards the close of the year ended in his death at Jordanhill on January 17, 1867. His end was peace. Surrounded by his family, in full possession of his faculties, in humble yet firm trust on 'Jesus Christ alone,' he fell asleep.

Mr. Smith had nine children; of these two daughters alone are living. His only son who survived infancy was the late Archibald Smith, F.R.S., formerly Fellow of Trinity College, Cambridge, and barrister-at-law.

INTRODUCTION.

Tradition, from time immemorial, has pointed out a bay in the island of Malta as the scene of St. Paul's shipwreck. It has never been known by any other name than 'Cala di S. Paolo,' or St. Paul's Bay. There is no more effectual mode of perpetuating the memory of events than that of naming places after them; but, although we can scarcely have a stronger case of traditional evidence than the present, in the following inquiry I attach no weight to it whatever. I do not even assume the authenticity of the narrative of the voyage and shipwreck contained in the Acts of the Apostles, but scrutinise St. Luke's account of the voyage precisely as I would those of Baffin or Middleton,[1] or of any

[1] At the commencement of this century the accounts of those two navigators were held to be apocryphal, and their discoveries expunged from our maps; but in both cases their veracity has been established by the same process to which I am subjecting the account of St. Luke: the localities have been examined by subsequent visitors, and found to agree with the narratives.

ancient voyage of doubtful authority, or involving points on which controversies have been raised. A searching comparison of the narrative, with the localities where the events so circumstantially related are said to have taken place, with the aids which recent advances in our knowledge of the geography and the navigation of the eastern part of the Mediterranean supply, accounts for every transaction, clears up every difficulty, and exhibits an agreement so perfect in all its parts as to admit of but one explanation, namely that it is a narrative of real events, written by one personally engaged in them, and that the tradition respecting the locality is true.

Although many volumes have been written upon a question connected with this voyage, whether St. Paul was wrecked at Malta or Meleda in the Adriatic, I am not aware that any such comparison as the one I am about to attempt has yet been made;[1] none, indeed, could have been made with success in the hitherto imperfect state of our knowledge of

[1] Boysen, *De difficili Pauli Itinere*, with a promising title, throws no light on the subject. Major Rennell's paper, *On the Voyage and Place of Shipwreck of St. Paul* (*Archæologia*, vol. xxi.), belongs to the series of works on the controversy above alluded to. He had no personal knowledge of the supposed locality, and therefore had to contend with imaginary difficulties. It is written with that caution and candour which distinguish him. The conclusion he has arrived at is, as might be expected, that Malta was the scene of the shipwreck.

the geography of the Levant, and of the ships and seamanship of the ancients. For all purposes of minute comparison, our acquaintance with either of these subjects was worse than useless, and only calculated to mislead. Nothing, for instance, could be more erroneous than the charts of the south coast of Crete, where so many events of importance to the right understanding of the occurrences of the voyage took place, or of Malta, where it terminated in shipwreck.[1]

Had the geographers of former days been contented without filling up conjecturally the spaces in their maps, about which they were ignorant, or only given us 'elephants instead of towns,' we should have had but little reason to complain; but they more frequently did the very reverse, and gave us towns instead of elephants. In one of the French Admiralty charts of 1738, the southern promontory of Crete, now called Cape Matala, and the great bight (the Gulf of Messara) to the west of it, are altogether omitted, and the line of the coast represented as nearly straight. On the other

[1] Dr. Bloomfield, in his 'Recensio Synoptica,' refers to the map of Malta of Cluverius, for the spit of land which forms the place where two seas meet (*τόπον διθάλασσον*). The spit, or 'ness,' is evidently the present site of Valetta; but the map has scarcely any resemblance to Malta.

hand, Sanson, in his great map of Crete,[1] 'E Conatibus Geographicis,' as it is entitled, exhibits projections and indentations where none really exist; and in particular he has represented an extensive promontory in the centre of the Gulf of Messara, upon which he has placed the town of Assos, evidently for the purpose of accommodating his geography to the narrative of St. Luke; so that, whether we translate the word ἆσσον (Acts xxvii. 13) into 'Assos,' as it is rendered in the Vulgate, or 'close by,' as in the English translation, we are sure that the account and map will agree with each other.

Recent surveys have, however, corrected these errors, and furnished us with a correct outline of the coasts of Crete.[2] The soundings are not yet filled in; but this is immaterial in the earlier proceedings of St. Paul and his companions. At Malta, where we require to know

[1] Appended to Meursii *Creta*, Opera iii. 143. In Dapper's map (*Description de l'Archipel*, p. 385) there is neither cape nor bight. Fair Havens and the city of Lasea are placed at the east end of Crete; and Claudos (the island of Clauda), according to the longitude of Ptolemy, at the opposite extremity.

[2] The British survey now carrying on has not yet extended to the south coast of Candia. I am, however, assured by officers engaged in it that the coast lines of the late French Admiralty chart are extremely accurate. I have accordingly made use of it in the chart of the south coast of Crete; I have also used it in that part of the general chart of the voyage which lies to the east of long. 24°, the meridian where Admiral Smyth's chart of the 'western division of the Mediterranean Sea' terminates.

not only the outline and peculiar features of the coast, but the soundings and nature of the bottom, we have Admiral Smyth's chart of the island, and above all his plan of St. Paul's Bay, to a scale of nine inches to the mile,[1] which leave nothing to be desired with regard to the hydrography of this part of the voyage.

Next in importance to a correct knowledge of the geography is that of the peculiarities of ancient navigation; but there is no department of classical antiquity about which we are so much in the dark. I have not met with any modern author on the subject who has not left it more obscure than he found it, chiefly from a want of practical knowledge of the science.[2]

[1] I question if modern science has ever done more to confirm an ancient author than Admiral Smyth's survey of St. Paul's Bay has done in the present case. The soundings alone would have furnished a conclusive test of the truth of the narrative. To the common reader, the mention of twenty fathoms and fifteen fathoms indicates nothing more than the decreasing depth which every ship experiences in approaching the land: but when we come to consider the number of conditions which must be fulfilled in both instances where the depth is mentioned, in order to make the chart and narrative agree, we must admit that a perfect agreement cannot be accidental. I refer the reader for the details of the coincidences to the Narrative of the Voyage.

[2] M. Jal, author of a late work entitled *Archéologie Navale*, and Captain Beechey, R.N., are to be excepted from this last remark; but M. Jal is rather a mediæval than a classical antiquary; and Captain Beechey's remarks on ancient ships, appended to his travels in Africa, are avowedly taken from Potter. His observations on the rate of sailing of ancient ships are, however, valuable, and I have availed myself of them.

Translators and commentators have necessarily had recourse to the writings of authors who have treated *de re navali antiqua* as authorities; and the consequence is that there is scarcely a single nautical term in the narrative which is correctly rendered, and even when one is, the reader has no certainty that the meaning is the right one, for he will rarely find two commentators agreed in opinion respecting it.

We are not, however, to suppose that men of learning and research offer conjectures at random; all of them have some grounds to go upon, and it is only by testing their conclusions by a careful examination of the data upon which they rest them, and by rejecting such as we can prove to be erroneous, that we can hope to arrive at the true explanation of the terms. This I have attempted; but I found it a work of much greater labour than I anticipated. Even the verification of quotations is anything but an easy task; we often meet with errors in the references, and every ancient author has not a verbal index to guide us in searching for passages.

But it is not enough to discover the passages, or even to assure ourselves, from the context, that we understand the meaning of the author; we must, by comparing him with other authorities, satisfy ourselves that he understood what he was writing about, and is correct in his terminology. Those who trust implicitly to ancient authors will not infrequently be led into error, particularly where the object is to arrive at the meaning of technical expressions. The ancient scholiasts and lexicographers, and writers *de omnibus rebus*, like Julius Pollux and Isidore of Seville, cannot always be right in their explanations; and I should consider inferences drawn from their works of little value, unless supported by independent collateral evidence. But if caution be requisite with regard to the writings of the ancients, it is still more so with regard to the engravings of representations of ancient ships on coins, marbles, and pictures. To the nautical antiquary the engraved figures, particularly of coins, are of little value, except to guide him to the originals.

It has been my object, in every instance where it was in my power, to get at the best evidence. I cannot accuse myself of want of industry in the research, and I have been placed in circumstances in some respects peculiarly favourable for prosecuting it.

A winter's residence in Malta afforded me ample opportunities for a personal examination of the localities. In the ships of war stationed there, I could consult with skilful and scientific seamen, familiar with the navigation of the

Levant, an advantage I did not fail to avail myself of; and as it is my object to put my readers in possession of my authorities, I have never scrupled to name them. In the Knights' Library I had access to an extensive collection of works, printed and manuscript, on the controversy as to the scene of the shipwreck, on the hydrography of the Mediterranean, and on local and classical antiquities. The following summer I spent on the Continent, and devoted my time almost exclusively to the investigation, with the advantages which the museums and libraries of Naples, Florence, Lausanne, and Paris afforded. Since my return, I have continued it with the advantages our own country possesses, particularly in the libraries and medal rooms of the British Museum and records of the Admiralty,[1] and with a private library which I may term rich in early sea voyages, formed in a great measure for the purpose of illustrating geographical and nautical antiquities, and with the means of testing experimentally the soundness of my conjectures as to the internal arrangements of ancient ships.

It is not enough, however, to be placed in a position favourable for observation in order to arrive at just conclusions; we must also know

[1] It will be seen that the record of the proceedings of a court-martial on the officers of a frigate wrecked in St. Paul's Bay furnished very important information, bearing directly on the subject.

'what to observe' and 'how to observe;' but the power of doing so with advantage depends in a great measure upon practice; and I think it is due to the reader to state that none of the channels into which my inquiries on the subject have branched are altogether new to me. I have, in the first place, endeavoured to identify the locality of a shipwreck which took place eighteen centuries ago. An attempt to do this would be of little value, unless the geological changes to which sea-coasts are liable, which may or must have occurred in the interval, are taken into account. Now it so happens that this is a department of geology which I have been engaged for many years in investigating.

In like manner, it would be hardly possible to reconstruct the history of a sea voyage out of such scattered and fragmentary notices as we find in the narrative of St. Luke, without some practical knowledge of navigation and seamanship. My knowledge of these subjects is only that of an amateur, yet a yacht sailor of more than thirty years' standing can scarcely fail to have acquired some skill in those principles of nautical science which are common to all times, though he may not always express them in the appropriate language of the quarter-deck. I find, at all events, that the knowledge I have thus acquired enabled me to consult my nautical friends with advantage. But nautical skill, whether original or borrowed, will not tell us how Greek and Roman vessels, so different from the modern in rigging and construction, should be managed under given circumstances. Here, also, former pursuits come to my aid. Nautical antiquities have long been a favourite study, and not a little practical experience in planning, building, and altering vessels, has given me definite notions both of external form and internal capabilities; whilst the opportunity of testing my conclusions by experiment, and the success of those I have made, give me confidence in their accuracy.

I have felt some hesitation in dwelling upon the advantages I possess for conducting such inquiries with success, which are in a certain degree personal, and I turn with satisfaction to those which I have derived from recent antiquarian discoveries, from the pictures and marbles exhumed at Herculaneum and Pompeii, and especially from the discovery of the inventories of the Athenian fleet, which were excavated at the Piræus in 1834. These last are inscribed upon marble tables: they have been published by Professor Böckh, of Berlin, well known for his researches on Attic antiquities, and his great collection of Greek inscriptions. Nothing can be more satisfactory than the manner in which he has edited these important fragments.

He has, in the first place, printed the tables in inscription characters. He has next printed them in the common Greek type, with the lacunæ filled up conjecturally within brackets, as far as that could be done with tolerable certainty, and he has accompanied them with notes and preliminary dissertations.[1] It will be seen that I frequently dissent from his nautical inferences, but this difference of opinion by no means lessens my sense of the care and fidelity with which he has executed his editorial labours. These tables contain, in the most authentic form, much information on nautical matters, calculated to throw light on difficult and unexplained passages, both in the sacred and profane writers of antiquity.

We are also indebted to M. Jal for having brought forward, in his 'Archéologie Navale,' some important documents respecting the shipping of the Middle Ages. They furnish a valuable link connecting the modern and ancient nautical language, which I have not failed to avail myself of.

If, therefore, I have succeeded in clearing up unexplained passages in the sacred historians, or other ancient writers, my success must

[1] The title of the work is 'Urkunden über das Seewesen des Attischen Staates, hergestellt und erläutert von August Böckh,' 8vo, Ber. 1840: i.e. Archives of the Navy of the Attic State. I have quoted them as 'Attic Tables.'

be ascribed, in a great measure, to discoveries unknown to the authors who preceded me in the same lines of inquiry.

My original intention was to have confined myself to the illustration of St. Paul's voyage, and that the work should have been, in the strictest sense of the word, a monograph ; that my antiquarian researches should have been confined to the wheat ships of Alexandria, and my critical researches to the nautical style of St. Luke. I could not, however, in searching for evidence regarding the merchant ships of the ancients, avoid noticing that which regarded the war galleys also ; and I could not resist the temptation of attempting a solution of what Dr. Arnold has called 'an indiscoverable problem,'[1] the internal arrangement of the rowers.

I have also extended my inquiries respecting the writings of St. Luke much beyond my original intention. In comparing his nautical style with that of other authors, ancient and modern, I was led to a minute examination of his account of the miracle of stilling the tempest on the lake of Gennesareth, as compared with those given of the same event in the Gospels of St. Matthew and St. Mark.

With this view I copied them out in the

[1] *Roman Hist.* iii. 572.

original in parallel columns, placing St. Luke's account, which it was my object to elucidate, in the centre. After repeated transcriptions, I succeeded in adjusting them so as to exhibit at a glance its relation to each of the other two. The results of this comparison were to me unexpected, but in the highest degree interesting and satisfactory. I found I had unintentionally been led to place in juxtaposition the passages which were, perhaps, the best calculated of all to show us what were the authorities which St. Luke has made use of in this part of his Gospel. In the parallel passages of St. Matthew and St. Mark, we have all the data, and nothing but the data, which he has employed. There is here no disturbing cause to perplex us, such as the employment of authorities which have perished, or of information procured by personal inquiry. We are thus introduced, as it were, into his study. We see the two works from which he composed his narrative open before us. One of these, which is in Greek, is the Gospel according to St. Matthew; the other is in the language of the country (Syro-Chaldaic or Aramaic, called by the fathers Hebrew). The original employed by St. Luke, it is true, is no longer extant, but we have what I believe to be a close and literal translation of it in the Gospel of St. Mark.

By thus placing the writings of the first three Evangelists in a new point of view, and employing a new instrument of examination, if I may be allowed the expression, I cannot help thinking that I have succeeded in throwing new light on the origin of their Gospels. I say a new instrument of examination; for it was the contrast between the *landsmanlike* style in which St. Matthew describes the storm and its effects, and the accurate but provincial style of the fisherman of the lake apparent in St. Mark's account, and the equally accurate but less provincial and more historical style in which St. Luke, in a narrative evidently constructed from the other two, relates the same occurrence, which first arrested my attention. This led me to examine into the nature of the connection of the accounts given of this miracle by St. Luke and St. Mark. The conclusion at which I arrived was that St. Mark is the translator of a contemporary account by an eye-witness, and that St. Luke has based his account of the miracle, not upon St. Mark's translation, but upon this original narrative, supplying some particulars from St. Matthew's Gospel in Greek.

An important question here presented itself: if St. Mark be a translator, whom did he translate? The answer which I have endeavoured to establish, both by internal and external evidence, I give in the words of Papias and other ancient fathers :—'Mark is the translator of Peter' (*Μάρκος ἑρμηνευτὴς Πέτρου*), not, as some of those writers have, as I think, erroneously supposed that he was the translator of what St. Peter remembered and dictated at a distance of years, but that a considerable part of St. Mark's Gospel is a translation of an account of the transactions in which St. Peter was personally engaged, written by St. Peter himself upon the spot, immediately after the events took place which he has recorded.

Since writing the above I have seen some remarks on this subject by the translator[1] of Schleiermacher's 'Critical Essay on the Gospel of St. Luke,' in which he points out the importance of examining it from every point of view, and anticipates the probability that the right clue may thus be discovered. He says :—

> That a problem so complicated may not yet have been viewed from every possible side, and, therefore, that the right clue may still be discovered, is not in itself improbable.[2]

Now, independently of all the proofs which I have brought forward in support of my view of the authorship of the original documents, and the use which has been made of them by St. Luke, I cannot help thinking that I have got possession of the right clue, when I feel

[1] Dr. Thirlwall, now Bishop of St. David's.

[2] Introduction, p. xxii.

the ground so firm under me, when I feel that in every step I have taken, difficulties have disappeared, when I feel assured that I am not wandering amongst the mists of myths, legends, or early traditions, but amidst the clear light of the best of all historical evidence, that of the contemporary accounts of the persons actually engaged in the transactions which they have recorded.

Although it does not come within the plan of this work to discuss the bearing of the conclusions I have arrived at, on the question of the genuineness or authenticity of the writings of St. Luke, there is one remark which, as it depends on the peculiarities of the nautical style of the Acts of the Apostles, I wish here to make. That style, as I shall have occasion more than once to observe, though accurate, is unprofessional. No sailor would have written in a style so little like that of a sailor; no man not a sailor could have written a narrative of a sea voyage so consistent in all its parts, unless from actual observation. This peculiarity of style is to me, in itself, a demonstration that the narrative of the voyage is an account of real events written by an eye-witness. A similar remark may be made on the geographical details. They must have been taken from actual observation, for the geographical knowledge of the age was not such as to enable a writer to be so minutely accurate in any other way.

There is one objection to the locality assigned by the Maltese tradition as the scene of the shipwreck, which meets us at the very threshold of our inquiry, and which it is necessary to obviate in a work which aims at exhausting the subject. It is maintained by Giorgi, Bryant, Falconer, and others, that it did not take place at Malta at all, but at Meleda, in the Gulf of Venice, an island which was anciently known by the same name as Malta, namely, Melita.

But for the above-mentioned reason, I should have been much inclined to have noticed this objection very briefly, thinking, with Joseph Scaliger, 'that it would not deserve to be confuted, if it had not had supporters.'[1] But when I find it adopted by modern commentators[2] and biographers,[3] and read such passages as the subjoined,[4] I feel called upon to subject the

[1] 'Hæc ridicula opinio, si non sectatores nacta esset, indigna erat quæ vel confutaretur.' (*De Emendatione Temporum*, p. 536.)

[2] Dr. Valpy, in his edition of the New Testament.

[3] Chalmers's *Biog. Dict.* art. 'Bryant.'

[4] 'On sait bien aujourd'hui, à ne plus en douter, que c'est l'île de Meleda dans la Mer Adriatique, sur la côte de la Dalmatie, et qui faisait autrefois partie de la république de Raguse, où St. Paul fit naufrage.' (Corresp. de Bar. Zach, ix. 78.)

'The most celebrated treatise with which we are acquainted is that of Mr. Bryant, who has defended his opinion at great length with all

arguments by which it is supported to a minute and sifting examination. This I have attempted to do, following the reasoning of Bryant and Falconer, as best known in this country. I have not, however, left any of the arguments of foreign writers on the subject, who have adopted the same side of the question, unnoticed or unanswered.

JORDANHILL: *March* 12, 1848.

his usual learning, and more than his usual judgment, and in the general opinion, I believe, has been supposed to have established his position.' (Townsend's *New Testament arranged in Chronological Order*, ii. 445.)

'The course of this voyage, related Acts xxvii., in which the Apostle was shipwrecked on the island of Melita, Acts xxviii. 1, has been mistaken by the first geographers and commentators, and their maps of it erroneously constructed, in consequence of the vulgar error that the island in question was the African Melita or Malta, instead of the Adriatic Melita or Meleda. This correction of the received geography we owe to the sagacious Bryant; and it has recently been established with much learning and ability by a layman, in a dissertation on this voyage, Oxford, 1817, the ingenious Dr. Falconer, the physician of Bath, who has furnished a correcter map of the voyage.' (Hales, *Chronology*, iv. 406.)

'The supposition (that Malta was the scene of the shipwreck) is quite absurd. Not to argue the matter at length, consider those few conclusive facts. The narrative speaks of the barbarous people and barbarians of the island; now our Malta was at the time fully peopled and highly civilised, as we may surely infer from ancient and other writings. A viper comes out of the sticks upon the fire being lighted; the men are not surprised at the appearance of the snake, but imagine first a murderer, and then a God from the harmless attack. Now in our Malta there are, I may say, no snakes at all.' (Coleridge's *Table Talk*, p. 185.)

'This (Malta) is not the Melita where St. Paul was shipwrecked.' (Lord Lindsay's *Letters from Egypt and the Holy Land*, i. 19.)

'I am bound to express my entire certainty that Melita is Meleda.' (Neale's *Notices of Dalmatia*, etc.)

THE VOYAGE AND SHIPWRECK

OF

ST. PAUL.

DISSERTATION ON THE LIFE AND WRITINGS OF ST. LUKE.

PERHAPS no point in ancient literature is more thoroughly established than that Luke the physician was author of the third Gospel and the Acts of the Apostles; the external evidence reaching through the early Christian authors back to the fragment discovered by Muratori, which contains a date showing that it was written less than a century after the Acts, and therefore within the limits, with respect to time, of direct evidence; not that the author could remember the first publication of the Acts, but he must have known many who did.

The proofs drawn from St. Luke's own writings, and those of St. Paul, are not less conclusive.

In the Epistles he is mentioned as a fellow-labourer (Philem. 24), as one who was with him at Rome (2 Tim. iv. 11), and as a physician (Coloss. iv. 14). Here, then, are three conditions, which if shown to be fulfilled in St. Luke, and in him alone of all the companions of St. Paul, necessarily involve the conclusion that he is the author of the works in question. I shall therefore endeavour to show that they are all fulfilled in the writer of the third Gospel and the Acts of the Apostles.

1st. He was a fellow-labourer. This is proved by the text (Acts xvi. 10), wherein he states himself as one of those called 'to preach the Gospel in Macedonia.'

2nd. He was with Paul on his first visit to Rome, proved by Acts xxviii. 16, 'And when *we* were come to Rome,' &c.

3rd. He was a physician.

From the simplicity of St. Luke's style, and entire absence of anything like professional pedantry, his professionalisms are never obtrusive ; when, however, we subject his accounts of the cures of diseases to a searching examination, we find that he is always careful to state their precise nature and extent, and that he does so in the technical language of the Greek physicians. I content myself with one from the Gospel, and one from the Acts. In the account of the cure of Peter's wife's mother, she is said to be *labouring under* a *great* fever (iv. 38, ἦν συνεχομένη πυρετῷ μεγάλῳ). Now we are expressly told by Galen, in his treatise on the difference of fevers, that physicians were accustomed to distinguish fevers as the *great* and small fevers.[1] In an excellent paper on the medical style of St. Luke, signed J. K. Walker ('Gent. Mag.' June 1841, p. 585), the author remarks :—

[1] Καὶ συνηθὲς ἤδη τοῖς ἰατροῖς ὀνομάζειν ἐν τούτῳ τῷ γένει τῆς διαφορᾶς τὸν μέγαν τε καὶ μικρὸν πυρετόν. (*De Feb. Diff.* lib. i. c. 1.)

'Nor does he (St. Luke) fail, as often as he has occasion to mention diseases or their cure, to select such appropriate language as none but a professional man could have used . . . . In speaking of Simon's wife's mother, who was taken with a *great* fever (Luke iv. 38), he uses the term συνεχομένη in the same sense as the Greek writers do.'

Compare the above-quoted text with that describing the disease of the father of Publius, at Melita (Acts xxviii. 8), where we are told that he was '*labouring under fevers* and dysentery,' πυρετοῖς καὶ δυσεντερίῳ συνεχόμενον. Here also we have the testimony of Hippocrates, who uses πυρετοί, fevers, in the plural. In both these cases we have the best evidence as to the technical character of St. Luke's medical terminology, but we know also from St. Jerome, that ecclesiastical authors who wrote before him had borne the strongest testimony to the medical skill of St. Luke.

'Evangelistam Lucam tradunt veteres ecclesiæ tractatores medicinæ artis fuisse scientissimum.' (Com. in Isaiam, xliii. 6.)

I may add that modern medical authors familiar with the works of the Greek physicians have observed, that when he mentions diseases he uses the appropriate language correctly. He also exhibits professional feeling in his account of the cure of the woman with the issue of blood (viii. 43), taken, as I have elsewhere shown, from the original of St. Peter, evidently from personal knowledge. In St. Mark's Gospel we are told that the woman had suffered many things of many physicians, and had wasted[1] (δαπανήσασα) all

[1] It is not clear that προσαναλώσασα, the word used by St. Luke, is milder than that which Mr. Smith renders 'wasted' in St. Mark's

she had, and was nothing bettered by them, but rather grew worse (Mark v. 26). Strong language, but no doubt true, and what might have been expected from the doctors in a fishing village. In St. Luke's account, whilst he removes the implied reflection on the profession, there is no *suppressio veri*;—he adheres rigidly to the facts of the case. He tells us that the woman 'had expended her whole living upon physicians, neither could be healed by any' (viii. 43). We may conclude therefore with confidence, that the fact of his having been a physician is established, and that the conditions which identify Luke, the friend of St. Paul, with the author of the Gospel and Acts are fulfilled.

I come now to consider the evidence as to his country. The first indication occurs in his enumeration of the seven deacons (Acts vi. 5); in relating their names he stops to tell us that Nicolas was a proselyte of Antioch, but does not mention the country of any of the others. Now if St. Luke was himself an Antiochean, nothing could be more natural than such a notice, just as I find in my own library eight accounts of the Russian campaign of 1812, three by French, three by English, and two by Scotch authors. The two last, Scott and Alison, tell us that the Russian General Barclay de Tolly was of Scotch extraction; none of the others take any notice of it. In both cases, the authors I have no doubt were prompted by national feelings, of which they were probably unconscious, and I attribute the notice of the country of

account. The difference is probably only an example of the familiar phenomenon of the same Aramaic word translated differently by St. Mark and St. Luke. [See *Dissertation on the Origin and Connection of the Gospels*, p. xxiii.]

Nicolas to the same cause. Another case of the same kind is where he tells us that the disciples were first called Christians at Antioch. Whatever may have been the place of his birth, we have direct evidence that he was resident at Antioch when St. Paul *first* visited that city. The internal evidence for this is drawn, first from the autopticity of his style, or in other words, from his relating events with the circumstantiality of an eye-witness. His account of this part of the early history of Christianity is so minute and circumstantial as to have satisfied me that he was present at the events related in this part of the history, even before I was aware that there was conclusive external evidence to prove that he was, as I stated in the first edition of this work.

The earliest notice of Antioch connected with the history of Christianity occurs in Acts xi. 19, where we are informed that 'they who were scattered abroad upon the persecutions that arose about Stephen travelled as far as Antioch.' St. Luke's account is here so minute and circumstantial as to indicate the pen of an eye-witness: he mentions the places from whence the disciples came, and distinguishes those who addressed the Jews from those who addressed the Grecians. He also mentions the names of certain Antiocheans—men of consequence, no doubt, in their own city, but never heard of elsewhere. The manner, too, in which he relates the events which took place at Antioch at this time, indicates no less clearly that his is the narrative of an eye-witness. Thus, in speaking of the men of Cyprus and Cyrene, he tells us that when they were come to Antioch, they spake unto the Grecians (xi. 20); that Barnabas *departed* (from

Antioch), and brought him (Paul) to Antioch, prophets came *from* Jerusalem, relief is sent *to* Jerusalem. And at the end of the following chapter, after narrating the persecutions of Herod and his death, he tells us, without prefatory explanation, that St. Paul and Barnabas *returned from* Jerusalem (xii. 25). This is the language of a person who was at Antioch at the time; any other would have said they returned to Antioch.

The proof that St. Luke was present at Antioch is confirmed by a passage from the Acts, xi. 28, contained in one of the so-called interpolations in the Codex D. The passage is as follows:—'And in those days came prophets from Jerusalem unto Antioch, and *there was great joy; and when we were assembled*[1] there stood up one of them, named Agabus,' &c. This passage, although it does not form part of the received text, is better supported by evidence than some that do, for it is expressly quoted by St. Augustine a century at least earlier than the date of the manuscript in question. The testimony of Augustine[2] is so clear and precise as to leave no doubt that the passage was contained in other and older MSS. than Codex D.

Lardner opposes the opinion of Irenæus to the direct evidence of Augustine, a later Father, but

[1] Ἦν δὲ πολλὴ ἀγαλλίασις συνεστραμμένων δὲ ἡμῶν.

[2] 'Item in Actibus Apostolorum *scriptum est*, ea quæ ad victum sunt necessaria procurata esse in futuram famem, *sic enim legimus*: "In illis autem diebus descenderunt ab Ierosolymis prophetæ Antiochiam, *eratque magna exultatio. Congregatis autem nobis*, unus ex illis, nomine Agabus," &c.' (*De Serm. Domini*, lib. ii. c. 57.) [The passage is rejected by the best modern critics, as also are others which are peculiar to Codex D, such as that quoted on p. 53.]

there is no question between them. The question, if there be one, is between Irenæus and Luke himself. Augustine could not be mistaken in the direct assertion that such was the text of the Acts; and if he told the truth, then we have the authority of Luke himself that he was present when Agabus visited Antioch.

The testimony of Irenæus, however, has no reference to the time when St. Luke first joined St. Paul, but to the fact that he was his companion on his journeys and fellow-labourer; it is in the following terms:—'Lucas inseparabilis fuit a Paulo et cooperarius ejus in evangelio; ipse fuit manifestum non glorians, sed ab ipsa productus veritate. Separatis enim inquit a Paulo et Barnaba et Joanne, qui vocabatur Marcus, et cum navigassent Cyprum, nos venimus ad Troadem' (c. Haer. iii. 14, 1). Irenæus quotes from memory, and, as might be expected, falls into mistakes, but in this case they do not affect any inferences drawn from his incidental expressions. St. Luke certainly was not with St. Paul on his journey after he parted with Barnabas and Mark; neither was he with him when he first visited Troas (Acts xvi. 8), for he was already there, and his notice of his arrival at Troas with St. Paul refers to his second visit to that city many years afterwards (Acts xx. 6). Tillemont's objection, adduced by Lardner to the authority of Codex D, that it is 'plein d'additions et altérations contraires au véritable texte de S. Luc' (Mém. Eccl. t. ii. 2 S. Luc. note), is mere assumption, as, I believe, is the character very generally given of this manuscript, that it abounds in interpolations; a character which, at least in the two pregnant instances brought under consideration in the present inquiry, neither of which form part of the received text,—I mean the one in question, and another shortly to be considered—is without foundation.

I am therefore satisfied, from the concurring evidence just stated, that St. Luke was a resident inhabitant of Antioch when St. Paul first visited it, and from that time was a fellow-labourer with him in the spread of the Gospel, and joined with him in many of his missionary journeys.

The circumstantiality of the accounts of St. Paul's first missionary journey to Cyprus and Asia Minor in company with Barnabas (Acts xiii. 4 to xiv. 23), affords strong presumption that he accompanied him; the places they passed through, and the particular species of blindness which affected Elymas the sorcerer, mentioned in medical language, and his groping for assistance, mark at once the physician and the eye-witness.

I conclude therefore from the evidence I have stated, that St. Luke was a resident at Antioch when St. Paul first visited it, and from that time was a fellow-labourer with him in the spread of the Gospel. After the return of Paul and Barnabas to Antioch (xiv. 26), he appears to have remained there till Paul and Silas finally left it (xv. 40). There is nothing in the account of the journey which Paul and Barnabas made to Jerusalem to indicate that he accompanied them; but from his mentioning that they passed through Phenice and Samaria, where we do not hear of anything being done, except that 'they were brought on their way by the church' (xv. 3), it is probable he accompanied them so far; at all events, such details show that he was still at Antioch.

After St. Paul left that city, we hear nothing of St. Luke till they again met at Troas (xvi. 8), and here it falls from him that he was engaged with St. Paul in preaching the Gospel, for he infers from his vision 'that the Lord had called *us* to preach,' &c. From Troas he accompanies the Apostle and his party to Philippi; the circumstantiality with which he relates this short voyage and the events at Philippi would have assured us of his presence, even if it had not been confirmed by the use of the first person plural. These proofs of his presence cease with the departure of Paul and his companions from Philippi, and although, as usual, he is silent as to his own proceedings, there is good reason to suppose that he laboured in that city and the adjoining regions till St. Paul's return to Macedonia (Acts xx. 2); his entire silence as to the events of the circuit made by the Apostle on this occasion would of itself assure us that he did not join in it. It is during this period that a circumstance took place which is mentioned by St. Jerome, namely, that he was 'the brother whose praise was in the Gospel throughout all the churches, who was sent by St. Paul along with Titus to receive the contributions of the church there' (2 Cor. viii. 18).

As the circumstance above alluded to is an important event, and throws much light upon a portion of his life about which he is entirely silent, it becomes desirable to ascertain how far the statement of Jerome is confirmed by other and independent authorities. Origen, in noticing St. Paul's praise of Luke's Gospel, evidently understands that he was 'the brother,' &c., and it is expressly so stated in the (longer) epistle of Ignatius to the Ephesians.

But these are not the only authorities which have come down to us which prove that St. Luke was one of the companions of Titus in the mission in question. In the subscription to the Second Epistle to the Corinthians, it is expressly stated that he was; this is not indeed canonical authority, but it is one of great antiquity, and quite independent of that of Jerome. He has not introduced it into the Vulgate, and he cannot have taken his statement from it, for it says nothing about Luke being 'the brother whose praise is in the churches;' whilst, on the other hand, Jerome says nothing about Luke being the companion of Titus.

It is true that several of the subscriptions to the Epistles have been shown by Paley to be erroneous; but this is not one of them. Those which are shown to be erroneous are evidently the conclusions which transcribers have drawn from the matter of the Epistles; but as the name of Luke is not mentioned in the body of the epistle, its insertion in the subscription must either be the record of a fact, or an arbitrary interpolation,—a supposition in which there is not a shadow of probability.

The manner in which St. Paul's second visit to Macedonia is related in the Acts is precisely what might have been expected from St. Luke, on the supposition that he was sent to Corinth upon St. Paul's arrival in Macedonia. He was too intimately connected with the Apostle, and too anxious to record his proceedings, to have noticed them in so cursory a manner, had he not been absent at this time. Now, we know that St. Luke was at Philippi at the time of this visit, for he left it with St. Paul on his departure from Macedonia. We must infer, from his usual style of writing when with St. Paul, that he neither was with him during his stay at Philippi, nor accompanied him in his progress through Macedonia, the whole of which is related in these words :—'He departed (from Ephesus) for to go into Macedonia ; and when he had gone over those parts, and had given them much exhortation, he came into Greece' (Acts xx. 1, 2). St. Luke, therefore, although in Macedonia, was not with St. Paul either during his stay at Philippi or on his journey through Macedonia. I account for his absence by the supposition that St. Paul's first business, on his arrival, was to despatch him with Titus to Corinth, and that he returned to Philippi before St. Paul (xx. 2). We can thus explain the manner in which he describes St. Paul's proceedings on this occasion, so different from that which he uses when he was in his company.

The next peculiarity I would advert to is the remarkable contrast between the writings of St. Paul and St. Luke respecting the contributions. It is quite obvious, from both of his Epistles to the Corinthians and that to the Romans, that St. Paul attached the highest importance to them : the very circumstance of his declining to take charge of them is a proof that they were of great importance ; and yet, were it not that it incidentally drops from him in his address to Felix (Acts xxiv. 17), that he came to Jerusalem to bring alms and offerings, nothing whatever respecting this matter would have been known from the Acts. I attribute this silence on the part of St. Luke to the entire abnegation of self, which characterises his writings. I believe that the history of the contributions belongs in a great measure to the history of St.

Luke, and that he was not merely the selected trustee, but a principal mover in the contributions of the earliest European churches, both to St. Paul personally, and to the church at Jerusalem. Assuming then, as I do, that the fact mentioned in the subscription to the 2 Corinth. with respect to Luke is established, it follows that he is 'the brother whose praise is in the Gospel in all the churches' of Macedonia. I do not, with Jerome and many commentators, suppose that St. Paul, in mentioning the Gospel, alludes to the Gospel written by St. Luke, but to his success in preaching the Gospel, and adopt the translation of Mr. Conybeare :—

'The brother whose praise, in publishing the glad tidings, is spread throughout all the churches.'

Agreeing with this view, let us revert to the circumstances under which St. Luke first visited Philippi. We learn from Acts xvi. 10, that the members of St. Paul's mission, of whom St. Luke was one, proceeded to Philippi, where St. Paul founded the first European church ; Paul, Silas, and Timothy then left Philippi, or rather were driven from it (Acts xvi. 40, and xvii. 14) ; but St. Luke certainly did not, as I have already shown, accompany them. This church, notwithstanding the absence of St. Paul, and all the other members of the mission except St. Luke, continued to flourish. Immediately after leaving it, St. Paul proceeded to Thessalonica ; and here we learn that he repeatedly received relief to his necessities from the Philippian church. I cannot doubt but that this assistance was mainly due to the devoted friend who remained with that church,—who knew his wants, and who exerted himself to supply them. St. Luke felt he was called upon to teach the Gospel to the Macedonians, and we must suppose that he obeyed the call, and laboured assiduously and successfully, as every indication connected with the Macedonian churches proves.

Years roll on, and St. Paul again visits Macedonia. St. Luke, after fulfilling the mission to Corinth, returns to Philippi with the contributions, and is there joined by St. Paul, whom he accompanies to Jerusalem ; his journey thither is circumstantially related in the Acts, xx. 6 to xxi. 17, and need not be repeated here.

St. Luke, as usual, is entirely silent respecting his own proceedings. There are, however, the strongest reasons for believing that, during the two years of St. Paul's imprisonment at Cæsarea, he composed his Gospel.

There are several indications in that work which tend to prove that it was written in Judea. In the first place, he tells us in his preface that his object was to give an account 'of the things which had been accomplished *amongst us*' (περὶ τῶν πεπληροφορημένων ἐν ἡμῖν πραγμάτων), showing that he was then writing in the scene of the events. In the next place, his descriptions are those of a person familiar with the localities, and who was upon the spot at the time of writing ; thus, in relating the triumphal entry of our Lord into Jerusalem, he informs us of the exact place where the attendant multitudes burst out into Hosannas,—it was on 'the descent of the Mount of Olives' (Luke xix. 37), a circumstance only noticed by him. The last proof of the Judean origin of the Gospel is the manner in which he makes use of the national denomination, 'the Jews,' as compared with the use he makes of it in the Acts. A person writing in the country does not think of giving the national denomination to its inhabitants, except in cases where it is unavoidable; but writing out of it he very naturally does. Now in the Gospel St. Luke only uses the word 'Jew' five times, and that in cases where he could not help it,—namely, 'the King of the Jews,' 'the elders of the Jews,' 'a city of the Jews;' but he never uses it when speaking of the people in general. In the Acts, on the other hand, it is used no less than eighty-two times.

I infer from these indications that St. Luke's Gospel was written in Judea; but if so, it must have been written before he quitted it with St. Paul on his voyage to Rome, for there is no later period to which its composition can be referred. It was therefore written between A.D. 58 and A.D. 60, under circumstances of all others the most favourable for historical investigation, on the spot where the transactions took place, and with constant opportunities of intercourse with those chiefly engaged in them. To this beloved friend of the Great Apostle of the Gentiles, himself, as I have shown, a leading member of the mission which first bore the light of the Gospel into Europe, every means of information at that time in the possession of living witnesses must have been accessible.

In the narrative of the voyage we have a minute account of the events of the life of St. Luke till the arrival of St. Paul at Rome, and we learn from the Epistles to the Colossians and Philemon that he was still there when they were written. The only subsequent notice in Scripture respecting him is that in

2 Tim. iv. 11, where we are told that he alone was with the Apostle in the very crisis of his fate, 'when the time of his departure was at hand,' and when all but Luke had forsaken him. From his not being included in the greetings to the Philippians, it has been inferred that he had previously left Rome. This is confirmed by his silence as to the events alluded to in Phil. i. 12, as 'having fallen out unto the furtherance of the Gospel.' St. Luke mentions the results of these events when he states that St. Paul taught 'those things which concern the Lord Jesus Christ with all confidence, no man forbidding him' (Acts xxviii. 31). We can only account for this silence by supposing that he was not present when they took place. The change of style also, from that of an eye-witness, when he relates what took place on their arrival at Rome, to that of an historian, when he gives an account of the two succeeding years, points to the same conclusion. Thus he devotes thirteen verses to the proceedings of the first few days, and only two to the remaining two years.

When St. Paul ascertained that his case could not come before the Emperor for a considerable length of time, and that till it was decided he was in no personal danger, we find that his first care was to dispatch Tychicus to the churches in Asia Minor. We may suppose that St. Luke would be sent on a similar mission; but if so, the church of Philippi is clearly the one to which conjecture would lead us. Now, there is, I think, very strong reason for believing that he actually was there when the epistle to that church was written, and that the 'true yoke-fellow' (iv. 3), addressed in it, was no other than St. Luke, to whose care the epistle would be naturally addressed. Had it been a Philippian presbyter that was meant, we must suppose that he would have named him; whereas, if he sent Luke to the Philippians, as he did Tychicus to the Asiatic churches, it would be unnecessary. The terms in which the message is expressed show clearly that it was addressed to one of the class of St. Paul's friends to which St. Luke belonged; and from the evident allusions to what took place on his former visit to Philippi (compare Phil. iv. 3, with Acts xvi. 13), it must have been one of those who were with him at the time. Now, we know very accurately those who were the members of the mission. It consisted at first of Paul and Silas. Timothy joined them at Lystra (Acts xvi. 1), and the author of the Acts at Troas (ib. xvi. 10). There is no mention of any other of the Apostle's companions; nor does St. Luke's style of narration afford any warrant for supposing that there were any except those mentioned. The true yoke-fellow must, therefore, have been either Timothy, Silas, or Luke. Timothy it could not be, for he was at Rome when St. Paul wrote the epistle (Phil. i. 1). Neither, I apprehend, could it be Silas; he disappears from the page of sacred history at least ten years before the date of the epistle, a circumstance which could not have happened had he continued a fellow-labourer of St. Paul. The last time we hear of him is about A.D. 56, when St. Paul wrote the Second Epistle to the Thessalonians, from Corinth, in which city he preached along with St. Paul, and where he appears to have remained (see 2 Thess. i. 1, and 2 Cor. i. 19). After St. Paul's departure, he probably returned to Jerusalem, and joined St. Peter, for next time we hear of him is in connection with that Apostle (1 Peter v. 12). We are thus led to fix upon St. Luke. The very terms of the message point to one who was a beloved friend as well as a fellow-labourer.

Assuming that the true yoke-fellow and the author of the Acts are identical, we are furnished with the date of the Acts, both with respect to time and place. It was written, or any rate finished, at Philippi, and sent from thence to Theophilus, in the summer of A.D. 63. It ends in one respect abruptly, as every history written by a contemporary inevitably must; but in so far as respects the history of the progress of the Gospel, which it was the author's object to record, the work is brought down to a period at that time certainly the brightest which had yet occurred in its annals. In order to estimate its importance, we must lay aside our knowledge of subsequent events, and view it from the same point as the author did, and, as far as we can, enter into it with the same feelings. His object in the Acts was to record the progress of Christianity, as it had been his object in his 'former treatise' to record its rise. He begins the Acts when the number of Christians together was about a hundred and twenty, and traces the progress of the Gospel throughout Syria, and Asia Minor, into Europe. At the first planting of a Christian Church in this quarter of the globe St. Luke himself assisted; and we have every reason for believing that he continued to labour with success in the same field; that the church at Philippi, with which he was more immediately connected, had received the unqualified approbation of St. Paul; that other churches had sprung up in Macedonia and the more distant regions of Greece; and that the Great Apostle of the Gentiles, he whose career it was his special object to narrate, was then in the capital of the civilised world, 'preaching the kingdom of God, and teaching those things which concern the Lord Jesus Christ with all confidence, no man forbidding him.' If we can divest ourselves of our knowledge of the persecutions which were so soon to follow, it is difficult to imagine a conjuncture which afforded brighter prospects of the success of the cause in which he laboured.

As a history therefore 'the Acts' concludes at a well-marked epoch, and bears the most perfect evidence of having been finished two years after St. Paul's arrival at Rome, which was in spring A.D. 61, and thereby furnishes a date of the utmost importance, for it establishes the earlier date of his Gospel; and that, in its turn, as I shall endeavour to show, establishes the still earlier date of the Gospels of Matthew and Mark. The works of the first three evangelists were therefore written within thirty years after the death of Christ, and the events recorded were within the memory of the then existing generation.

I have stated that Luke concludes the history of the Acts of the Apostles as all contemporary historians must. Let us compare it with one in modern times. Elliot's 'Life of Wellington' contains no mention of the Battle of Waterloo. What modern critic, applying the usual rules of critical research, but would at once explain this omission, by assuming that the book must have been written before the battle was fought, although there is nothing in the date (1815) to prove that it was? But Biblical critics, misled by their own preconceived views, have exhausted their ingenuity to explain away so obvious an inference. What would be said of a modern critic who would account for this author's silence as to the Battle of Waterloo by saying it was an event so well known as to render any notice of it superfluous? yet the same is actually said of St. Luke's silence as to the release of St. Paul. It is interesting to compare the last notices of the career of Wellington given by this author with that of St. Paul as given by St. Luke. After informing us that he went as Ambassador to Paris, the author adds, 'since which period he has resided in that capital, fulfilling the important duties of his station with a degree of judgment and skill which prove that he is no less qualified to support the honour of his country by his diplomatic talents than by his military ones' (p. 572).

Having thus traced St. Luke to what I believe to have been the great scene of his labours, we hear no more of him till near the conclusion of St. Paul's course, when, he (St. Paul) says, he had fought the good fight, and finished his course; when Demas and others had forsaken him, and only Luke was with him. (2 Tim. iv. 7, 10, 11.) Such was the termination of the public life of one who but for his modesty would have ranked as high as a man of action, as he ever must as an able and faithful historian. We have no other well-authenticated notice of him, but tradition says that he died, at an advanced age, a natural death. St. Jerome, in his life of St. Luke, says that he died, unmarried, at the age of eighty-four, and that his bones were transported from Achaia to Constantinople, in the twenty-eighth year of the reign of Constantius.[1]

The style of St. Luke as an historian is clear, animated, and picturesque. This last attribute is of course most obvious when he describes scenes which fell under his own observation.

Combined with these excellences, we find the total want of anything like display or attempt at fine writing, his sole object being to convey the truth to his readers, not to enhance his literary reputation.

When he describes events on the authority of others, his style is purely historical; when he describes those which fell under his own observation, it is eminently autoptical, and has all the minuteness and circumstantiality which almost unavoidably characterise the descriptions of eye-witnesses.

We are indebted to the autopticity of his style for the numerous facts which, combined with the inferences we draw from them, enable us to reconstruct the narrative of the Voyage and Shipwreck. It enables us also to judge with great certainty as to the presence or absence of the author in the transactions which he has recorded. I may here observe that nothing but the most perfect truthfulness could have enabled us to draw conclusions in every instance consistent with themselves, and in numerous cases with facts, the knowledge of which we arrive at by recent discoveries, and which could only have been known to the author from personal observation.

As a voyage-writer St. Luke is possessed of another most essential qualification,—he is thoroughly

[1] *Hieronymi Vita D. Lucæ.*

versed in nautical matters, and describes them in the appropriate language of seamanship.

No man could by any possibility attain so complete a command of nautical language who had not spent a considerable portion of his life at sea—not, however, as a seaman, for his language, although accurate, is not professional. The difference in the manner of describing nautical events by seamen and landsmen is too obvious to require remark; but there is a third class of authors who are, properly speaking, neither seamen nor landsmen. I mean those who from some cause or other have been much at sea, who from living with the officers of the ship, and hearing nautical matters constantly discussed, necessarily acquire the use of the technical language of seamen. An attentive examination of St. Luke's writings shows us that it is to this class of authors that he belongs. How he acquired this knowledge we have no means of knowing; but I cannot help thinking that he must, at some period of his life, have exercised his profession at sea. From the great number of persons which we often hear of in ancient ships,[1] we must suppose that they carried surgeons. Whether St. Luke ever served in that capacity or not is, of course, mere matter of conjecture: one thing is certain, no one unaccustomed to a sea-life could have described the events connected with it with such accuracy as he has done.

But although his descriptions are accurate, they are, as I have already observed, *unprofessional.* The seaman in charge of the ship has his attention perpetu-

[1] The ship in which Josephus went to Rome carried 600. (*Life.*)

ally on the stretch, watching every change or indication of change of wind or weather. He is obliged to decide on the instant what measures must be taken to avail himself of favourable changes or to obviate the consequences of unfavourable ones. Hence in describing them he naturally dwells upon cause and effect. He tells us not only what was done, but why it was done. The impression produced by incidents at sea upon the mind of the passive observer is altogether different, and of course his mode of describing them equally so. He tells us what has happened, but rarely tells us how or why the measures connected with it were taken. In doing so he often mentions circumstances which a seaman would not think of noticing from their familiarity, or from their being matters of course ; and is frequently silent as to those which are of the greatest importance, and which no seaman would pass over.

Now these are exactly the peculiarities which characterise the style of St. Luke as a voyage-writer ; for instance, when the ship was run ashore, he tells us that they loosed the bands of the rudders. A seaman would rather have told us, in the previous stage of the narrative, how the rudders were secured,—a matter of necessity in an ancient ship when anchored by the stern ; and when we remember that it was in the face of a lee shore, in a gale of wind, it must have been one of difficulty, whereas loosing them when they made sail was a mere matter of course. Thus, also, when the shipmen became aware of the proximity of land, no seaman would have neglected to mention what were the indications which led them to 'deem that they drew near to some country' (xxvii. 27).

It would be easy to multiply instances from the

narrative, or to cite analogous ones from the published works of medical men who have written narratives of their voyages; for those who are led by the love of science or adventure to make long voyages frequently become their historians. I prefer, however, making the comparison with a fragment of a journal of an officer in Captain Cook's ship, from the 'United Service Magazine' (May 1842, p. 46). There can be no doubt but that in this case the author was a medical man.[1] The correspondent who communicates it infers that he is so, from the circumstance of a medical case being in the same book. The professional manner in which he describes Captain Cook's remains would have been proof sufficient to me that he was one. I prefer this as a case in point, because we have it as it was written on the spot, without being pruned or worked up for effect, and because we can compare it with the published accounts of the same events written by professional seamen. It exhibits the same peculiarities which I have alluded to, as characterising the style of St. Luke.[2] The author relates the events as they fell

[1] I have no doubt that the author of this interesting fragment is Mr. Anderson, surgeon of the Resolution, Captain Cook's ship, for the following reasons:—He calls the other ship the Discovery, but does not name his own. I find his description of Captain Cook's remains in Captain King's narrative of the voyage. Now it was natural that he should apply to the surgeon of the ship for it; and he accompanies the two captains when they land on a newly-discovered island,—circumstances which clearly point to the principal surgeon of the expedition.

[2] In this respect the fragment presents a curious contrast with Captain King's eloquent account of the recovery and solemn committal to the deep of Captain Cook's remains. By the surgeon's account, some of the bones could not be those of Captain Cook, but he adds, 'We said nothing about it; and some of the bones were brought to the ship the day after the funeral, and dropped into the sea as near as possible to the spot where the other bones were dropped the day before,' a circumstance Captain King says nothing about.

under his observation in correct nautical language, but offers no explanation of the reasons which induced the officers to take the measures which he narrates. Take the following examples :—

'24th Feb. (1779).—In the evening hauled our wind, and stood out clear of the islands.' ('Journal,' p. 46.)

Compare this with Captain King's account :—

'At sunset, observing a shoal which appeared to stretch a considerable distance to the west of Mowee, towards the middle of the passage, and the weather being unsettled, we tacked and stood to the south.' (King's 'Voyage,' p. 84.)

Or the following :—

'28th.—Hauled our wind, and are to stand off and on for the night.' ('Journal,' p. 46.)

'It being too late to run for the road on the south-west side of the island, where we had been last year, we passed the night in standing on and off.' (King's 'Voyage,' p. 88.)

Here it will be observed that the nautical language is quite as correct in the one case as in the other, the only difference being, that the seaman relates the causes of their proceedings, whilst the medical author of the journal omits them.

When St. Luke mentions the incident of hoisting the boat on board, he informs us that it was a work of difficulty (*μόλις*, xxvii. 16), but he does not tell us wherein the difficulty consisted. In like manner, when the author of the journal notices the incident of getting the Resolution's foremast into its place, he merely says :—

'The mast after much trouble and risk was got in.'

Compare this with the accounts given by seamen of the same circumstance :—

'We had the satisfaction of getting the foremast shipped. It was an operation attended with great difficulty and some danger, our ropes being so exceedingly rotten that the purchase gave way several times.' (King's 'Voyage,' p. 79.)

This mode of writing accounts for the omission in the narrative of St. Luke of circumstances which, nautically speaking, were of much importance, and the insertion of others which were of none. But notwithstanding these omissions it is the style of all others best calculated to give us a clear idea of the events of the voyage. We can, generally speaking, infer the causes of the events from the effects, provided they are stated truthfully and accurately ; while the familiarity which a professional man acquires, leads him to pass over circumstances which he knows others with professional knowledge will conclude must have taken place. Walter Scott in one of his letters notices the description of one of the battles in Spain by a volunteer officer who was present, thus :—

'The narrative was very simply told, and conveyed better than any I have seen the impressions which such scenes are likely to make when they have the effect (I had almost said the charm) of novelty. I don't know why it is, I never found a soldier could give me an idea of a battle.' ('Life,' vol. ii. p. 324.)

Had St. Luke's object been to describe a sea-voyage, this style of narrating the events would no doubt have been liable to objections ; but it was no part of his intention to do so, except in so far as the events of the voyage illustrated passages in the life of St. Paul; and but for his circumstantiality when relating events at which he was present, we should probably have known no more than that the Apostle was shipwrecked at Melita on his voyage from Syria to Italy. His notices of events are altogether accidental and fragmentary. He records them simply because he observes them, not because they are intrinsically important. They drop unintentionally from his pen, and are never thrown in for the purpose of heightening the effect, although no doubt they very often do so, as in the account of the visit to Philippi, for it is impossible to write autoptically without at the same time writing graphically. Still less are the circumstances thrown in for the purpose of lending probability to his narrative. On the contrary, they often detract from it—'*Le vrai n'est pas toujours le vraisemblable.*' The most important circumstances probably did not fall under his notice, and he never stops to offer explanations. St. Luke, however, possesses two qualifications as a voyage-writer, which in a great degree compensate for his omissions, and which enable us to supply many of them with the greatest certainty. The first of these is his perfect acquaintance with nautical matters, and the second his accuracy. No man who was not in an eminent degree gifted with this quality could have given a narrative capable of being tested as his has been in the following examination. He must not only have been an accurate observer, but his memory must have been accurate, and his habits of thought and reasoning not less so. Hence his facts afford the firmest grounds for resting inferences upon, and these, in their turn, furnish data for mathematical reasoning. The reader may give an incredulous smile at working the dead reckoning of a ship from such disjointed and apparently vague notices : yet I have done so, and the result is nearer than I could have expected beforehand, had it been the journal of a modern ship, and had her log-book been lying before me.[1]

[1] Extraordinary as is the coincidence above alluded to, it has received a confirmation not less extraordinary. My friend Dr. Howson found amongst the papers of the late Admiral Sir Charles Penrose a calculation of the course and distance. 'With respect to the distance,' Admiral Penrose observes, 'allowing the degree of strength of the gale to vary a little occasionally, I consider that a ship would drift at the rate of about one mile and a half per hour, which at the end of fourteen complete days would amount to 504 miles. But it does not appear that the calculation is to be made for fourteen entire days. It was on the fourteenth night the anchors were cast off the shores of Melita. The distance from the south of Clauda to the north of Malta, measured on the best chart I have, is 490 miles ; and is it possible for coincident calculations of such a nature to be more exact? In fact, on one chart, after I had calculated the supposed drift, as a seaman, to be 504 miles, I measured the distance to be 503.' (Conybeare and Howson's *St. Paul*, vol. ii. p. 346, note.)

Before comparing Admiral Penrose's calculation with mine, it will be right to estimate, as nearly as the narrative will allow, the time elapsed from the departure of the ship from Fair Havens till her departure from Clauda, and from thence till 'the shipmen deemed they drew near to some country' (Acts xxvii. 27). The departure from Clauda must have been on the first day, after mid-day and before midnight ; taking the mean, the time is about thirteen days and six hours. Now the distance of the point at the entrance of St. Paul's Bay from Clauda is, according to the accurate determinations of longitude and latitude of Admiral Smyth, 476·6 miles, which, at the rate of drift assumed by Admiral Penrose, would take 13 days, 5 hours, 47 min. According to my calculation it would take 13 days, 1 hour, 21 min. ; or, reckoning the distance, that given by the rate assumed by Admiral Penrose is 477 miles, by mine $483\frac{1}{2}$, the actual distance from Clauda to St. Paul's Bay being $476\frac{1}{2}$ miles. I may well say with Admiral Penrose, 'Is it possible for coincident observations of such a nature to be more exact?' Certainly none could have been more independent of each other, as my calculations, which were first published, were made in entire ignorance of the previous calculations of Admiral Penrose.

The care which St. Luke takes, on all occasions, to select the most appropriate expressions, and the precision which results from it, are very remarkable; thus, to express the progression of a ship, we have not only the substantive πλοῦς (xxvii. 9), but not less than fourteen verbs expressing the same thing, but with a distinction indicating the particular circumstances of the ship at the time. I may add that, with the exception of the last three, they are all nautical expressions. They are also peculiar to the writings of St. Luke, occurring both in the Gospel and the Acts, but are not used by any of the other New Testament writers. The following is the list:—

1. Πλέω. Luke viii. 23; Acts xxi. 3, &c. &c.
2. Ἀποπλέω. Acts xiii. 4, xiv. 26, xx. 15, xxvii. 1.
3. Βραδυπλοέω. Acts xxvii. 7.
4. Διαπλέω. Acts xxvii. 5.
5. Ἐκπλέω. Acts xv. 39, xviii. 18, xx. 6.
6. Καταπλέω. Luke viii. 26.
7. Ὑποπλέω. Acts xxvii. 4, 7.
8. Παραπλέω. Acts xx. 16.
9. Εὐθυδρομέω. Acts xvi. 11, xxi. 1.
10. Ὑποτρέχω. Acts xxvii. 16.
11. Παραλέγομαι. Acts xxvii. 8, 13.
12. Φέρομαι. Acts xxvii. 15.
13. Διαφέρομαι. Acts xxvii. 27.
14. Διαπεράω. Acts xxi. 2.

The reader cannot fail, in perusing his writings, to remark how much precision is thus given to his descriptions, and in how few words they are expressed.

It may be asked, how can we be certain that the nautical language of St. Luke is so correct?

The reply is, in the first place, that it must be a real language and correctly used, which admits of being deciphered as it has been. In the account of the voyage I have cited the case of a German physician, who made a voyage in the same seas, and in some part of it under very similar circumstances; but although he obviously intended to give an account of his voyage, his statements are not only confused, but impossible, and we have no difficulty in seeing that he does not understand what he is writing about.

Independently however of this consideration, it so happens that although ancient literature is scanty in the department of voyages, it is not so in the terminology of seamanship. Julius Pollux, in his 'Onomasticon,' has given many pages of Greek nautical terms and phrases. It will be seen by the notes that a large proportion of those employed by St. Luke are to be found in this author.

I now proceed to inquire into the nature of the materials from which St. Luke drew up his historical works; but before I do so, it will be convenient to state shortly what I believe were the historical records of Christianity when St. Luke visited Judea, *circa* A.D. 58, and when, as I have already stated, there is good reason to believe that he wrote his Gospel.

In my 'Dissertation on the Origin and Connection of the Gospels,' I have stated the evidence from which I conclude—first, that several of the Apostles, including Matthew, Peter and John, drew up memoirs of our Lord's transactions immediately after they took place, some of which, certainly Peter's, were in the language of the country, i.e. Syro-Chaldaic, or Aramaic, known in the New Testament and works of the Fathers as Hebrew, or as the *native* language (πατρίῳ); second, that St. Peter's memoirs were the original, which, being afterwards translated by St. Mark, now forms the Gospel of Mark; third, that when the apostles were driven by persecution from Judea, St. Matthew drew up from these memoirs a history of our Lord's life in Hebrew and Greek; the Greek version being the same as our first Gospel.

That several such narratives had been written when St. Luke composed his Gospel, may be gathered from his preface, in which he informs us—first, that 'many had undertaken to draw up a digest of the things which had been accomplished' (v. 1); and, next, that 'those who from the beginning were eye-witnesses and ministers of the word had delivered such accounts unto us' (παρέδοσαν ἡμῖν); or in other words, that he was in possession of such accounts, for the word 'us' must include St. Luke. Eusebius clearly understands that St. Luke means himself in particular, for he quotes the passage in the third person, παρέδοσαν αὐτῷ, 'delivered to him,'—and rightly concludes that he meant to assure Theophilus that such were the authorities which he had made use of. He tells us—

'One of these (St. Luke's writings) is his Gospel, in which he testifies that he has recorded as those who were from the beginning eye-witnesses and ministers of the word delivered *to him*, whom also, he says, he in all things followed.' (H. E. iii. 4. Cruze's Translation.)[1]

[1] Origen also tells us that Luke wrote what he had received (παρέλαβε) from eye-witnesses and ministers of the word (Homil. in *Luc.* opp. iii. 932); and Irenæus, that he wrote his Gospel, as he himself testifies, saying 'Quemadmodum tradiderunt nobis qui ab initio contemplatores et ministri fuerunt Verbi.'

The word 'many' is a relative term, and has reference probably to the literary habits of Judea, and the time which had elapsed since the events which he has recorded occurred : just as Alison, in his preface to the history of the French Revolution, speaks of his authorities : 'Although so short a time has elapsed since the termination of these events, the materials which have been collected for their elucidation have already become, beyond all precedent, interesting and ample. (Vol. i. p. 29.) Neither St. Luke nor Alison says that they made use of such materials. Why should they? Is it possible that St. Luke should write to Theophilus that he was anxious that he should know the certainty of the things in which he had been instructed ; that he had carefully investigated everything from the beginning, and that he was in possession of the accounts of those personally engaged in the transactions ; and yet that we should be in doubt as to whether or not he made use of such authorities? I conclude therefore that St. Luke's preface was meant to assure his readers that his authorities were eye-witnesses and ministers of the word. St. Matthew was an eye-witness and minister of the word ; and it becomes a question, whether St. Luke made any use of his Gospel in drawing up his own.

This can only be ascertained by comparing the two accounts. Now we have not to go far before we have evidence to prove that he did make use of St. Matthew's Gospel. The parallelism between the Gospels begins with the public life of our Lord (Matt. iii. 1, Luke iii. 1) ; and at the 7th verse of the 3rd chapter of St. Luke we find a passage, extending to three verses, agreeing verbally with four verses of the same account in the Gospel of St. Matthew (vv. 7, 8, 9, 10). Here, at least, St. Luke must have taken from a *written* account in the same language; and when I find such a passage in the work of an eye-witness and minister of the word, I am satisfied that I have traced it to its source. We have not to go far for another example of the same kind, for the 16th and 17th verses of the same chapter correspond verbally with the 11th and 12th verses of St. Matthew's account. There are many others of the same nature. If examples can be adduced where similar agreements arise from any other cause than transcription from a work in the same language, I am quite ready to abandon my hypothesis; but as I am confident that no such case can be adduced, I feel entitled to call the attention of the reader to the consequences which flow from the establishment of a point of such importance in the evidences of the origin of the Christian religion. Had St. Luke's writings never been heard of till now, had they been discovered for the first time among the papyri of Herculaneum, would any doubt have been entertained, with such evidence before us, that the author had made use of the Gospel of St. Matthew as one of his authorities? It would have been held as the most valuable of all the ancient external evidences of the authenticity of that Gospel, as indeed it is, because it is at once the fullest and the most ancient, and because the author had the most ample means of knowing that it was indeed the work of an eye-witness. It proves that the Gospel of St. Matthew, as we now have it, was known to an author who wrote less than thirty years after the transactions, and when they must have been within the memory of a large portion of the then existing generation.

My present object, however, is not to look at the consequences of my researches, but to consider the evidences upon which my conclusions rest. I must therefore, if I can, obviate the objections which have been made to the supposition that St. Luke made use of the Gospel of St. Matthew. They all resolve themselves into the negative one, that if St. Luke had known of the previous Gospel he would have written differently from what he has done. Arguments which rest upon the opinion of critics never can overthrow positive proofs. Amongst those who have called my conclusions respecting the connection between Luke and Matthew in question, I may mention Mr. Alford, and Professor Thiersch of Marburg. Both of these critics admit the identity of the above-cited passages. Mr. Alford in his note observes that the agreement 'indicates a common origin;' and Professor Thiersch, who agrees with me entirely as to the originality of the second Gospel, and the use made of it by St. Luke, observes in a letter to me that—

'There were more written accounts than St. Mark's Gospel which they could make use of; and it is in this way that I should like to explain those coincidences in Matthew and Luke for which there are no parallels in Mark. In Germany we are in a continual struggle with Strauss and other sceptical antagonists of sacred history; and therefore we feel more of that difficulty, with which you are less urged in England, viz.: If Luke had before his eyes the two first chapters of Matthew, how could he neglect them entirely?—If he did so, he must have ascribed very little value to them.'

The explanation of the connection between St. Luke and St. Matthew which I have to offer is, that the former meant to make his Gospel at once supplementary for those who possessed St. Matthew's Gospel, and intelligible to those who did not. But it would not have been intelligible had he resolutely admitted everything in St. Matthew ; whilst, on the other hand, had he included everything in St. Matthew, his Gospel would have exceeded the length consistent with a wide circulation, when the only means of multiplying copies depended on transcription. Admitting this conjecture, which at least is a probable one, it furnishes us with a reason for the omissions in St. Luke's Gospel of important matter which we find in St. Matthew's Gospel. St. Luke leaves it out because St. Matthew had already recorded it.

Both Professor Thiersch and Mr. Alford adduce the difference in the two first chapters of St. Matthew's and St. Luke's Gospels as proofs that St. Luke could not have seen that of St. Matthew. But there is nothing contradictory in the two accounts. Mr. Alford observes truly enough that 'The *only* inference from the account in these two chapters, *which is inevitable*, is that they are wholly independent of one another.' It is quite true that in their accounts of the early portion of our Lord's life they are independent of one another ; but independence is no proof that the later writer was ignorant of the work of his predecessor. Selection is the rule of all the evangelists. St. John repeatedly tells us that there were many things which Jesus did that are not written in his Gospel. It has been supposed, and, I think, with much probability, that St. Luke's authority for the first two chapters in his Gospel was the mother of our Lord. The events related are such as His mother must have known and was likely to narrate; they relate to private and domestic matters, whilst those in Matthew relate to public and historical events—events about which St. Luke was silent, because they were already related by St. Matthew.

The conclusion to which a minute comparison between the two Gospels has led me is, that St. Luke was in possession of the present Greek Gospel of St. Matthew; that he did make occasional use of it, chiefly for the purpose of rendering his own account of the transactions and sayings of our Lord more complete, thereby proving that it (the Greek Gospel) was the work of 'an eye-witness and minister of the word.'[1]

This is no contradiction to the patristic evidence that St. Matthew wrote in Hebrew; nor do I hold the supposition that he wrote in two languages to be a compromise between competing evidence. The state of Judæa with respect to language at the time required that any work meant for all classes of its inhabitants should be bi-lingual. Josephus, who was the contemporary of St. Matthew, and who wrote like him for the use of the Jews, informs us in his preface to his Greek history of the Jews' Wars, that he had also written it in his native language (*πατρίῳ*, the word used by Eusebius for the original language of St. Matthew), for the use of those who did not understand Greek (*οἱ βάρβαροι*).

The conditions of the agreements which subsist

[1] The discovery of the Curetonian Syriac MS. satisfies me that Luke was also possessed of the original Aramaic Gospel of Matthew, and made use of it in the composition of his Gospel; for proof of this, see the concluding pages of this article.

between Luke and Mark are altogether different from those between Luke and Matthew. In Luke and Matthew we have two historians writing in the same language; but in Luke and Mark we have an historian (Luke) who uses an original autoptical memoir in another language (Peter), which is translated by Mark, and which had also been made use of by the preceding historian (Matthew). These are the agreements of contemporary historians, and are so simple in themselves, and of such every-day occurrence, that I question if we can examine any series of contemporary writers who narrate the same transactions in a language different from that of the persons engaged in them, without meeting with them all. I have elsewhere[1] illustrated this view of the connection of the three first Gospels by examples from the historians Alison, Napier and Suchet, who hold the same relation to the events of the Peninsular campaigns in respect to time, which Luke, Matthew and Mark hold to the events in the life of our Saviour; Alison being an historian who takes as his authorities the accounts of those who witnessed the transactions; and when it suits his purpose to give extracts from the originals, he transcribes from Napier and translates from Suchet; just as Luke, when he extracts from the originals, transcribes where the language is the same, translates where it is different. Now I find, when I compare the passages peculiar to Luke and Matthew, the phenomena are those of transcription; when I compare the passages peculiar to Luke and Mark, the phenomena are those of translation. Hence I arrive at the conclusion that Mark is a translator. But it may

[1] *Dissertation on the Gospels*, pp. xxvii, xxxii.

be asked, if the Gospel of Mark be a translation of memoirs written by Peter, why is it not called the Gospel of Peter? To this I answer, that the title it bears is only that affixed to it by tradition, for the work itself is anonymous; and I cannot admit that traditional evidence can supersede that which is the result of inductive reasoning.

In holding that Mark is the translator of Peter's memoirs, I do not rest altogether on the evidence drawn from the study of the phenomena, for the earliest quotation from the second Gospel is that by Justin Martyr, who gives it expressly *as it is written* in his (Peter's) memoirs—*γεγράφθαι ἐν τοῖς ἀπομνημονεύμασιν αὐτοῦ* (Πέτρου).[1] So also Jerome, in speaking of Mark's Gospel, says it is called *his* (Peter's).[2]

Assuming that we have in the three first Gospels a case of contemporary historians, the same as the very common one of Alison, Napier and Suchet, the nature of the agreement between them ought to be the same as that which we find between the modern historians. I have already adduced one between Luke and Matthew. As an example of that between Luke and Mark, I take that which I have alluded to in the introduction, as having first called my attention to the subject. It is perhaps the most instructive I

[1] *Apol.* ii. p. 333.

[2] *Cat. Sacr. Eccl.* c. i.: 'Evangelium juxta Marcum . . . hujus (sc. Petri) dicitur.'

Bishop Pearson says on this point, 'Marci evangelium credebant veteres nihil aliud fuisse quam Petri ἀπομνημονεύματα' (Vindiciæ Ignatianæ). And Bishop Gleig, 'I am inclined to think likewise, that the Gospel by St. Mark contains little more than similar notes and memorandums which had been made by St. Peter, which will sufficiently account for many of the ancients calling it St. Peter's Gospel. (*Directions for the Study of Divinity*, p. 409.)

could select, because it is entirely free from the complication which arises from being mixed up with matter drawn from other authorities. It is also one of the few cases in which St. Matthew makes no use of the original of St. Mark, i.e. the memoir of St. Peter. We have here, then, the very simple case of an historian drawing up an account of an event from two preceding works, one of which is in a different language.

CHRIST STILLS THE TEMPEST.

MATT. VIII.	LUKE VIII.	MARK IV.
	22 'Εγένετο δὲ	35 Καὶ λέγει αὐτοῖς
	ἐν μιᾷ τῶν ἡμερῶν,	ἐν ἐκείνῃ τῇ ἡμέρᾳ,
		ὀψίας γενομένης,
23 Καὶ ἐμβάντι αὐτῷ	καὶ αὐτὸς ἀνέβη	
εἰς πλοῖον,	εἰς πλοῖον	
ἠκολούθησαν αὐτῷ	καὶ	
οἱ μαθηταὶ αὐτοῦ.	οἱ μαθηταὶ αὐτοῦ·	
	καὶ εἶπεν πρὸς αὐτούς,	See first line.
See v. 18.	Διέλθωμεν	Διέλθωμεν
	εἰς τὸ πέραν τῆς λίμνης·	εἰς τὸ πέραν.
		36 Καὶ ἀφέντες τὸν
		ὄχλον παραλαμβάνουσιν
		αὐτὸν ὡς ἦν ἐν τῷ
		πλοίῳ καὶ ἄλλα
		πλοῖα ἦν μετ' αὐτοῦ.
	Καὶ ἀνήχθησαν.	
	23 Πλεόντων δὲ αὐτῶν	
	ἀφύπνωσεν.	
24 Καὶ ἰδοὺ	καὶ κατέβη	37 καὶ γίνεται
σεισμὸς μέγας	λαῖλαψ	λαῖλαψ μεγάλη
ἐγένετο	ἀνέμου	ἀνέμου,
ἐν τῇ θαλάσσῃ,	εἰς τὴν λίμνην·	
ὥστε τὸ πλοῖον καλύπ-		
τεσθαι ὑπὸ τῶν κυμάτων·		
		καὶ τὰ κύματα ἐπέβαλλεν
		εἰς τὸ πλοῖον, ὥστε ἤδη
	καὶ συνεπληροῦντο,	γεμίζεσθαι τὸ πλοῖον.
	καὶ ἐκινδύνευον.	
αὐτὸς δὲ		38 Καὶ ἦν αὐτὸς
		ἐν τῇ πρύμνῃ
		ἐπὶ τὸ προσκεφάλαιον,
ἐκάθευδεν.		καθεύδων,

MATT. VIII.	LUKE VIII.	MARK IV.
25 Καὶ προσελθόντες	24 Προσελθόντες δὲ	καὶ
ἤγειραν αὐτὸν	διήγειραν αὐτόν,	ἐγείρουσιν αὐτόν,
λέγοντες,	λέγοντες,	καὶ λέγουσιν αὐτῷ,
Κύριε,	Ἐπιστάτα, ἐπιστάτα,	Διδάσκαλε,
σῶσον,		οὐ μέλει σοι ὅτι
ἀπολλύμεθα.	ἀπολλύμεθα.	ἀπολλύμεθα;
26 Καὶ λέγει αὐτοῖς,		
Τί δειλοί ἐστε,		
ὀλιγόπιστοι;		
τότε ἐγερθεὶς	Ὁ δὲ διεγερθεὶς	39 Καὶ διεγερθεὶς
ἐπετίμησεν τοῖς ἀνέμοις	ἐπετίμησε τῷ ἀνέμῳ	ἐπετίμησεν τῷ ἀνέμῳ,
καὶ	καὶ	καὶ εἶπεν
τῇ θαλάσσῃ,	τῷ κλύδωνι τοῦ ὕδατος,	τῇ θαλάσσῃ,
		Σιώπα, πεφίμωσο.
	καὶ ἐπαύσαντο	Καὶ ἐκόπασεν ὁ ἄνεμος
καὶ ἐγένετο γαλήνη	καὶ ἐγένετο γαλήνη.	καὶ ἐγένετο γαλήνη
μεγάλη.		μεγάλη.
	25 Εἶπεν δὲ αὐτοῖς,	40 Καὶ εἶπεν αὐτοῖς,
		Τί δειλοί ἐστε;
	Ποῦ ἡ πίστις ὑμῶν;	οὔπω ἔχετε πίστιν;
27 Οἱ δὲ ἄνθρωποι		
	Φοβηθέντες δὲ	41 Καὶ ἐφοβήθησαν
		φόβον μέγαν,
ἐθαύμασαν,	ἐθαύμασαν,	
λέγοντες,	λέγοντες πρὸς ἀλλήλους,	καὶ ἔλεγον πρὸς ἀλλήλους,
Ποταπός ἐστιν οὗτος,	Τίς ἄρα οὗτός ἐστιν,	Τίς ἄρα οὗτός ἐστιν,
ὅτι καὶ οἱ ἄνεμοι	ὅτι καὶ τοῖς ἀνέμοις	ὅτι καὶ ὁ ἄνεμος
	ἐπιτάσσει	
καὶ ἡ θάλασσα	καὶ τῷ ὕδατι,	καὶ ἡ θάλασσα
αὐτῷ ὑπακούουσιν;	καὶ ὑπακούουσιν αὐτῷ;	ὑπακούει αὐτῷ;

TRANSLATION.

MATT. VIII.	LUKE VIII.	MARK IV.
	22 And it came to pass	35 And
	on one of the days,	on that day,
		when even was come,
23 And when he was	that he	
entered into a boat,	entered into a boat	
his disciples	and his disciples;	
followed him.	and	
	he said to them,	he saith unto them,
	Let us go over to the	Let us go over to the
	other side of the lake.	other side.

MATT. VIII.	LUKE VIII.	MARK IV.
		36 And having sent
		away the people, they
		take him just as he
		was in the boat ;
		and there were
	And they put off.	other boats with him.
	23 And as they sailed	
	he fell asleep.	
24 And, behold,	And	37 And
	there came down	there arises
a great disturbance	a squall	a great squall
arose	of wind	of wind ;
in the sea,	into the lake,	
so that the boat		
was being covered with		
the waves :		and the waves were
		beating into the boat
	and	so that the boat
	they were being filled	was now filling.
	and were in jeopardy.	
but he slept.		And he was sleeping
		at the stern, on the
		seat cover :
25 And having gone	24 But having gone to	And
to him	him	
they awoke him,	they woke him up,	they awake him,
saying,	saying,	and say to him,
Lord,	Master, Master,	Teacher,
save *us*,		carest thou not that
we perish.	we perish.	we perish ?
26 And he saith to		
them,		
Why are you afraid,		
O ye of little faith ?		
Then he arose, and	But he rose up, and	And he rose up, and
rebuked the winds	rebuked the wind	rebuked the wind,
and	and the raging of	and said unto
the sea ;	the water ;	the sea,
		Peace, be still.
	and they ceased,	And the wind fell,
and there was	and there was	and there was
a great calm.	a calm.	a great calm.
	But he said to them,	And he said to them,
		Why are you afraid ?
	Where *is* your faith ?	Have ye
		not yet faith ?

MATT. VIII.	LUKE VIII.	MARK IV.
27 But the men	But they	41 And they
	being afraid	feared with great fear,
wondered,	wondered,	
saying,	saying one to another,	and said one to another
What man is this,	Who then is this,	Who then is this
that even the winds	that even the winds	that even the wind
	he commandeth	
and the sea	and the water,	and the sea
obey him?	and they obey him?	obeys him?

Here the accounts of Sts. Luke and Mark are obviously too closely connected to admit the supposition that they are separate and independent accounts of the same event; one of them must therefore be taken from the other, or both from a common source. This last supposition is so far true that the accounts bear internal proofs of being derived from an original in another language. But St. Mark's account bears the strongest internal evidence of having been written by an eye-witness. It must, therefore, be a translation of an autoptical memoir; and a literal translation of an autoptical memoir may be held as an original authority where the original itself is lost.

It is right, however, to observe that the second Gospel is held by Griesbach and others to be a compilation from the Gospels of Sts. Matthew and Luke. According to this view, what I hold to be omissions on the part of St. Luke are additions on the part of St. Mark, and what I hold to be additions on the part of St. Luke are omissions on the part of St. Mark.

I come first to the matter which is peculiar to St. Mark. He states—

1st. The particular day on which the miracle took place.

2nd. The time of day.

3rd. The dismissal of the multitude.

4th. That the disciples took our Lord into the boat 'even as he was.'

5th. That there were other boats in company.

6th. That our Lord was in the stern of the boat.

7th. That he was reposing on the seat cover.

8th. The words with which he rebuked the storm.

Here are no less than eight facts mentioned in this short account, not one of which could possibly be taken from either of the other evangelists; for they are neither expressly noticed, nor can they be inferred from their accounts. With the exception of the date, they are all purely autoptical, such as an eye-witness would very naturally relate, but such as an historian would omit, because they do not affect the main event, neither do they render the other accounts clearer.

Let us subject the matter which is peculiar to St. Luke's account to a similar examination—

1st. He leaves the date undetermined.

2nd. He adds that it was 'the lake' to which the expression 'the other side' refers.

3rd. The nautical expression, 'They shoved off, and when under way.'

4th. That the squall 'came down on the lake.'

5th. That they were in danger.

6th. That the disciples were astonished at the events as well as terrified.

1st. With regard to the date, when we examine the context carefully, it will be found that there is a difference between Sts. Matthew and Mark with respect to the time when the event took place. I have already shown that St. Luke made use of St. Matthew's Gospel. I am now showing that he also made use of St. Mark's. Had he in this case adopted the arrangement of St. Matthew, he must have differed from that of St. Mark; with both before him, by using the expression 'on one of the days,' he differs from neither. We have, therefore, an obvious reason why he left the exact day undetermined.

2nd. The expression *τὸ πέραν*, 'the other side,' applied to the eastern side of the lake, is a provincialism, or rather Capernaumism, which St. Luke corrects by explaining that it is 'the other side of the lake' which is meant. Here also the reason for the addition is obvious.

3rd. The nautical expressions are characteristic of St. Luke's style of describing nautical events; they give great clearness to the narrative, and they can be inferred with certainty from the other accounts.

4th. By the expression *κατέβη*, St. Luke, by a single word, gives the effect of the particular kind of squall with perfect precision, and at the same time corrects the Hebraism of St. Matthew, who speaks of a great disturbance in the *sea*.

5th. 'They were in danger' (*καὶ ἐκινδύνευον*). St. Luke here supplies a qualification, the want of which in the other Gospels is remarked by Dr. Bloomfield in his notes on the passage.

6th. The effects of the miracle upon the disciples are described by St. Matthew as those of 'wonder,'—by St. Mark, of 'fear.' St. Luke combines them both, 'They, being afraid, wondered.'

There are none of these additions but what are either inevitable inferences from the statements in St.

Mark's account, or are taken from St. Matthew's, and in each of them we can see a reason for its insertion.

I hold, therefore, that in the preceding Gospels we have the materials from which St. Luke drew up his account of this miracle; that it is based upon that in the second Gospel, but completed from that in the first. I hold, also, that the original of the second Gospel existed in a different language from Greek when St. Luke wrote his.

In order to ascertain this point, we must lay out of sight all the changes made by St. Luke as an historian, and also the matter which he has taken from St. Matthew, and confine the comparison to passages in which he has adhered to the account in St. Mark. Where he has done so, I find twenty-one lines in which there is no change except that which arises from translation. Of these, eight lines are expressed in identical terms and thirteen in synonymous terms. This is about the usual proportion which we find in independent translations. Thus, in the example of independent translations from the French given in my former work, consisting of nineteen lines, I find that there are eight lines identical and eleven synonymous or translational. St. Mark then is a translator; but if a translator, he must be the translator of St. Peter, and by that designation he is known by the earliest Christian writers,—'Mark, the translator of Peter,' *Μάρκος ἑρμηνευτὴς Πέτρου*, being the designation given to him by Papias, the first writer by whom he is mentioned.

I have already glanced at the external evidence which would lead us to conclude that St. Peter was the original author of the second Gospel. The internal evidence furnished by a minute examination is not less conclusive. The author of the account of stilling the tempest, whoever he was, was a Galilean residing on the western shore of the lake; he must have been in the boat when the event happened, and he must have been familiar with the navigation of the lake: all of which characteristics agree with those of St. Peter. But we can come still nearer to him, for he relates, as an eye-witness would, things which could only be known to three of the disciples—Peter, James, and John; such as what took place in the house of Jairus (v. 37 ff.), at the transfiguration (ix. 2 ff.), and in the house of Peter (i. 29–31). In this last case we can strike off James and John. They are mentioned as being present, but only as spectators; and no mention is made of Peter, who must also have been present. But a man does not think it necessary to say he was in his own house. Lastly, he speaks of Peter's house exactly as the owner would. Who but Peter would think it necessary to tell us that Andrew was a joint tenant? I have elsewhere entered into the evidence at greater length; for my present purpose it is sufficient to show that St. Luke, in making use of such an authority as we find in St. Mark, was making use of the best historical evidence, that of 'an eye-witness and minister of the word.'

St. Luke's connection with St. Paul gave rise to an early tradition that he was indebted to that Apostle for the matter of his Gospel. Tertullian mentions it, but only as a tradition, which he accounts for by saying that 'it was natural to ascribe to the master what the disciple promulgated.'[1] Origen states that the

[1] 'Lucæ digestum Paulo ascribere solent. Capit magistrorum videri quæ discipuli promulgarint.' (*Adv. Marcion.* iv. 5.)

Gospel was praised by Paul.[1] Irenæus, indeed, goes further, and says that 'Luke wrote what Paul preached;' but he says elsewhere that 'Luke delivered to us what he had learned from the Apostles, as he himself testifies in his preface;'[2] we can lay no weight, therefore, upon this assertion, further than that when he wrote, the tradition alluded to was prevalent and in his mind at the time.

We must, however, suppose that Paul communicated to Luke accounts of his own transactions and spoken addresses; but we cannot suppose that St. Paul preached in the historical style in which St. Luke wrote. There is indeed one great historical event in the life of our Lord narrated by St. Paul, which he stated that he had received by revelation, namely the institution of the Lord's Supper (1 Cor. xi. 23 ff.), which, if my views of the time and place of writing the Gospel be correct, we should expect to find made use of by St. Luke as an authority. Now it has been long observed that St. Luke's account agrees more nearly with St. Paul's than with any of the others. There are indeed, or rather there were, difficulties which a minute comparison suggested, difficulties which have not escaped modern criticism; for example the passage in the received text—'*καὶ εἶπε, λάβετε, φάγετε,*' 'and said, Take, eat'—occurs in St. Matthew's account, but not in St. Luke's. Upon this, De Wette observes, 'It is not probable that Matthew was acquainted with Paul's

[1] Καὶ τὸ τρίτον τὸ κατὰ Λουκᾶν, τὸ ὑπὸ Παύλου ἐπαινούμενον εὐαγγέλιον. (Ap. Euseb. *H. E.* vi. 25.) Origin evidently alludes to 2 Cor. viii. 18, and supposes Paul meant the Gospel of St. Luke by the expression τὸν ἀδελφόν, οὗ ὁ ἔπαινος ἐν τῷ εὐαγγελίῳ.

[2] 'Lucas . . . ea quæ ab eis (Apostolis) didicerat tradidit nobis, sicut ipse testificatur, dicens,' &c.

account;' and it would contradict Paul's account that he had received it from the Lord, were we to suppose he got it from Matthew. In the early MSS., however, no such difficulty exists, for the passage does not occur in the account in the Epistle to the Corinthians. The agreement is then too close to admit of any supposition, except that one of the accounts must be taken from the other; and as St. Paul informs us that he had received his 'of the Lord,' St. Luke must have taken his from it.

Since the foregoing pages were written, new and important light has been thrown upon the writings of St. Matthew and St. Luke, by the discovery of a more ancient Syriac manuscript of the Gospels than any hitherto known, by the late Rev. Dr. Cureton; and a careful examination of the Gospel according to St. Matthew led that eminent scholar to conclude 'that this Syrian text of the Gospel of St. Matthew has, to a great extent, retained the identical terms and expressions which the Apostle himself employed.' Such a conclusion, cautiously, but as respects the author's own conviction decidedly expressed, and coming from such a quarter, if not a reason for adopting it, was at least one for giving it a most minute and searching examination. As a first step, and in order to ascertain the precise relations between the Syriac and the Greek, I transcribed the *textus receptus* of the Greek of Matthew, line for line, on paper of the same size and with the lines at the same distance as the printed text of the literal translation of the Syriac, so that by laying the columns beside each other I could see at a glance how far they agreed or disagreed; the result was sufficiently remarkable, both as to agreement and variation. I found that every line of the literal translation from the Syriac was represented in, and had the same meaning as the Greek version; there was, however, one striking exception at chapter xx. 28, where I found a gap of no less than eighteen lines. On consulting Dr. Cureton's preface, I found that the Codex Bezæ contained a Greek version of the missing lines with the exception of the two last, which, however, I discovered as forming the conclusion in the parallel passage in the Gospel of St. Luke (xiv. 8, 9, 10),—a proof, as I hope to show, that the original Syriac was known and used by that Evangelist. But before I do so I must first inquire how far the phenomena elicited by so minute a comparison confirm or disprove the conclusions of Dr. Cureton that the Syriac is virtually identical with the original Gospel of St. Matthew, written in the then vernacular language of Judæa, termed Hebrew in the New Testament and by the Fathers.

My present object is to elucidate the origin of St. Luke's historical works, but I must in the first place endeavour to show that the minute comparison to which I have subjected the Curetonian Syriac, with the Greek version of St. Matthew's Gospel, leads to the irresistible conclusion that we are now in possession of the original so-called Hebrew Gospel of St. Matthew, with no alterations but such as the gradual changes in a language unfixed by important literary works, must in the course of centuries inevitably produce. So far, the result of the present inquiry is in confirmation of Dr. Cureton's conclusions; but it goes further,—it furnishes fresh and independent evidence of what I have alluded to in the foregoing pages, but stated more fully in my 'Dissertation on the Origin and Connection of the Gospels' (p. lxi); I mean that we have in the first Greek Gospel what I would call an 'authorial' translation—that is, a translation made by an author of his own work. I may here add that I consider that the characteristic feature of such a translation is its combination with *revision.* I cannot indeed produce many cases in point where authors do as I suppose Matthew to have done,—first to write in one language and then translate their work into another,—but in every case in which I can, I find the translation is also revised. Thus, Mr. Beckford wrote his romance of 'Vathek' in French and afterwards translated it it into English, the English version having on its title, 'corrected and *revised.*' Lord Mahon, now Earl Stanhope, wrote the 'Life of Condé' in French and then translated it, at least superintended the translation. He states in the preface that it is *revised.* My friend Dr. Alexander Blair made a translation in correspondence with the author of the original, who insisted on its being revised; and another friend, the Rev. John M'Leod Campbell, wrote a tract in two languages, English and Gaelic, which he also revised. One can easily understand why it should be so.

I shall now inquire how far the phenomena indicated by a comparison of the Curetonian Syriac with the Greek version of the Gospel of St. Matthew contains evidence of revision as well as of translation.

This will be best illustrated by examples taken from Dr. Cureton's literal translation of the Syriac, compared with a literal translation from the Greek.

The following may serve as examples of the nature of the revision :—

SYRIAC.	GREEK.
Matt. i. 16, *To whom was espoused* Mary *the Virgin.*	The husband of Mary.
i. 22, By *the mouth of Esaia:* the prophet.	By the prophet.
ii. 7, Appeared *to them*	Appeared
ii. 20, Seeking the life of the boy *to take it away*	Seeking the life of the young child
iii. 5, *The children of* Jerusalem	Jerusalem
iii. 10, The axe is *arrived* upon the root	The axe is *laid* at the root
iii. 14, *John* forbade	*He* forbade
iv. 1, The spirit of *holiness*	The spirit
iv. 21, While they were *sitting* in the boat	In the ship
iv. 24, *Upon each one of them* he was *laying his hand and* was healing them all.	He healed them.
v. 18, One *letter* Yod.	One iota.
v. 23, Against thee *in enmity.*	Against thee.
vi. 30, *Gathered and falleth* into the oven	Cast into the oven
vii. 21, *He shall enter into heaven's kingdom*	Om. Gr.
vii. 22, Have we not *in thy name eaten and drunk, and* in thy name prophesied?	did we not prophesy in thy name?
viii, 9, I am a man that is under authority, *and there is to me authority also to me*	I am a man under authority

Or take an entire passage (Matthew xvi. 13–14).

SYRIAC.	GREEK.
He was asking his disciples,	He was asking his disciples,
and saying,	saying,
What say men concerning me	Whom do men say
that I am? who forsooth	that
is this Son of man?	The Son of man is?
His disciples say to him,	But they said

SYRIAC.	GREEK.
There are who say that	Some indeed (οἱ μέν),
he is John the Baptist ;	John the Baptist ;
others say that he is Elia ;	and some (ἄλλοι) Elias ;
others say he is Jeremia ;	and others (ἕτεροι), Jeremias
others say he is	or
one of the prophets.	one of the prophets.

This may be taken as an example of the revised translation we possess in the Greek version of the first Gospel.

I have now to inquire into the nature of the connection between the Curetonian Syriac and the Greek Gospel of St. Luke, which, as in the former case, will, be best illustrated by examples. In the first column of the following extracts we have short passages of the literal translation of the Syriac by Dr. Cureton. In the other two columns we have literal translations of the same passages of the Greek Gospels of St. Matthew and St. Luke.

MATT. SYRIAC.	MATT. GR.	LUKE.
iii. 3, *Written by*	spoken of by	iii. 4, *written* in the book of the words of
iv. 11, left him *for a season*	leaveth him	iv. 13, departed from him *till a season*
iv. 4, *Jesus* answered	he answered	iv. 4, *Jesus* answered
iv. 9, worship *before me*	worship me	iv. 7, worship *before me*
v. 12, be glad *in that day*	be glad	vi. 23, be glad *in that day*
v. 15, *no man*	neither do *they*	viii. 16, *no one*
v. 47, what is your *grace*	what do ye more	vi. 32, what *is your grace*
vii. 4, how *art thou* able	how *wilt thou*	vi. 42, how *art thou* able
viii. 16, *at the sun's setting*	when even was come	iv. 40, *at the sun's setting*
x. 33, before *his angels*	om. Matt.	xii. 9, before *the angels of God*

MATT. SYRIAC.	MATT. GR.	LUKE.
xii. 1, *rubbing in their hands*	om. Matt.	vi. 1, *rubbing with their hands*
xii. 10, whose *right* hand was withered	having a withered hand	vi. 6, and his *right* hand was withered
xii. 32, that shall *blaspheme* against	whoso speaketh against	xii. 10, having *blasphemed* against
xiii. 22, *fell* among the thorns	*sown* among the thorns	viii. 14, *fell* among the thorns
xxii. 25, left not *children*	not having seed	xx. 29, childless
xix. 13, lay his hand on them	put his hands on them	xviii. 15, *touch* them
xix. 16, that I may *inherit*	that I may have	xviii. 18, shall I *inherit*
xix. 20, since *I was a boy*	om.	xviii. 21, *from* (*my*) *youth*
xxi. 23, and say *to him*	saying	xx. 2, and spake *unto him* saying

It will be observed that Luke seldom adopts the emendations of Matthew. I shall now give what is in fact a synoptical section of a parallel passage in the Gospels of Matthew and Luke, which, from the passage in Matthew not being included in the received text, did not form part of the synopsis of the three first Gospels made by me, nor, as far as I am aware, in any other synopsis of the Gospels, and which only occurs in Greek in the Codex Bezæ. Dr. Cureton has however brought forward such a mass of external evidence as to leave no doubt in my mind that it did occur both in the original Aramaic and the earliest Greek version of St. Matthew's Gospel. In addition to Dr. Cureton's evidence, I have to add that of St. Luke. The passage in question is parallel with that in St. Luke's Gospel, xiv. 8, 9, 10, and the only two lines in Dr. Cureton's literal version which I could not find translated or at least represented in Greek, were as follows:—'Thou shalt have more glory in the eyes of the guests;' St. Luke's version being, *ἔσται σοι δόξα ἐνώπιον πάντων τῶν συνανακειμένων σοι.* St. Matthew, in the Greek version, merely says it will be profitable or useful (*χρήσιμον*) *scil.* not to assume a high place. In a Latin poetical translation of the passage by Juvencus in the first half of the fourth century, evidently from the Greek, he completes the somewhat abrupt conclusion of the Greek version by supposing that the reward of modesty was not 'glory in the eyes of the guests,' but a better place at the feast.

'Ad potiora pudens transibit strata tororum.'

The passage in question is as follows:—

SYRIAC.	GREEK, MATT. XX. 28	LUKE XIV. 8.
Whenever ye are invited	Παρακληθέντες	Ὅταν κληθῇς ὑπό τινος
to the house of a supper	δειπνῆσαι	εἰς γάμους,
be not sitting down	μὴ ἀνακλίνεσθε	μὴ κατακλιθῇς
in the honoured place,	εἰς τοὺς ἐξέχοντας τόπους,	εἰς τὴν πρωτοκλισίαν,
lest should come he	μήποτε	μή ποτε
that is more honoured	ἐνδοξότερός	ἐντιμότερός
than thou,	σου	σου
		ᾖ κεκλημένος ὑπ' αὐτοῦ,
and to thee	ἐπέλθῃ, καὶ προσελθὼν	καὶ ἐλθὼν
the lord of the supper	ὁ δειπνοκλήτωρ	ὁ σὲ καὶ αὐτὸν καλέσας
should say,	εἴπῃ σοι	ἐρεῖ σοι,
Come near below, and	ἔτι κάτω χώρει, καὶ	Δὸς τούτῳ τόπον· καὶ τότε
thou be ashamed	καταισχυνθήσῃ·	ἄρξῃ μετὰ αἰσχύνης τὸν ἔσχατον τόπον κατέχειν.
in the eyes of the guests.		
But if thou	Ἐὰν δὲ	Ἀλλ' ὅταν
		κληθῇς πορευθεὶς
sit down in the	ἀναπέσῃς εἰς τὸν	ἀνάπεσε εἰς τὸν
little place,	ἥττονα τόπον	ἔσχατον τόπον, ἵνα ὅταν
and he that is less than	καὶ	
thee should come,	ἐπέλθῃ σου ἥττων,	ἔλθῃ

SYRIAC.	GREEK, MATT. XX. 28.	LUKE XIV. 8.
and to thee the lord of the supper shall say,	ἐρεῖ σοι ὁ δειπνοκλήτωρ	ὁ κεκληκώς σε ἐρεῖ σοι, Φίλε
Come near and come up and sit down,	Σύναγε ἔτι ἄνω,	προσανάβηθι ἀνώτερον·
thou also shalt have	καὶ ἔσται σοι τοῦτο χρήσιμον.	τότε ἔσται σοι
more glory in the eyes of the guests.		δόξα ἐνώπιον πάντων τῶν συνανακεμένων σοι.

A glance at the above will show the condensed emendation of St. Matthew, with the disregard to condensation by St. Luke, whose evident object was to express the meaning of the original fully and clearly; hence his translation is somewhat paraphrastical, and he omits a circumstance not necessary for the elucidation of the object our Lord meant to inculcate—the entrance of an inferior person to the feast.

The general remarks of our Lord, which in Matthew precede, but in Luke follow what he terms 'a parable,' are expressed antithetically. In the former the contrast is between 'little and great;' in the latter between 'exalted and abased:' both cases refer to social position; in Luke this is expressed more clearly, and the antithesis more formally put. I have translated *γάμους* a feast, as I find it so used without reference to marriage. Commentators generally suppose that this passage, as it occurs in Codex Bezæ, is taken from Luke, and even Dr. Cureton acquiesces in this view, in the following passage:—'It certainly belongs to the most ancient times of Christianity; and the fact of the same advice of our Lord in very similar words being found in the Gospel of St. Luke would at least make it appear that it is to be *referred ulti-*

mately to him, whatever might have been the channel through which it has been derived' (p. xxxviii). I own I can see no difficulty in the case. If the manuscript in which it is found be the work of St. Matthew, then is the passage in question also his. Had I entertained any doubt of the priority of St. Matthew's Gospel to that of St. Luke, the comparison of his Gospel with the Syriac version would have settled the matter; there can be no more decisive proof of priority than the occurrence of unimportant facts naturally mentioned by an eye-witness, but also naturally omitted by a subsequent historian. Now, here we have a case of this kind. In the Syriac, mention is made of the entrance of an inferior person, in these words:—'And he that is less than thee should come.' Matthew shortly renders it, *καὶ ἐπέλθῃ σου ἥττων*. Luke omits it entirely. If we suppose he took the passage from Matthew, we can easily understand why, as an historian, he should leave out notice of a fact which is in itself of no importance. If, on the other hand, we suppose Luke's account to be the original, there is nothing whatever in it which could suggest its insertion. So far therefore as concerns the passage in question, it proves its priority to Luke's version; but such merely autoptical facts occur not unfrequently in the Gospel of Luke, and were, till the discovery of the Curetonian Syriac, inexplicable. In forming the synopsis of the first three Gospels, there were three which perplexed me in an especial manner: first, that the daughter of Jairus was an only daughter; second, that in the miracle of the cure of the withered hand, it was the right hand which was cured; and lastly, that when the disciples pulled and ate the ears of corn on the Sabbath 'they rubbed them with their hands' (vi. 1). In the first of these cases the passage is wanting in the Syriac, whilst in the other two they occur in St. Luke's Gospel, but are omitted in the Greek Gospel of St. Matthew, —obviously because it was immaterial in the miraculous cure of the withered hand which hand it was, and because the infringement of the observance of the Jewish Sabbath consisted in plucking and eating the ears of corn, and not in the necessary act of rubbing off the husks in their hands. I attempted to account for this conjecturally, and cite my explanation merely to show of how little value conjecture is in such inquiries: '"Rubbing them with their hands" is, I believe, a paraphrastic addition; the Evangelist mentions what must have been done in eating ears of corn.' The simple explanation is, that in the original Aramaic the passage occurs exactly as given by St. Luke, and that from that original he derived it.

I have already stated the very remarkable agreement between the Curetonian Syriac and the Greek so that every line of the Syriac was represented in the Greek. There are indeed here and there vacant lines for which there is no corresponding Greek text; nearly all of which can be accounted for by the condensation of revision, with the exception of the parable of the invited guests already explained and the names of the three kings in the line of our Lord's descent mentioned in 1 Chron. iii. 10, 11, viz. Ahaziah, Joash and Amaziah. Without pretending to explain the difference in the Old Testament line from that of the New, I refer to Dr. Cureton's remarks on the subject, and hold that this reading is a proof amongst others of the great antiquity of the Syriac.

Another class of phenomena elicited by the comparison I have made is the occurrence of passages in the received Greek which have no corresponding passages in the Curetonian Syriac. The explanation I have to give is, that the Syriac is in reality more ancient than the Greek manuscripts which contain the passages in question. But it is confirmed by the Greek MSS. of the same early age; nearly all the readings in which it is wanting agreeing with the most ancient textual authorities, especially with the recently discovered Codex Sinaiticus ℵ.

	ℵ	B	C	D
iv. 2. νύκτας τεσσαράκοντα				
v. 39. δεξιάν				D
vi. 25. ἢ τί πίετε	ℵ			
vi. 27. μεριμνῶν				
vi. 32. ὁ οὐράνιος	ℵ			
xii. 15. ὄχλοι	ℵ	B		
xii. 47. v. 47		B		
xiv. 13. ἐν πλοίῳ				
xv. 14. τυφλῶν	ℵ	B		D
xvi. 2. vv. 2, 3.	ℵ	B		
xvii. 21. v. 21	ℵ	B		
xviii. 35. τὰ παραπτώματα αὐτῶν	ℵ			D
xix. 9. καὶ . . . μοιχᾶται	ℵ			
xx. 17. μαθητὰς	ℵ			D
xx. 22. vv. 22, 23				
xxi. 12. τοῦ Θεοῦ				D
xxiii. 18. ὀμόσῃ . . . ὃς δ' ἂν				

The preceding table exhibits the agreements in this matter between the Curetonian Syriac and the most authoritative of the ancient Greek MSS., viz. the Vatican (B), Codex Ephraemi (C), Bezæ (D), and Sinaiticus (א). The Alexandrian (A) is not included in it, as it wants the greater part of the Gospel of St. Matthew.

Of this class of differences between the Curetonian and Greek, only four are unsupported by ancient MSS.

The next class of variations from the Greek text consists in the use of equivalents which are certainly not translations, in place of employing words having the same meaning, for instance, speaking of Joseph, it is said in the Syriac 'to whom was espoused Mary;' in the Greek it is 'the husband of Mary;' or in the Syriac, where Mary is spoken of, instead of naming her she is mentioned as his (Joseph's) wife.

Simon, in reference to such changes, observes, 'Ne pourroit-on pas même conjecturer que celuy qui a traduit d'Ébreu en Grec l'original de saint Matthieu, l'a abrégé en quelques endroits, et qu'il a quelquefois pris la liberté d'en traduire plutôt le sens que les mots?' ('Hist. Crit. du texte N. T.,' ch. ix. p. 98.) The answer is, that an author translating his own work may condense his narrative and translate the sense rather than the words, but a translator is not entitled to such liberties,—still less is he entitled to introduce circumstances which he did not find in the original, such as in the cure of the withered hand, the information that it was the right hand which was cured, or the fact that the disciples rubbed off the husks from the ears of corn before eating them.

Most of the above readings appear to be additions, the result of repeated transcriptions. The reader will observe that Codex Ephraemi C contains all the passages wanting in the earlier MSS.,—a proof that, whatever be the date of that particular manuscript, the text of the Vatican and Cambridge MSS. is older than it, and that in that of the Curetonian Syriac and Sinaitic MS. we have the oldest existing documentary evidence of the text of the Gospels. Neither of them can be altogether free from error. In ch. xxiii. 18, Dr. Tregelles explains the omission thus, 'per errorum librarii δι' ὁμοιοτέλ.'

In conclusion, the inference I draw from the phenomena presented by these most interesting and important discoveries is in entire accordance with that I formerly arrived at in my inquiry into the origin and connection of the Gospels—our Lord and his disciples spoke and wrote in the vernacular language of Judea, but when it became necessary to record their transactions in writing the task devolved upon St. Matthew, a Jew holding office under the Roman government, and therefore necessarily master of both languages spoken in Judea, namely Greek the language of government and of the more educated classes, and Aramaic, termed in Scripture and by the fathers Hebrew, by Eusebius and Josephus πατρίῳ. St. Matthew's object of communicating the Gospel to his countrymen could only be done in both languages, and accordingly we find from St. Luke's Gospel that St. Matthew's already existed in both languages. He tells us in his preface that his authorities were eye-witnesses and ministers of the word. We can trace in the Gospel three of his original authorities,—first, St. Peter's memoirs not yet translated by St. Mark; second, St. Matthew's Gospel in the original Aramaic; and lastly, the same in the language in which we now have it.

Having in my dissertation stated very fully the evidence upon which my conclusions rest, I can only add that the result of the inquiry into the sources of his writings goes to prove that on every occasion in which it is possible to trace them, we find that those sources are written accounts by Apostles; and we are warranted in supposing from his preface that those of his writings which we cannot trace to any existing authority were drawn from similar sources; and from the perfect fidelity with which he adheres to his authorities where we can put it to the test, we cannot entertain a doubt that he is a true and faithful historian of events which either fell under his own observation or which he derived immediately from those who were engaged in them.

CHART OF ST PAULS VOYAGE FROM CÆSAREA

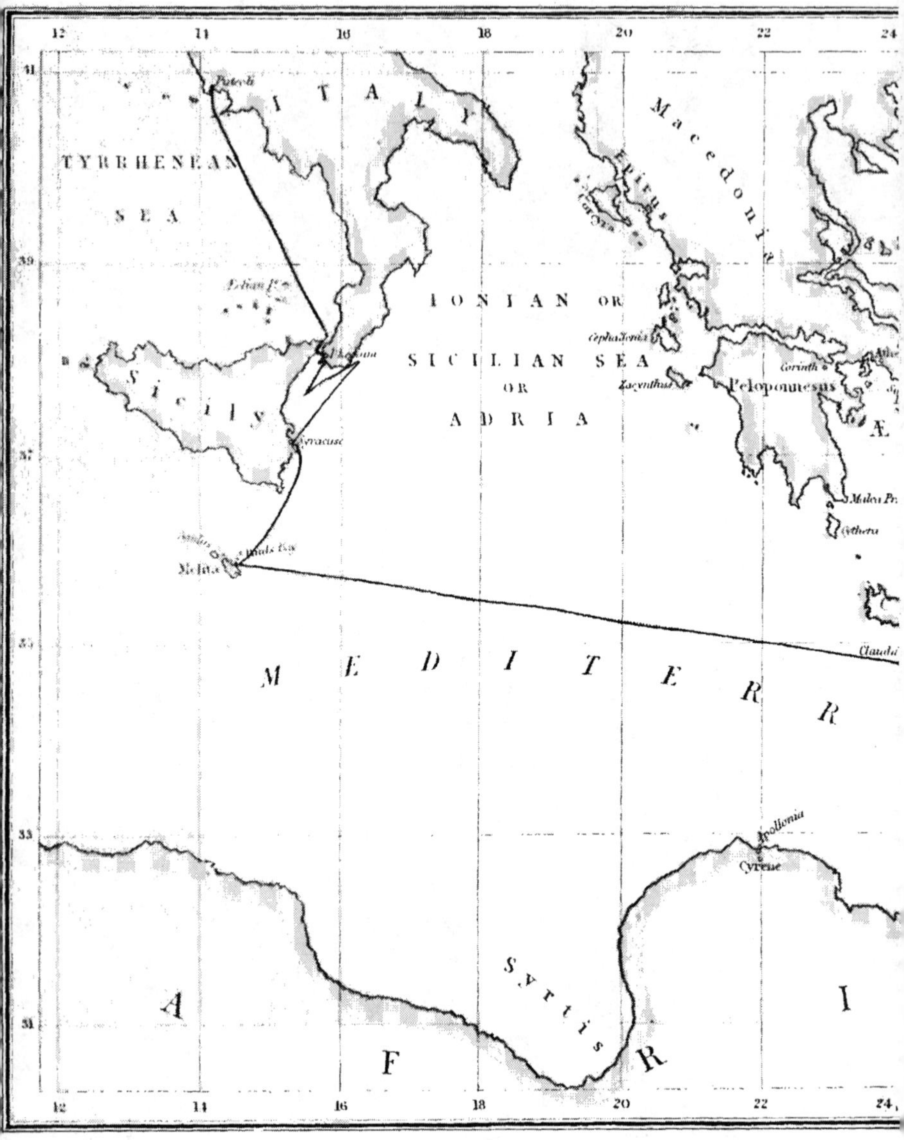

TO PUTEOLI BY JAMES SMITH ESQ^R F.R.S.

NARRATIVE OF THE VOYAGE.

CHAPTER I.

CÆSAREA TO MYRA.

(Acts xxvii. 1–6.)

AFTER two years' imprisonment at Cæsarea, and after repeated examinations before Felix and Festus, successive Roman governors of Judea, and before

1 Ὡς δὲ ἐκρίθη τοῦ ἀποπλεῖν[1] ἡμᾶς εἰς τὴν Ἰταλίαν, παρεδίδουν τόν τε Παῦλον καί τινας ἑτέρους δεσμώτας ἑκατοντάρχῃ ὀνόματι Ἰουλίῳ σπείρης Σεβαστῆς.

1 And when it was determined that we should sail into Italy, they delivered Paul and certain other prisoners unto *one* named Julius, a centurion of Augustus' band.

[1] Ἀποπλεῖν. Literally 'to sail from.' St. Luke, by his accurate use of nautical terms, gives great precision to his language, and expresses by a single word what would otherwise require several. Mitford observes, that 'we are often at a loss to render the verb πλέω otherwise than by our word *to sail*, though they are far from being of the same precise import. The use of oars, so prevalent in Grecian navigation, is so little known in our seas, that to sail is our only general term for going by sea.' (*Hist. of Greece*, ii. 362.) St. Luke alone of the sacred writers uses this nautical term, either simply or as in the present instance in composition.

King Agrippa the last of the Herod family, St. Paul appealed unto Cæsar.

In consequence of this appeal it was determined that he should be sent, along with other prisoners, by sea to Italy. He was accordingly committed to the charge of a centurion named Julius, of the Imperial band, a person who, upon all occasions, treated the apostle with humanity and consideration.

Cæsarea was at that time the principal seaport of Syria.[1] It would appear, however, that there were no ships bound for Italy in the harbour capable of accommodating the party of Julius, including the prisoners and their guard. He therefore embarked them in a ship of Adramyttium,[2] a seaport of Mysia, on the Eastern shore of the Ægean Sea, opposite Lesbos. This ship was evidently bound for her own port, and her course from Cæsarea thither necessarily led her close past the principal seaports of Asia.[3]

[1] See account of Cæsarea in Josephus, *Antiq.* xv. 13. Bryant, absurdly enough, supposes that Ptolemais (Acre) was the port of embarkation; and adds, as if it were a mere conjecture, 'Grotius is of opinion that they went from Cæsarea.' It would have been quite contrary to St. Luke's usual method to have omitted the land journey from Cæsarea to Ptolemais, had it actually taken place. (See Acts xxi. 7, 8.)

[2] See a very full account of the notices in ancient authors of this place, in Wetstein ad loc.

[3] By Asia St. Luke means proconsular Asia, of which Ephesus was the capital, i.e. the western part of Asia Minor, which, according to Cicero, comprehended Caria and Lycia; and, according to St. Luke, did not include Pamphylia. (Acts ii. 9, 10.) By attending to this, we are left in no doubt as to 'the places' (*τοὺς τόπους*) meant in the text, which they would arrive at by the route they pursued. The places '*κατὰ τὴν Ἀσίαν*,' which may be translated 'along the coast of Asia,' were then flourishing sea-ports, three of which are mentioned by St. Luke; namely, Myra (Acts xxvii. 5), Patara (xxi. 1), and Cnidus (xxvii. 7). For an account of the present state of Myra, see Spratt and Forbes,

Now this is also the course which a ship would take in making a voyage from Syria to Italy; they would therefore be so far on their voyage when they reached the coast of Asia, and in the great commercial marts on that coast they could not fail to find opportunities of being carried on to their ulterior destination. On St. Paul's former voyage from Philippi to Syria (Acts xx. 6 to xxi. 7) the same plan was adopted: they sailed to the places on the coast of Asia (*κατὰ τὴν Ἀσίαν*), and changed ship at one of them, Patara, just as we find was done in the present instance at Myra. We have, therefore, an obvious reason why they took their passage in this ship. The apostle was on this

---

2 Ἐπιβάντες δὲ πλοίῳ Ἀδραμυντηνῷ μέλλοντι πλεῖν εἰς τοὺς[1] κατὰ τὴν Ἀσίαν τόπους ἀνήχθημεν, ὄντος σὺν ἡμῖν Ἀριστάρχου Μακεδόνος Θεσσαλονικέως.	2 And entering into a ship of Adramyttium, which was about to sail by the coasts of Asia, we launched *one* Aristarchus, a Macedonian of Thessalonica, being with us.

Travels in Lycia, i. 125. It has been observed that the magnitude of ancient cities may be inferred from that of their theatres; the diameter of that of Myra is 360 feet and the 'arena is now a corn-field.' (*Ib.* 132.) The theatre of Patara is also a magnificent structure. See a view of it in the *Ionian Autiquities*, published by the Dilettante Society (vol. ii. pl. 56, 57), and an account of it in Beaufort's *Caramania*, p. 5. For an account of Cnidus, see Clarke's *Travels*, vol. ii. p. 216.

[1] Μέλλοντι πλεῖν εἰς τοὺς. &c., is the reading of the Vatican, Sinaitic, and Alexandrian MSS., the earliest, and, in a case like the present, the best authorities, and is that adopted by Lachmann and Tregelles; the common reading is *μέλλοντες πλεῖν εἰς τοὺς*, &c.: the preposition *εἰς* renders the meaning obvious, by showing that the ship was to touch at 'the places' &c.

occasion accompanied by Aristarchus, a Macedonian of Thessalonica, and St. Luke, the historian of the voyage. The former appears to have been a prisoner, for St. Paul, in his epistle to the Colossians, designates him as his fellow-prisoner.[1] (iv. 10.)

On the day after they left Cæsarea they touched at Sidon. From the distance accomplished, sixty-seven geographical miles, we must infer that they had a fair, or at least a leading wind, probably westerly, which is the wind which prevails in this part of the Mediterranean.[2] We are not informed of the cause of their stopping at Sidon; probably, however, it was for the purposes of trade.[3] Whatever was the cause

---

2 *Τῇ τε ἑτέρᾳ κατήχθημεν εἰς Σιδῶνα,*

3 *Φιλανθρώπως τε ὁ Ἰούλιος τῷ Παύλῳ χρησάμενος ἐπέτρεψεν πρὸς τοὺς φίλους πορευθέντι ἐπιμελείας τυχεῖν.*

2 And the next *day* we touched at Sidon.

3 And Julius courteously entreated Paul, and gave *him* liberty to go unto his friends to refresh himself.

---

[1] This companion of St. Paul is very unceremoniously mentioned by our English translators, by the gratuitous insertion of the word '*one.*' He is twice previously noticed in the Acts, once as a Macedonian (xix. 29), and once as a Thessalonican (xx. 4); here he is mentioned as both.

[2] 'The wind continues to the westward. I am sorry to find it almost as prevailing as the trade winds.' (4th July 1798, near Alexandria.—*Life of Lord de Saumarez*, i. 210.) 'We have just gained sight of Cyprus, nearly the track we followed six weeks ago, so invariably do the westerly winds prevail at this season.' (19th Aug. 1798.—*Ib.* i. 243.) A westerly wind would be fair between Cæsarea and Sidon, as the bearing of the coast line between the two places is about N.N.E. See *Sailing Directions for the Coast of Syria*, by Capt. E. Smith, R.N.

[3] According to Strabo, Sidon was situated on the finest harbour of the Continent, and contested with Tyre the supremacy of the Phœnician

of the delay, it afforded the centurion an opportunity of showing kindness to St. Paul, for we are told in the narrative that he 'gave him liberty to go unto his friends to refresh himself' [or rather 'to receive their attention;' i.e., perhaps, 'to obtain from them that outfit for the voyage which, on account of the official precision of his custody at Cæsarea, he could not there be provided with.'—ALFORD.]

Loosing[1] from thence they were forced, by con-

4 Κἀκεῖθεν ἀναχθέντες ὑπεπλεύσαμεν τὴν Κύπρον διὰ τὸ τοὺς ἀνέμους εἶναι ἐναντίους,

4 And when we had launched from thence, we sailed under Cyprus, because the winds were contrary.

---

cities (lib. xvi. c. 2). Achilles Tatius calls it the metropolis of the Phœnicians, μήτηρ Φοινίκων ἡ πόλις; he describes it as having two harbours, one of which is large with a narrow entrance, where merchant ships can winter in safety (lib. i.). To judge from its present state, the shelter was afforded by a ridge of rocks, parallel to the coast, forming a natural breakwater. The harbour was filled up during the wars of the Middle Ages. For an account of its present state, see Robinson's *Biblical Researches*, and Wilson's *Lands of the Bible*. The latter author gives a plan of the harbour. See a view of it in Carne's *Syria and the Holy Land Illustrated*, vol. iii. p. 6.

[1] 'Αναχθέντες is one of those nautical terms about which there is no doubt as to the meaning—which is, to depart from a place; it is used by St. Luke both in the Gospel and Acts, and is rendered in the authorised version, 'to launch,' 'to loose,' 'to sail,' 'to set forth,' 'to depart.' 'Ανάγεσθαι is amongst the nautical terms of Julius Pollux. There is no precisely corresponding term in English. Mitford observes, that in rendering it 'we must risk the sea phrase *to get under way*, or content ourselves with the inaccurate expression *to set sail*.' (*Hist. of Greece*, vol. ii. p. 232, note.)

St. Luke uses the words ἀποπλέω, ἐκπλέω, and αἴρω, to express the same thing. The last is an elliptical expression: it occurs in verse 13 of this chapter, and is translated 'loosing.' It would have been more accurately rendered 'weighed,' τὰς ἀγκύρας, the anchors, being under-

trary winds, to run under the lee of Cyprus.[1] A question here arises, which was the lee side of Cyprus? In passing it, did they leave it upon their right or upon their left? Commentators are divided upon the subject, but it is generally supposed that they left it on their right; that is, that they passed to the south of that island. This opinion is evidently founded upon the erroneous suppositions that the coast of Syria is comprehended by St. Luke in the term *Asia*, and that the ancients only made coasting voyages. The question is not one of importance, further than that it is desirable to leave nothing uncertain where certainty can be attained, and because, in the next place, if we are sure of the meaning of the author in this case we can compare the proceedings of the ancient navigators with those of modern ones, who have been placed under similar circumstances in the same locality, and can thus form a more correct estimate of their seamanship.

As I dissent from the generally-received opinion

stood. Thus, in Plutarch (Pompey, p. 1208), ἀραμένοι τὰς ἀγκύρας. It is, however, generally used absolutely, as in the present case, and as its English equivalent to weigh. See *Wetstein* ad loc. The corresponding word for coming to land, κατάγεσθαι, Jul. Pollux, *Onom*. i. 102, occurs in the preceding verse.

[1] Ὑπεπλεύσαμεν, 'we sailed under the lee.' Dr. Falconer, in his Dissertation on St. Paul's Voyage, supposed it meant to sail to the south of a place, because the maps of the ancients, like those of the moderns, were constructed with the north point uppermost. The explanation of Wetstein is, however, unquestionably the true one: 'ubi navis vento contrario cogitur a recto cursu decedere, ita ut tunc insula sit interposita inter ventum et navem, dicitur ferri *infra* insulam.' We meet with the same word again in the seventh verse, where ample proof will be given that this is the meaning of the term. Kuinöl erroneously supposes that it means to sail close to the shore: 'sublegere, oram *cominus* legere.'

that they sailed by the south of Cyprus, I shall, in the first place, state the arguments upon which that opinion is founded. Dr. Falconer, in his 'Dissertation on St. Paul's Voyage,' says,—

'On their loosing from Sidon, they found that their intention of continuing their voyage along the coasts of Asia Minor would be frustrated by contrary winds, which obliged them to pursue their voyage under or on the southern side of the island of Cyprus, instead of the northern, as according to their plan of sailing along the coast they had at first proposed.'

Dr. Bennet, a late commentator on the Acts, expresses himself thus:—

'Sailed under or to the south of Cyprus, on account of the winds being contrary, when they would otherwise have taken them to the north, along the Asiatic coasts.' ('Lectures,' p. 399.)

When we hear of contrary winds, and wish to ascertain their direction, the chief points to be determined are the ship's actual position and intended course. Now, when St. Luke talks of contrary winds, we know that the ship had left Sidon, and must have been in sight of Cyprus, for he tells us that the winds forced them to leeward of that island. Their ultimate object was Italy and their proximate one was one or other of the 'places in Asia,' which I have already shown lay in the same direction. As St. Luke does not include Pamphylia in Asia, the nearest part of that region to Syria is Lycia, and a ship's course from Sidon thither is W.N.W., leaving Cyprus on the right. St. Luke was perfectly aware of this, for upon the former voyage, in which he accompanied St. Paul, he tells us that on their passage from Patara, one of the 'places in Asia,' to Phœnicia, 'they left Cyprus on the left hand,' i.e. on the north. (Acts xxi. 3.) The winds therefore which prevented them from taking the straight course to the places in Asia must have been from the westward. Now these are the very winds which might have been expected in this part of the Mediterranean at this season (summer). Admiral de Saumarez writes, 19th August, 1798:—

> 'We have just gained sight of Cyprus, so invariably do the westerly winds prevail at this season.' ('Life,' i. 243.)

Under these circumstances, sailing under Cyprus is equivalent to saying that they left Cyprus on their left hand; but this point is put out of doubt by St. Luke himself, for he tells us in the 5th verse that they *sailed through* the sea of Cilicia (διαπλεύσαντες), not *over*, as in the authorised version; but as this sea lies altogether to the north of Cyprus, they could not have sailed through it without leaving the island on their left.

In pursuing this route they acted precisely as the most accomplished seaman in the present day would have done under similar circumstances; by standing to the north till they reached the coast of Cilicia, they might expect when they did so to be favoured by the land wind, which prevails there during the summer months, as well as by the current, which constantly

---

5 Τό τε πέλαγος τὸ κατὰ τὴν Κιλικίαν καὶ Παμφυλίαν διαπλεύσαντες κατήλθαμεν εἰς Μύρρα τῆς Λυκίας

5 And when we had sailed over the sea of Cilicia and Pamphylia, we came to Myra, a city of Lycia.

runs to the westward, along the south coast of Asia Minor.[1]

M. de Pagès, a French navigator, who made a voyage from Syria to Marseilles, took this course, and has given the reasons why he did so. He informs us, that after making Cyprus,

'The winds from the west, and consequently contrary, which prevail in these places during the summer, forced us to run to the north. We made for the coast of Caramania (Cilicia) in order to meet the northerly winds, which we found accordingly.' [2]

Fynes Moryson, in his 'Itinerary,' narrates a sea voyage from Syria to Crete, in which the circumstances of wind and weather bear a still more marked resemblance to those experienced by the ancient mariners than any of the above. He sailed from Scanderoon the port of Aleppo, with the intention of disembarking at the city of Candia on the north side of Crete, and therefore his course so far was the same as that of St. Paul and his companions. At first he tells us,—

'We sayled prosperously, but after the winds grew so contrary as we were driven to the south of Candia.' (p. 251.)

Here, in the seas where I infer from the silence of

[1] 'From Syria to the Archipelago, there is a constant current to the westward.' (Beaufort's *Description of the South Coast of Asia Minor*, p. 39.) Dr. Pococke found this current running so strong between Rhodes and the Continent, that it broke into the cabin windows even in calm weather. (*Description of the East*, ii. 236.)

[2] 'Nous fîmes route sur l'île de Chypre. Après l'avoir côtoyée, les vents de l'ouest, par conséquent contraires, qui règnent pendant l'été dans ces parties, nous firent élever au nord; nous cherchions la côte de la Caramanie, pour rencontrer les vents du nord, que nous y trouvâmes en effet.' (*Voyages autour du Monde*, tom. i. p. 406.)

St. Luke that the circumstances of St. Paul's voyage were favourable, they 'sayled prosperously;' and in the seas where St. Paul's ship met with contrary winds, *μὴ προσεῶντος ἡμᾶς τοῦ ἀνέμου*, 'the winds grew contrary,' and had precisely the same effect upon the ship, which it drove to the south of Crete; and, what is still more remarkable, Moryson is carried to Fair Havens. It is not, perhaps, easy to recognise in 'the wild rocks called Calis Miniones' the Fair Bays which give the harbour its name, and which it still retains in Calos Limeones. There is no doubt, however, of the identity of the places, for Moryson marks the position of Calis Miniones by saying it is

> 'Some three miles distant from a monastery called Santa Maria Aggidietra,'

just as St. Luke marks it, as 'nigh unto the city Lasea.' The monastery still remains: in Pashley's map it is spelt Hodhetria, and is exactly three miles above the 'rocky promontory' which separates the two bays upon which Moryson was landed. (See the account of a visit to the monastery, by the Rev. George Brown, Appendix i.)

Favoured, as they probably were, by the land wind and currents, they arrive without any recorded incident at Myra of Lycia, then a flourishing seaport, now a desolate waste. The stupendous magnitude of its theatre attests the extent of its former population; the splendour of its tombs,[1] its wealth. But it is not

[1] 'Sepulchres, which for the elegance of their design, costliness of execution, and size, seem to have been suited rather for the keeping of the ashes of rulers and kings, than of common citizens.' (Spratt and Forbes, i. 132.) See a view of Myra in the above work, frontispiece to vol. i.

my intention to describe the ancient or modern state of the places visited, farther than as they illustrate the events of the voyage.

This city is situated, according to Admiral Beaufort, about three miles from the sea; according to Strabo, the distance is twenty stadia, or about two geographical miles, the difference being probably caused by the silting up of the river Andriaki, which flows past it into a spacious bay. This river, which Appian calls the port of the Myrians (Μυρέων ἐπίνειον), 'Bell. Civ.' lib. iv. cap. 82, was navigable to Myra, for he informs us that Lentulus, having broken the chain of the harbour, ascended to that city.

The voyage has hitherto been prosperous, and the object which the party had in view in proceeding to 'the places in Asia' is attained. At the first of them which lay in their way, the centurion found a ship of Alexandria, loaded, as we afterwards learn, with wheat, bound for Italy, in which he embarked his charge. Egypt was at this time one of the granaries of Rome, and the corn which was sent from thence to Italy was conveyed in ships of very great size.[1] From the dimensions given of one of them by Lucian,[2]

6 Κἀκεῖ εὑρὼν ὁ ἑκατοντάρχης πλοῖον Ἀλεξανδρινὸν πλέον εἰς τὴν Ἰταλίαν ἐνεβίβασεν ἡμᾶς εἰς αὐτό.	6 And there the centurion found a ship of Alexandria sailing into Italy; and he put us therein.

[1] After the capture of Jerusalem the Emperor Titus returned to Italy in one of these ships, touching at Rhegium, and landing at Puteoli. (Sueton. *Vit.* ch. 5; see also *Vit. Augusti*, 98; and Seneca, *Epist.* 77.)

[2] In the Dialogue Πλοῖον ἢ Εὐχαί. See the Dissertation on Ancient Ships, *post*.

they appear to have been quite as large as the largest class of merchant ships of modern times. We need not be surprised, therefore, at the number of souls which we afterwards find were embarked in this one,[1] or that another ship of the same class could after the shipwreck convey them to Italy, in addition to her own crew.

Some commentators have supposed that Myra lay so much out of the track from Alexandria to Italy that the term Alexandrian must mean the particular 'build' of the ship, just as we say Liburnian galleys, and not as marking the port to which she belonged. Now it is quite true that Myra is out of the direct course from Alexandria to Italy, which is by the south of Crete. But with the westerly winds which prevail in those seas, ships, particularly those of the ancients, unprovided with a compass and ill calculated to work to windward, would naturally stand to the north till they made the land of Asia Minor, which is peculiarly favourable for navigation by such vessels, because the coast is bold and safe, and the elevation of the mountains makes it visible at a great distance; it abounds in harbours, and the sinuosities of its shores and the westerly current would enable them, if the wind was at all off the land, to work to windward, at least as far as Cnidus, where these advantages ceased.[2] Myra lies due north from Alex-

[1] Granville Penn, on the authority of the Vatican MS., reads 'seventy-six,' instead of 'two hundred and seventy-six' See his note on the subject; the Sinaitic, and other uncial MSS., however, have two hundred and seventy-six [except the Alexandrian, which reads 'two hundred and seventy-*five*.' Westcott and Hort follow the Vatican, and read 'about seventy-six '].

[2] We learn from Thucydides (viii. 35), that Cnidus was frequented by merchant ships from Egypt, ἀπ' Αἰγύπτου ὁλκάδες.

andria,[1] and its bay is well calculated to shelter a windbound ship. The Alexandrian ship was not, therefore, out of her course at Myra, even if she had no call to touch there for the purposes of commerce.

We may suppose that the same westerly winds which forced the Adramyttian ship to the east of Cyprus, drove the Alexandrian ship to Myra. The land wind on the Cilician coast appears to be quite local, and therefore might enable St. Paul's ship to reach Myra, although the prevalent wind did not admit of the ships in that harbour proceeding on their voyage.

[1] According to Ptolemy it lies just east of the meridian of Alexandria, which is precisely its position. I have never had occasion to consult this great geographer without being astonished at the extent and accuracy of his information. It is easy, for modern writers to find fault with him; the very precision he introduced into the science enables them to detect errors unavoidable in the state of knowledge which the ancients had of distant regions, or caused by errors in transcription. The edition of Tauchnitz, which I have used, though unpretending in form, is I believe the most correct.

CHAPTER II.

VOYAGE FROM MYRA TO FAIR HAVENS IN CRETE.

(Acts xxviii. 7, 8.)

In this ship of Alexandria, in which the centurion and his party embarked, they proceeded on their voyage. Their progress after leaving Myra was extremely slow; for we are told that it was 'many' days before they were 'come over against Cnidus,' that is before they reached the entrance of the Ægean Sea. As the distance between the two places is not more than 130 geographical miles, which they could easily have accomplished with a fair wind in one day, they must either have met with calms or contrary winds. I infer that the delay was caused by contrary winds, from the expression *μόλις*, which is translated in our authorised version 'scarce,' producing the impression that the ship had scarcely reached Cnidus when the winds became contrary; but which ought to be rendered 'with difficulty,' expressing the difficulty which ships experience in contending with adverse winds. The same word

7 Ἐν ἱκαναῖς δὲ ἡμέραις βραδυπλοοῦντες καὶ μόλις γενόμενοι κατὰ τὴν Κνίδον, μὴ προσεῶντος ἡμᾶς τοῦ ἀνέμου, ὑπεπλεύσαμεν τὴν Κρήτην κατὰ Σαλμώνην,

7 And when we had sailed slowly many days, and scarce were come over against Cnidus, the wind not suffering, as we sailed under Crete, over against Salmone,

occurs in the following verse, where it is translated 'hardly,' where there can be no doubt as to its meaning, for the general trending of the south coast of Crete, which they were navigating (*παραλεγόμενοι*, v. 8), was the same as that of Asia, east and west; and we are now told that the winds were contrary (v. 7). Cicero, in one of his epistles, uses very similar terms to express the effects of contrary winds:—

> 'Quum sane adversis ventis usi essemus, *tardeque et incommode* navigâssemus.'[1]
>
> 'Having met with contrary winds, and *sailed slowly and with difficulty.*'

I am satisfied, therefore, that the words in the original, *βραδυπλοοῦντες καὶ μόλις γενόμενοι*, 'sailing slowly and with difficulty were come,' &c., express the delays which a ship experiences in working to windward.

The question now occurs, what was the direction of the wind which produced the effects recorded in the narrative. We are told, that when they 'were come over against Cnidus, the wind not suffering us, we sailed under Crete, over against Salmone.' (v. 7.) The direct course of a ship on her voyage from Myra to Italy, after she has reached Cnidus, is by the north side of Crete, through the Archipelago, W. by S. Hence a ship which can make good a course of about seven points from the wind, which I have shown elsewhere[2] cannot be far from the truth, would not have been prevented from proceeding on her course, unless the wind had been to the west of N.N.W. We are

[1] *Epist. ad Familiares*, lib. xiv. epist. v.

[2] Dissertation on Ancient Ships, *post.*

next told that she ran 'under Crete, over against Salmone,' which implies that she was able to fetch that cape, which bears about S.W. by S. from Cnidus; but unless the wind had been to the north of W.N.W., she could not have done so. The wind was, therefore, between N.N.W. and W.N.W. The middle point between these points is North-West, which cannot be more than two points, and is probably not more than one, from the true direction. The wind therefore would in common language have been termed north-west. Now, this is precisely the wind which might have been expected in those seas towards the end of summer. We learn from the sailing directions for the Mediterranean, that

> 'Throughout the whole of the Mediterranean, but mostly in the eastern half, including the Adriatic and Archipelago, the north-west winds prevail in the summer months;'[1]

which agrees with Aristotle's account of these winds.[2] According to Pliny, they begin in August, and blow for forty days.[3]

With north-west winds the ship could work up from Myra to Cnidus; because until she reached that point she had the advantage of a weather shore, under the lee of which she would have smooth water, and as formerly mentioned, a westerly current; but it would be 'slowly and with difficulty.' At Cnidus these advantages ceased; and unless she had put into

[1] Purdy's *Sailing Directions for the Mediterranean* (1841), p. 197.

[2] Οἱ Ἐτησίαι λεγόμενοι μίξιν ἔχοντες τῶν τε ἀπὸ τῆς ἄρκτου φερομένων καὶ ζεφύρων. (Arist. *de Mundo*, cap. iv. 15.)

[3] 'Perflant diebus quadraginta quos Etesias vocant.' (Plin. lib. ii. cap. 4.)

that harbour, and waited for a fair wind, her only course was to run under the lee of Crete, in the direction of Salmone[1] (κατὰ Σαλμώνην), which is the eastern extremity of that island. After passing this point, the difficulty they experienced in navigating to the westward along the coasts of Asia would recur; but as the south side of Crete is also a weather shore, with north-west winds, they would be able to work up as far as Cape Matala. Here the land trends suddenly to the north, and the advantages of a weather shore cease, and their only recourse was to make for a harbour. Now Fair Havens is the last harbour before arriving at Cape Matala, the farthest point to which an ancient ship could have attained with north-westerly winds.

The delays experienced by navigators proceeding westward in this part of the Mediterranean during the summer months, are of such constant occurrence that I have scarcely found an instance in which they have not been encountered.

Rauwolf, a German physician, who travelled in the Holy Land in the sixteenth century,[2] passed and repassed by the same track which St. Paul did. On his voyage eastward, the winds were favourable, i.e. westerly. The ship touched at and watered at a port which he calls Calismene (p. 16), which is evidently Fair Havens. After passing Cape Salmone, they met with a ship coming from the eastward, which had

[1] This promontory still retains its ancient name. (See Strabo, lib. ii. cap. 14. Apol. Rhod. lib. iv. ver. 1693. Ptol. lib. iii. cap. 17.)

[2] *Leonharti Rauwolfen Raiss in die Morgenländer*, Augsburg, 1582. It is translated by Ray, and included in his *Collection of Travels*, vol. ii.

been seven weeks on her passage from Tripoli, having been delayed by the prevailing westerly winds, and which they were obliged to supply with biscuit. On their return they met with the same contrary winds which that ship, as well as St. Paul's, had encountered when off the coasts of Lycia and Pamphylia. At length when they had reached the small mountainous island of Scarpanto, he tells us that a *north* wind sprang up which he says drove them *on their right course* towards Salmone.[1]

It is interesting to compare the confused and blundering account of the physician of Augsburg with the few but accurate notices of the physician of Antioch. In the first place, had the wind been northerly, no ship bound for the westward would have run down from Scarpanto to the south side of Crete; and in the next place, this was not 'the right course,' which was W. by S. across the Ægean Sea, to the north of Crete, for which a northerly wind would have been favourable. Rauwolf's ship could, as we learn, lie within about six points of the wind;[2] hence a northerly wind would have been quite fair. St. Luke, in a ship in the same position between Carpathus (Scarpanto) and Cnidus, and meeting with the same winds, says shortly but correctly that the winds did not permit of their proceeding on their course,[3] and that they ran to leeward of Crete (v. 7).

[1] P. 465.

[2] He tells us that, as they were proceeding eastwards, there were only three out of eight winds that were contrary: Sirocco, Levante, and Gregale (p. 18); hence the ship could lie within six points of the wind.

[3] Commentators very generally suppose that μὴ προσεῶντος ἡμᾶς τοῦ ἀνέμου, meant that the winds defeated the purpose of taking shelter in the harbour of Cnidus. Dr. Hacket in his *Commentary on the Acts*

It appears to me that in the ancient ship they had, not only a more correct historian, but more skilful seamen. St. Luke tells us that they succeeded in reaching Fair Havens, although it was with difficulty. Rauwolf says that, although they got into smooth water under the lee of Crete, in their apprehensions of being driven towards Africa, they kept so close to the high land that they had much difficulty in avoiding being shipwrecked on Candia;[1] a proceeding which argues anything but good seamanship.[2] They saved their ship, but failed in their attempt to reach a harbour, which could be no other than Fair Havens, and were obliged to put back to the Calderon Islands.

Sir James, afterwards Lord de Saumarez, returning from Aboukir, after the battle of the Nile, with a detachment of Lord Nelson's fleet, stood to the north till he discovered the island of Cyprus, from whence he intended to pass by the north side of Candia (Crete);

observes, 'That προσεάω does not occur in the classics. Πρός cannot well mean *farther*, as some allege, since they would have no motive to continue the voyage in that direction, even if the weather had not opposed it.' Admiral Penrose, however, a better authority in such a matter, takes the same view as I have done. He explains the passage thus: '*The wind not suffering them to get on in the direct course.*' (See Conybeare and Howson, ii. p. 326, note.) We are not told wherein the difficulty of entering Cnidus, if they wished it, lay. Mr. Alford takes what I have no doubt is the correct view; see his note on the passage.

[1] 'Also wurden wir des Getöses und Rauschen der Winden und Wellen wol loss: dargegen cam unser Schiff den Gestadten Candiæ so nahe, das wir alle Augenblicke müsten eines Schiftbruchs gewartig sein.' (p. 465.)

[2] Ships standing too close to high land in stormy weather, with the wind off shore, are apt to be caught in what may be called eddy squalls. This was evidently the case in Rauwolf's ship.

but the winds proved contrary, and he was forced, like the ancient voyagers and Rauwolf,[1] to run to the south of that island. His delightful journal, addressed to Lady Saumarez, and written from day to day, throws much light upon the circumstances which affect the navigation of this part of the Mediterranean, and shows how perfectly they agree with those experienced by St. Paul and his companions.

On August 28, 1798, he writes :—

'We are still off the island of Rhodes, which appears fertile and well cultivated. We have also sight of Candia, at the distance of above thirty leagues ; our present route is different from any of the former, as we go to the northward of Candia, amidst the innumerable islands that form the Archipelago.'[2]

This was precisely the course which St. Paul's ship was pursuing. The contrary winds, however, forced Sir James Saumarez, as they had forced the ancient navigators, to run to the south of Crete. On September 1, 1798, he thus writes to Lord Nelson :—

'After contending three days against the adverse winds which are almost invariably encountered here, and getting sufficiently to the northward to have weathered the small islands that lie more immediately between the Archipelago and Candia, the wind set in so strong from the westward that I was compelled to desist from that passage, and was compelled to bear up between Scarpanto and Guxo (Carpathus and Casus).[3]

It is to be observed, that the fleet could not 'fetch' Salmone with the wind at west ; which shows that in

[1] P. 465. [2] *Life*, p. 248. [3] *Life*, p. 253.

FAIR HAVENS, CRETE.

the apostle's case the wind must have been to the north of west.

I have already adduced the case of Fynes Moryson, whose ship was also forced to deviate from the original intention of going to the north of Crete, and take the same course as St. Paul's.

After these instances, it will scarcely be thought necessary to have recourse to an ancient scholiast for the reasons which induced the navigators of St. Paul's ship to pass by the south of Cape Salmone; yet recent commentators assure us that 'this question is resolved by the account of Eustathius, who on another occasion mentions that there were no good ports on the northern side of that island (Crete)—*δυσλίμενος ἡ Κρήτη πρὸς τὴν βοῤῥᾶν.*'[1] In fact, it so happens that there are two excellent harbours on the north side of Crete—Souda and Spina Longa.

After working up along the southern coast of Crete, they reached Fair Havens, which we have seen is the farthest point which an ancient ship, navigating under the lee of Crete, could reach with north-west winds. As this is an important point in the voyage, it becomes necessary to ascertain precisely its situation, as well as that of the port of Phenice and the

---

8 Μόλις τε παραλεγόμενοι αὐτὴν ἤλθομεν εἰς τόπον τινὰ καλούμενον Καλοὺς Λιμένας, ᾧ ἐγγὺς ἦν πόλις Λασέα.

8 And hardly passing it, came unto a place which is called the Fair Havens; nigh whereunto was the city of Lasea.

---

[1] Valpy's edit. of N. Test. *ad loc.*, quoted from Dr. Falconer. Even Barthélemy, in his Anacharsis, is misled by Eustathius, and assures us there are no harbours on the north side of Crete.

island of Clauda. St. Luke marks the position of Fair Havens by its vicinity to the city of Lasea; but neither Fair Havens nor Lasea are noticed by any other ancient authority, nor have the ruins of the city been discovered in modern times.[1] Commentators have generally supposed that *Καλοὶ Λιμένες*, or Fair Havens, of St. Luke, is the same as *Καλὴ 'Ακτή*, or Fair Strand,[2] of Stephanus Byzantinus.[3] This, however, is said to be a city of Crete; but St. Luke, by mentioning Fair Havens as in the vicinity of a city, seems to show that there was no city there. Mr. Pashley found a district in Crete bearing the name of Akté, and supposes with probability that the city mentioned by Stephanus was situated there. This district is however at the west end of Crete, and cannot be the same as Fair Havens, which from the context must be on the south coast.

Mr. Pashley afterwards visited the place, which still bears the ancient name, and which I am prepared to show is identical with the Fair Havens of St. Luke; but unfortunately the work terminates with-

[1] Since the above was written, the ruins of this city have been discovered by my friend and relative the Rev. George Brown. (Appendix No. 1.) It lies just east of Fair Havens, and still retains its name. [The ruins, but not the name, seem to have been discovered by Captain Spratt in 1853. He writes (Feb. 13, 1855): 'Lassea was discovered by me on the coast about two miles east of Fair Havens.']

[2] 'Ακτὴ ὁ αἰγιαλὸς, καὶ ὁ παραθαλάσσιος τόπος, 'ἀκτή, the beach, and place along the sea.' (*Hesych.*) Notwithstanding the authority of Hesychius, which, however, is not great in such matters, I suspect that ἀκτή and αἰγιαλός are not synonymous; that the latter means a sandy beach (see note on v. 39); the former, a more general term, equivalent to the English strand. Julius Pollux distinguishes the χωρία ἐπιθαλαττίδια into ἀκτή, ἠών, αἰγιαλός, χηλή, ὕφορμος, ὅρμος, λιμήν. (Lib. i. 99.)

[3] Καλὴ 'Ακτὴ πόλις Κρητῶν, &c.

out any account of his observations. I am however indebted to Signor Antonio Schranz,[1] the able artist who accompanied him, for the view of this interesting locality taken upon the spot.

Dr. Pococke appears to have been the first who ascertained its exact situation ; he says—

'In searching after Lebena farther to the west, I found out a place which I thought to be of greater consequence, because mentioned in Holy Scripture, and also honoured by the presence of St. Paul, that is, the Fair Havens, near unto the city of Lasea ; for there is another small bay, about two leagues to the east of Matala, which is now called by the Greeks Good or Fair Havens (Λιμέονες Καλούς).'[2]

Dr. Pococke found no ruins here, nor is there reason to suppose that it ever was more than it is at present —an open roadstead, or rather two roadsteads contiguous to each other.

Its retention of its name is owing, no doubt, to its appropriateness. In the old sailing directions, 'Licht der Seevaert' (Amst. 1621), and 'Miroir de la Mer,' it is thus described :—

'Right to the coast of Cabra (an islet) lies a fair bay (een schoone bay, Dutch ; une belle baie, Fr.), where there is good anchorage ; there is also one immediately to the west of it, where there is also good anchorage.'[3]

---

[1] It will be seen that this view enabled my friends Messrs. Tennent and Brown to identify the locality. (Appendix No. 1.)

[2] *Travels in the East*, vol. ii. p. 250.

[3] 'Recht beeosten Cabra leygt een schoone bay, daer seer goed trede is, desheliger ook een der recht bewesten daer't saer goedte legghen is.' (*Licht der Seevaert*, p. 217.)

'Il y a, droit à l'est de Cabra, une belle baie, où il y a une fort bonne rade, comme aussi encore une autre droit à l'ouest de là, où il fait aussi bon d'ancrer.' (*Miroir de la Mer*, p. 80.)

The most conclusive evidence, however, that this is the Fair Havens of Scripture is that its position is precisely that where a ship, circumstanced as St. Paul's was, must have put in. I have already shown that the wind must have been about N.W., but with such a wind she could not pass Cape Matala; we must therefore look near to this promontory, but to the eastward of it, for an anchorage well calculated to shelter a vessel in north-west winds, but not from all winds, otherwise it would not have been in the opinion of seamen an unsafe winter harbour. Now, here we have a harbour which not only fulfils every one of the conditions, but still retains the name given to it by St. Luke.[1]

Here, we learn, they were detained till 'navigation had become dangerous,'[2] in consequence of the advanced state of the season. The fast, supposed of the Expiation, which took place about the period of the autumnal equinox, was now past. It would appear that by this time all hope of completing the

[1] 'We have now examined the journeys and voyages of St. Paul and his companions; and of the numerous places named therein, we find but seven which are omitted by Strabo, the chief of the ancient geographers that are come down to us. The rest are described by him in exact agreement with the history of the Acts. Of the seven omitted by him, five are fully and clearly spoken of by other ancient authors. There remain only two, therefore, of which a doubt can be admitted.' (*Biscoe*, p. 383.) He adds in a note, 'The two are *the Fair Havens* and *Lasea*, of which the former it is probable is the Καλὴ 'Ακτή of *Stephanus*, the latter the *Lasos* of *Pliny*.' The position of *Lasea* agrees with the Lisia of the Peutingerian tables, i.e. about the centre of the south coast of Crete. (See note, p. 82.)

[2] V. 9, ἐπισφαλοῦς τοῦ πλοός, the appropriate nautical term, πλοῦς ἀσφαλής, Jul. Pollux, i. 105.

voyage during the present season[1] was abandoned; and it became a question whether they should winter at Fair Havens, or move the ship to Port Phenice, a harbour on the same side of Crete, about forty miles further to the westward.

St. Paul assisted at the consultation, and strongly urged them to remain, addressing them in the following terms:—'Sirs, I perceive that this voyage will be with hurt and much damage, not only of the lading and ship, but also of our lives.' The officers of the ship were, however, of a different opinion, and the centurion naturally deferred to it. The event justified St. Paul's advice. At the same time it may be observed that a bay open to nearly one-half of the compass could not have been a good winter harbour.[2]

[1] According to Vegetius, the sailing season did not close so early; he states that 'ex die igitur tertio iduum Novembris, usque in diem sextum iduum Martiarum, maria clauduntur. Nam lux minima noxque prolixa, nubium densitas, aeris obscuritas, ventorum, imbrium, vel nivium geminata sævitia. Non solum classes a pelago, sed etiam commeantes a terrestri itinere deturbat.' (Lib. v. 9.) These dates correspond better with their stay in the island of Melita: chap. xxviii. v. 11. Μετὰ δὲ τρεῖς μῆνας ἀνήχθημεν, &c.

[2] I have allowed this passage to remain as it stood in the first edition; for it is interesting to observe how each addition to our knowledge of the scene of the narrative confirms its authenticity and accuracy. It now appears, from Mr. Brown's observations and the late surveys, that Fair Havens is so well protected by islands, that though not equal to Lutro, it must be a very fair winter harbour; and that considering the suddenness, the frequency, and the violence with which gales of northerly wind spring up, and the certainty that, if such a gale sprang up in the passage from Fair Havens to Lutro, the ship must be driven off to sea, the prudence of the advice given by the master and owner was extremely questionable, and that the advice given by St. Paul may probably be supported even on nautical grounds.

It was determined at this consultation to attempt to reach Phenice, a harbour of Crete, which looked, according to St. Luke, *κατὰ Λίβα καὶ κατὰ Χῶρον*, which is rendered in our version, 'lieth toward the south-west and north-west.' The intermediate point between these two winds is west ; and it is generally understood that the harbour looked to, or was open to, the west. Father Giorgi, aware that if it could be

---

9 Ἱκανοῦ δὲ χρόνου διαγενομένου καὶ ὄντος ἤδη ἐπισφαλοῦς τοῦ πλοὸς διὰ τὸ καὶ τὴν νηστείαν ἤδη παρεληλυθέναι, παρῄνει ὁ Παῦλος

10 Λέγων αὐτοῖς Ἄνδρες, θεωρῶ ὅτι μετὰ ὕβρεως καὶ πολλῆς ζημίας οὐ μόνον τοῦ φορτίου καὶ τοῦ πλοίου ἀλλὰ καὶ τῶν ψυχῶν ἡμῶν μέλλειν ἔσεσθαι τὸν πλοῦν.

11 Ὁ δὲ ἑκατοντάρχης τῷ κυβηρνήτῃ καὶ τῷ ναυκλήρῳ μᾶλλον ἐπείθετο ἢ τοῖς ὑπὸ Παύλου λεγομένοις.

12 Ἀνευθέτου δὲ τοῦ λιμένος ὑπάρχοντος πρὸς παραχειμασίαν οἱ πλείονες ἔθεντο βουλὴν ἀναχθῆναι ἐκεῖθεν, εἴ πως δύναιντο καταντήσαντες εἰς Φοίνικα παραχειμάσαι, λιμένα τῆς Κρήτης βλέποντα κατὰ Λίβα καὶ κατὰ Χῶρον.

9 Now when much time was spent, and when sailing was now dangerous, because the fast was now already past, Paul admonished *them*,

10 And said unto them, Sirs, I perceive that this voyage will be with hurt and much damage, not only of the lading and ship, but also of our lives.

11 Nevertheless the centurion believed the master and the owner of the ship, more than those things which were spoken by Paul.

12 And because the haven was not commodious to winter in, the more part advised to depart thence also, if by any means they might attain to Phenice, *and there* to winter ; *which is* an haven of Crete, and lieth toward the south-west and north-west.

proved Phenice was on the south side of Crete, a ship could not be driven off the island towards the Adriatic Gulf, infers from this that it was at the west end of the island,[1] and that the situation of Clauda is uncertain. Dr. Falconer, a man of undoubted learning, admits that it is not easy to determine the exact import of this passage; but supposes it to be 'open to both quarters of the heavens from whence these winds proceed, and of course unsheltered from these winds:' he then observes that 'this would, according to Vitruvius, leave 105° open to the west.'[2] Such a harbour would certainly not be 'commodious to winter in,' and would not have warranted the attempt which was made to move to it.

Although they never reached this harbour, it becomes of importance to ascertain its position; because, unless we do so, we can draw no safe inferences respecting the ship's place when she encountered the gale, a point which it is of importance to determine. The harbour of Phenice no longer retains its name;[3] there is, indeed, a place named Phœnikias in Pashley's map, not far from the position assigned to it by Strabo and Ptolemy; but this cannot be the port of Phenice, for it is not on the coast; although it may possibly be the city of that name, for Ptolemy

[1] 'Quo modo Phenice Australis si ad eam ex Bonis Portibus Paulus secundo Austro tendebat . . . incertus est Claudæ situs' (p. 195).

[2] Grotius takes the same view of the meaning of this passage; he remarks, 'Βλέποντα κατὰ Λίβα, respicientem *ad* Africum . . . . καὶ κατὰ Χῶρον, et *ad* Caurum.'

[3] So in the first edition. But this is a mistake; Lutro is still known by the name Phenice: see Mr. Brown's letter, App. i., and the chart of Port Lutro (Phenice).

mentions both a city and port of Phenice, or rather Phœnix.

Lutro, Sphakia, and Franco Castello, places on the south coast of Crete, have each been supposed to be Port Phenice. For our present purpose of ascertaining the ship's course, it is not very material which of them is meant; I am, however, satisfied that it is the harbour of Lutro.

This harbour, however, looks to the east. I have already shown that the words of St. Luke in the original are generally supposed to indicate a harbour open in the opposite direction; unless, therefore, we get over this difficulty, we must give up the idea that Lutro is meant. The question as to the import of the passage must depend on the meaning we affix to the preposition *κατά*, in connection with the winds. I apprehend it means '*in the same direction as*' (in Latin, secundum); if I am right, *βλέποντα κατὰ λίβα* does not mean, as is generally supposed, that it is open to the point *from* which that wind (Libs) blows, but to the point *towards* which it blows—that is, it is not open to the south-west but to the north-east.

Herodotus speaks of a ship being driven *κατὰ κῦμα καὶ ἄνεμον*;[1] now it is quite clear that, in this sense, a ship driven *κατὰ Λίβα* must be driven to the north-east. There is a passage in Arrian still more apposite to this point. In his Periplus of the Euxine he tells us, that when navigating the south coast of that sea, towards the east, he observed during a calm

[1] Lib. iv. c. 110; in the Latin translation, 'secundum fluctus et ventum.'

a cloud suddenly arise, 'driven before the east wind'[1] —ἐξεῤῥάγη κατ' εὖρον. Here there can be no mistake; the cloud must have been driven to the west. When St. Luke, therefore, describes the harbour of Phenice as looking κατὰ Λίβα καὶ κατὰ Χῶρον, I understand that it looks *to* the north-east, which is the point towards which Libs blows; and to the south-east, that *to* which Caurus blows.[2] Now this is ex-

[1] Ἄφνω νεφέλη ἐπαναστᾶσα ἐξεῤῥάγη κατ' εὖρον. (*Periplus Euxini*, p. 3.)

[2] Professor Hacket, in his *Commentary on the Acts*, p. 358, contests the above view of the meaning attached to κατά in the following note:— 'This mode of explaining κατὰ Λίβα involves, I think, two incongruities: first, it assigns opposite senses to the same term, viz. *south-west* as the name of a wind, and north-east as a quarter of the heavens; and, secondly, it destroys the force of βλέποντα, which implies certainly that the wind and the harbour confronted each other, and not that they were turned from each other. Mr. Smith adduces κατὰ κῦμα καὶ κατὰ ἄνεμον, from Herod. iv. 110; but the expression is not parallel as regards either the preposition or the noun; κατά there denotes conformity of motion, and not of situation, where the objects are at rest; and ἄνεμος does not belong to the class of proper names like Libs and Corus, which the Greeks employed in such geographical designations.' Professor Hacket then quotes the passage in which I refer to Arrian, and observes that, 'to quote the passage in that manner assumes the point in dispute,' and adduces the authority of Professor Felton, of Cambridge, U.S., in support of the view he takes respecting the meaning of the passage in Arrian. To these remarks I would reply, that εὖρος means either a point of the compass, or the wind which blows from that point. If Arrian meant the bearing of the phenomenon which he has recorded, then no doubt the meaning attached to the passage by Professors Hacket and Felton is the correct one; but it was of no consequence in what quarter of the heavens it was observed, and a seaman who draws his inference from the observed effects of the action of the winds upon clouds, would be more apt to notice the direction in which the clouds were flying, than the direction in which he first observed them.

Professor Lushington of the University of Glasgow, also a high authority in such questions, observes to a friend who applied to him on

actly the description of Lutro, which looks or is open to the east; but having an island in front which shelters it, it has two entrances, one looking to the north-east which is *κατὰ Λίβα*, and the other to the south-east, *κατὰ Χῶρον*. The island is not laid down in Pashley's map; I find it, however, in Lapie's map, and in the

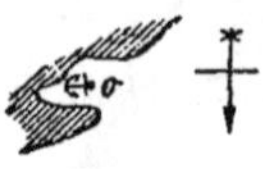

French admiralty chart of 1738. There is an anchor laid down inside, showing that it is a harbour. I cannot discover in sailing directions, ancient or modern, any hy-

the subject, 'I think the *κατά* question is very fairly dealt with by Mr. Smith; to pronounce positively, one should have hunted the maritime usages of wind language, of which blasts probably constitute a great portion with all nations. The phrase *κατ' εὖρον* is favourable, and also a passage in Thucyd. vi. 104, where a wind from the north is called *κατὰ βορέαν ἑστηκώς*.'

Dr. Howson, in his *Life of St. Paul*, considers 'my criticism quite tenable though unnecessary,' and cites a passage from Josephus, who, in speaking of the places between Joppa and Dora, says they were all *δύσορμα διὰ τὰς κατὰ λίβα προσβολάς*. Dr. Howson's explanation is that 'sailors speak of everything from their own point of view, and that such a harbour does "look," *from the water towards the land which encloses it*, in the direction of south-west and north-west.' (Vol. ii. p. 333.)

The fact that the harbour is open to the east admits now of no doubt; and as *κατά* is admitted to imply 'conformity of motion,' I am still of opinion that looking *in conformity with* the motion of the winds mentioned is what is meant. The island shelters the harbour, but it does not lie exactly in front of it, and the water between it and the land is too shallow to have formed an entrance. Mr. Brown observes, 'that there is only from three to six feet between it and the land.' (See Appendix No. 1.) It may indeed have been used as an entrance by small craft; and as St. Luke did not visit it, it might have been so described by native coasting seamen, from whom we must suppose St. Luke derived his information. Captain Spratt has shown, however, that an elevation of the land in this part of Crete has taken place within the human period, and therefore a passage may have existed when St. Luke wrote.

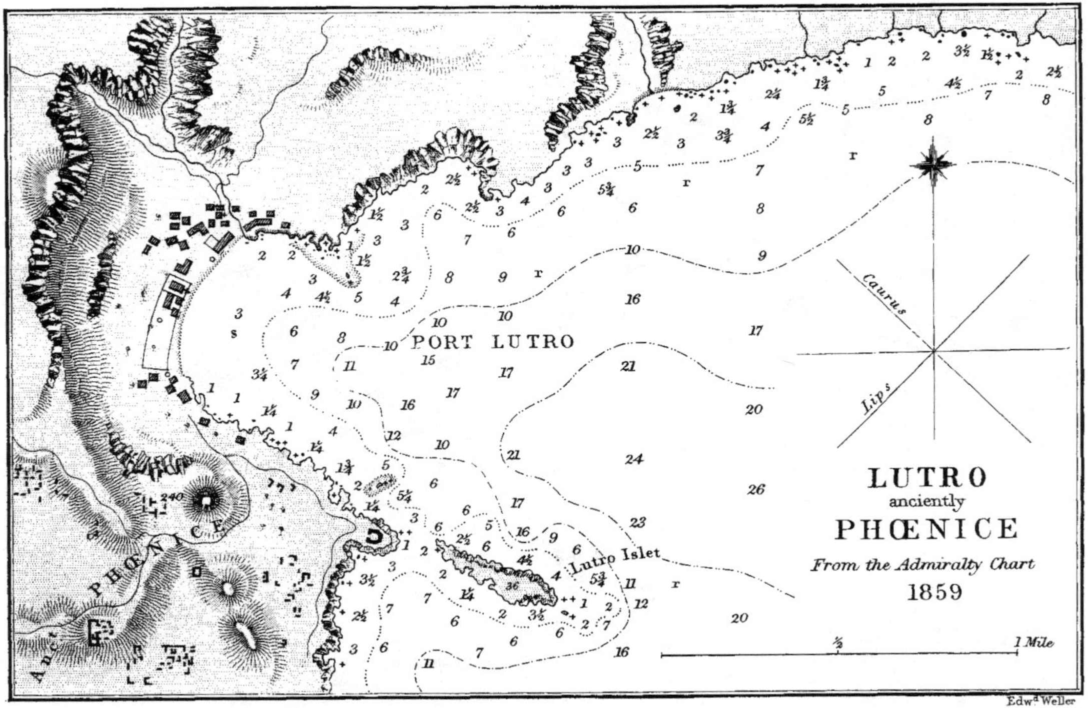

London: Longman & Co.

drographical description of it.[1] I have found it to be the general impression amongst naval officers acquainted with the navigation of these seas, that there are no ship harbours on the south side of Candia; but this is one of those harbours which, from the configuration of the land, must inevitably fill up in time. A mountain stream flows into it; and it is only necessary to look at the view given in Pashley's 'Travels'[2] to see in the ravine which in the course of ages it has hollowed out for itself, a proof that if the harbour could shelter the smallest craft in 1738, it must have been capable of sheltering the largest ships seventeen centuries before.[3]

[1] Since the above was written, the Admiralty survey and chart, of which the accompanying chart is a copy, have been completed, and leave nothing to be desired with regard to the hydrography of this harbour. Captain Spratt observes that 'it is the only bay where a vessel would be quite secure in winter . . . . It is represented to be safe in winter, as the south winds never blow home against the lofty precipitous mountains which rise above it; and the swell which then reaches the shore is consequently merely a dead swell, causing only motion to the vessel without strain to their ground-tackle.

'The head of a port has a narrow slip of shingle beach in front of a small garden, and a few houses. The position seems to confirm the statement of the natives regarding the safety of the port; for one of the houses is built within ten feet of the sea, and shows no indication of the sea ever reaching its foundation, consequently no damaging sea can ever exist within the port.' (*Sailing Directions for Crete*, p. 26.) I may add that the health officer at Lutro assured the Rev. George Brown that it (Lutro) was the only secure harbour in all winds on the south coast of Crete. (See Appendix No. 1, p. 253.)

[2] Frontispiece to vol. ii.

[3] When the above was written, the harbour may be said to have been unknown except to the native navigators. Upon reading the passage, Mr. Urquhart, M.P., well known for his writings on the East, kindly wrote to me that he had, when cruising with Lord Cochrane, during the Greek war, visited it, and thus expresses himself: 'Loutro is an excellent harbour. It opens like a box: unexpectedly the rocks

The next question is, does Lutro agree with the notices of Phenice which we find in the narrative of the voyage, and in ancient writers? In order to

stand apart, and the town opens within . . . . Excepting Loutro, all the roadsteads looking to the southward are perfectly exposed to the south or east.' Captain Spratt, R.N., also writes to me: 'Having in 1853 examined generally the south coast of Crete, I was fully convinced that Lutro was the Phenice of St. Paul, for it is the only bay to the westward of Fair Havens in which a vessel of any size could find any shelter during the winter months . . . . By hauling inside of the island (see chart of the south of Crete) and securing to the south shore of the bay a vessel is nearly land-locked. South-east and east only could endanger her; but with the former, where the fetch is greatest, the wind would not blow home against such a mountain as the White Mountains, so immediately over the bay, and rising to an elevation of 9,000 feet.' It will be seen from Mr. Brown's letter (Appendix No. 1) how completely Captain Spratt's conclusions respecting the goodness of this harbour are verified by the information he received upon the spot. The health officer informed him 'that though the harbour is open to the east, yet the easterly gales never blow home, being *lifted* by the high land behind, and that even in storms the sea rolls in gently (*piano, piano*); he says *it is the only secure harbour in all winds on the south coast of Crete.*' When we add to all this evidence the fact that the name of Phenice is still preserved by the natives, the evidence confirmatory of the conclusions respecting this locality is complete.

Canon Wordsworth, in his edition of the Acts, is inclined to adhere to the meaning attached to the passage by former editors and translators, on the ground that it is so rendered in the Vulgate. He supposes that a harbour may still be discovered to fit the description. He observes that there is a bay on the west side of the promontory, which contains Lutro, named Phineka, open to the west; but in the first place the south coast of Crete is now so well known, that we can say with certainty that there is no other harbour than Lutro in which a ship could winter to the west of Fair Havens, and that Phineka Bay is not open to Caurus. Dr. Wordsworth however adds, that 'if Lutro is Phœnix, the true rendering of the passage is this:—"If by any means they might reach Phenice and winter in it, being a Cretan harbour, which, *as approached by them*, entering it from the sea, looks towards the south-west and north-west, and is therefore sheltered from those winds by the land."'

agree with the narrative, the south wind must be a fair wind for a ship going from Fair Havens towards it. The first part of the course must lead a ship 'close past the land of Crete (v. 13);' and the last part must be at a certain distance from the land; for the expression in the fourteenth verse, *οὐ πολύ*, 'not long,' shows that they had passed the point where they were close to the land. On consulting the chart of the south coast of Crete, it will be seen that the position of Lutro agrees perfectly with every one of these notices.

Phenice, or rather Phœnix, is mentioned by Strabo, Ptolemy, Stephanus Byzantinus,[1] and in the Synecdemus of Hierocles. The last two authors merely mention it as a city of Crete. Hierocles, however, mentions it along with the island of Clauda;[2] now that island is exactly opposite to Lutro. According to Strabo, Phœnix is situated on the south side of the narrow part of Crete, which he calls an isthmus, on the north side of which is Amphimalla,[3] which also agrees with the situation of Lutro.

Ptolemy mentions both a city and port of Phenice. His longitudes, although they cannot be depended upon for the absolute position of places on

[1] Φοινικοῦς πόλις Κρήτης. (Steph. Byz.)

[2] Φοινίκη ἤτοι 'Αράδενα, νῆσος Κλαῦδος. (Hierocles.)

[3] Τὸ δὲ ἔνθεν ἰσθμός ἐστιν ὡς ἑκατὸν σταδίων, ἔχων κατοικίαν πρὸς μὲν τῇ Βορείῳ θαλάττῃ 'Αμφιμάλλαν, πρὸς δὲ τῇ νοτίῳ Φοινίκην τῶν Λαμπέων. (Lib. x. c. 4.) 'From thence is an isthmus of about a hundred stadia, having Amphimalla on the North Sea, and Phœnix of the Lampeans on the south.' The isthmus is, as nearly as possible, ten geographical miles, or one hundred stadia across.

the surface of the earth, are extremely useful in giving the relative positions of places with respect to places situated to the east or west. Now the difference of longitude between the eastern and western extremities of Crete, Κριοῦ μέτωπον ἄκρον (Cape St. John), and Σαμμώνιον ἄκρον (Cape Salmone), is according to him, 3° 5′: the actual distance is about 140 geographical miles. Hence the mean length of a degree of longitude in Crete is, according to Ptolemy, 45½ miles. Port Phenice is placed by him three-quarters of a degree to the east of Κριοῦ μέτωπον, which is equal to thirty-four geographical miles; the actual distance of Lutro from the same point is thirty-two. He places it 2° 20′ to the west of Salmone, which is equal to 106 miles; the actual distance on the French chart is 108 miles.[1]

The only traveller who has collected evidence upon the spot, bearing upon this point, is Mr. Pashley. It is not so complete as could have been wished, because that part of his work has been left unfinished; he has, however, stated enough to confirm the foregoing evidence. He found, a short distance above Lutro, two villages, bearing the names of Anopolis and Aradhena, and observes that,—

> 'The mention of an ancient city called Aradena, along with Anopolis and Port Phœnix in the Synecdemus of Hierocles, seems to point plainly to Lutro as the site of the last-named city.' (Vol. ii. p. 257.)

Mr. Pashley subsequently visited Lutro, and has marked on his map ruins near it, to which he gives the name of Port Phœnix.

[1] Ptol. lib. iii. c. 17.

If we compare his map with the notices in Hierocles and Stephanus, it will be found that they throw light on each other. According to Hierocles, Phenice was also named Aradena.[1] According to Stephanus,

> 'Araden, a city of Crete, also called Anopolis, or Upper Town, because it is upper.'[2]

Now upon the map these three places are little more than a mile from each other, and Anopolis is *above* Lutro. I think that we may conclude, therefore, with certainty, that the port of Phenice is the present port of Lutro.

With regard to the position of the island of Clauda there is no difficulty; it is unquestionably the same as the Claudos of Ptolemy, which he places to the south-west of Crete, and the Gozzo of the modern charts. Ptolemy, it is true, places it a degree too far to the west, which is perhaps a clerical error; but there is no island near his position, or for which it can be mistaken. The mention of it in the Synecdemus of Hierocles along with Port Phenice points very clearly to its true position. In many manuscripts it is spelt Cauda, which agrees with the spelling of Pliny and Suidas. Pomponius Mela spells it Gaudos, which is its present Greek name, Gaudonesi, or Island of Gaudos, which has been Italianized into Gozzo.[3] We have, therefore, the relative positions of

[1] Hierocles merely says, *Φοινίκη ἤτοι Ἀράδενα*, which implies that Phenice was also called Aradena.

[2] *Ἀράδην πόλις Κρήτης· ἡ δὲ Ἀνωπόλις λέγεται, διὰ τὸ εἶναι ἄνω.*

[3] Mr. Brown was informed upon the spot that the island still retained its ancient name Chlauda or Clauda Nesi, **Χλαῦδα** or **Κλαῦδα**

the three places mentioned in the proceedings of the day on which the Apostle and his companions left Crete, the events of which I shall now take into consideration.

Νῆσι. (See Appendix No. 1.) [The MSS. are much divided as to the spelling of this name. Westcott and Hort as well as Tregelles follow B. and the Vulgate in reading **Καῦδα.**]

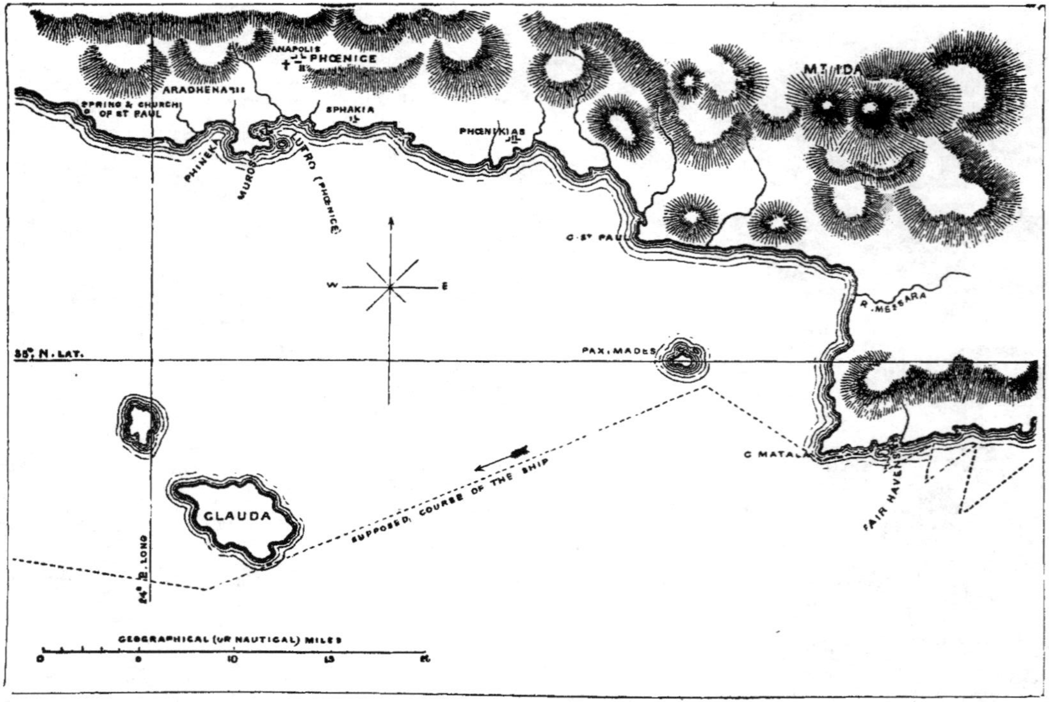

PART OF THE SOUTH COAST OF CRETE.

CHAPTER III.

CRETE TO MELITA.—THE GALE.

(Acts xxvii. 13.)

THE ship, as we have seen, remained wind-bound at Fair Havens till the advanced state of the season rendered navigation dangerous. They had however resolved, at the consultation mentioned in verses 10 and 12, to move to Port Phenice, as a more secure winter harbour; and a moderate breeze from the south having sprung up, it was considered favourable for their purpose. They accordingly weighed anchor.[1] After clearing the harbour, their course, till they had passed Cape Matala, was close to the land. A ship

13 Ὑποπνεύσαντος δὲ Νότου δόξαντες τῆς προθέσεως κεκρατηκέναι ἄραντες ἆσσον παρελέγοντο τὴν Κρήτην.

13 And when the south wind blew softly, supposing that they had obtained *their* purpose, loosing *thence* they sailed close by Crete.

[1] Ἄραντες may be translated either 'weighed' or 'set sail;' for ancient authors sometimes supply τὰς ἀγκύρας, 'anchors,' and sometimes τὰ ἱστία, 'sails.' (See note on ver. 4, and by Dindorf on Xenophon, *Hellen.* vi. 2.) Julius Pollux, however, like St. Luke, supplies neither, which is certainly the most nautical way of expressing it; he says, αἴροντες ἀπὸ τῆς γῆς. (Lib. i. 103.)

which could not lie nearer to the wind than seven points would just weather that point which bears W. by S. from the entrance of Fair Havens. We see therefore the force and propriety of the expression, 'they sailed *close* by Crete' (*ἆσσον*[1] *παρελέγοντο τὴν Κρήτην*), which the author uses to describe the first part of their passage. From the anchorage at Fair Havens to Cape Matala the distance is three or four miles, and from thence to Port Phenice the distance is thirty-four miles; and as the bearing of the course is W.N.W., the south wind was as favourable as could be desired, being two points abaft the beam. They had every prospect, therefore, of reaching their destination in a few hours. Their course lay across the great southern bight to the west of Cape Matala. They had not proceeded far (*οὐ πολύ*), however, when a sudden change in the weather took place.

> 'The flattering wind that late with promis'd aid
> From Candia's bay th' unwilling ship betray'd,
> No longer fawns beneath the fair disguise,
> But like a ruffian on his quarry flies.'
>
> (Falconer's 'Shipwreck,' canto ii.)

The ship was 'caught' (*συναρπασθέντος*) in a typhoon (*ἄνεμος τυφωνικός*), which blew with such violence that they could not face it,[2] but were forced,

[1] Ἆσσον, πλησίον, ἐγγύς· ἆσσον ἴτε, ἐγγὺς ἔρχεσθαι. (Hesych.)

[2] Ἀντοφθαλμεῖν, 'to look in the face.' The meaning of the expression is sufficiently obvious; the origin of it is probably drawn from the practice of the ancients of painting an eye on each side of the bow of their ships: a practice which still prevails in the coasting craft in the Mediterranean.

in the first instance, to scud before it,[1] for such is the evident meaning of the expression—*ἐπιδόντες ἐφερόμεθα*—'yielding to it we were borne along by it.' It follows from this that it must have blown off the land, for had it not they must have been stranded upon the Cretan coast, if they had been unable to gain their harbour. The expression, therefore, *ἔβαλεν κατ' αὐτῆς*, 'there arose against it,' cannot mean that it 'arose against Crete,' as some writers contend. The most obvious meaning is, that the typhoon struck the ship. It is quite true that according to strict grammatical rule the pronoun should stand for the last-mentioned noun; yet in it practice frequently refers to what is uppermost in the mind of the person who uses it at the time. St. Luke, who was in the ship, could not avoid thinking of its effect on the ship, but would certainly never dream of its effects upon an

14 *Μετ' οὐ πολὺ δὲ ἔβαλεν κατ' αὐτῆς ἄνεμος τυφωνικὸς ὁ καλούμενος Εὐρακύλων·*	14 But not long after there arose against it [or came down from it] a tempestuous wind called Euroaquilo.
15 *Συναρπασθέντος δὲ τοῦ πλοίου καὶ μὴ δυναμένου ἀντοφθαλμεῖν τῷ ἀνέμῳ ἐπιδόντες ἐφερόμεθα.*	15 And when the ship was caught, and could not bear up unto the wind, we let her drive.

[1] The appropriate nautical term, equivalent to the English one, to scud, is *ἀνακωχεύειν*, 'dicitur cum exorta tempestate in mari demptis velis navigium ventis sine repugnatione permittitur.' (Suidas.) The translation of Giorgi expresses the same meaning, 'non potente aspicere contra ventum, concedentes ferebamur.' Canon Wordsworth quotes with approval, 'We gave the ship to the gale and scudded before it.' The action of scudding before the wind could not be more clearly described than it is in the text.

island.[1] We know that it blew them out of their course towards the island of Clauda; if therefore we know whereabouts the ship was when the gale overtook her, we can form a tolerable estimate of the

[1] It is objected to this interpretation of κατ' αὐτῆς that πλοῖον, a neuter noun, has hitherto been used to designate the ship, and therefore had the ship been in the mind of the writer, it would have been κατ' αὐτοῦ. Now, without pretending to know the reason, I think it not improbable that there may be occasions in which ναῦς would be a more appropriate term than πλοῖον, and that this may be one of them, just as in modern language there are cases in which the less general term 'ship' would be used in preference to the more general one 'vessel.' In verse 41, St. Luke says 'they ran the ship ashore,' ἐπέκειλαν τὴν ναῦν, although in verse 39, where this measure was only contemplated, he speaks of 'thrusting the vessel (τὸ πλοῖον) into a creek.' Assuming this to be the case, I do not consider that we must of necessity refer the pronoun to the last preceding noun.

I, however, defer to the opinion of better scholars than myself, and admit the interpretation of Mr. Alford, Mr. Howson, and, I may add, the Rev. Mr. Drake of Coventry, and the Rev. Dr. Miller of Glasgow, who did me the honour to write to me on the subject; the former of whom, alluding to my explanation of κατὰ λίβα, &c., observes, 'exactly according with your views, κατ' αὐτῆς means *down from it*, down from the mountain-gorges of the island.' So also Mr. Alford understands it as '*down the highlands forming the coast.*' Mr. Alford supposes that when they had doubled, or were perhaps now doubling Cape Matala, the wind suddenly changed, and the typhoon '*came down upon them from the high lands.*'

When I compare what Mr. Alford supposes must have happened to St. Paul and his companions, with what did happen to my friend Captain Spratt, R.N., and in the same circumstances, I am more persuaded that his view of the passages is the right one. Captain Spratt thus writes me: 'In respect to the gale of wind I met with after starting from Fair Havens for Messara Bay, we left *with a light southerly wind* and clear sky—every indication of a fine day, until we rounded the cape (Matala), to haul up for the head of the bay. Then we saw Mount Ida covered in a dense cloud, and met a strong northerly breeze—one of the summer gales so frequent in the Levant, but which in general are accompanied by terrific gusts from those high mountains, the wind blowing direct from Mount Ida.'

direction of the wind which drove them thither. According to the narrative, it was not long, *οὐ πολύ*, after the ship was close to Crete, which can only mean that she had not passed over much of the space interposed between that point and the intended termination of her voyage, Port Phenice. The term employed by the Evangelist is a relative one, and must mean less than the half. Hence the ship must have been somewhere between Cape Matala, and a point bearing W.N.W., distant seventeen miles. But the former point bears E. 7° N. from Clauda, to which they were driven, and the latter E. 43° N. The wind, therefore, which drove them thither, must have been to the north of E. 7° N., but to the east of E. 43° N. The intermediate point, which cannot be so much as a point and a half from the true direction, is E. 25° N., or E.N.E. ¼ N. Another circumstance mentioned in the narrative indicates the direction of the wind within still narrower limits. When under Clauda they were apprehensive of being driven towards the Syrtis (v. 17); but the winds which blow from Clauda towards the Syrtis range between E. 18° N. and E. 37° N., the mean of which is E. 27° 30′ N., and the mean of both deductions is E. 26° 15′ N., or about E.N.E. ½ N., which cannot deviate so much as one point from the true direction of the wind, and does not differ a quarter of a point from the former determination.

Writers, such as Bentley and Penn,[1] who have drawn their conclusions from etymological reasons, infer that the wind was from the point between Eurus and Aquilo, or E.N.E. We have therefore three separate modes of estimating the direction of the gale

[1] See Appendix for the remarks of these writers.

perfectly independent of each other, and none of them differing from the other so much as half a point. Now there is not one circumstance mentioned in the subsequent part of the narrative which is not perfectly accounted for upon the supposition that this was the true direction of the wind; I differ, therefore, from the commentators who think that it was not a 'point wind,'—that is a wind blowing steadily from one point,—for I consider that no change took place in its direction during the remainder of the voyage.

The sudden change from a south wind to a violent northerly wind is a common occurrence in these seas.[1] The term '*typhonic*,' by which it is described, indicates that it was accompanied by some of the phenomena which might be expected in such a case, namely the agitation and whirling motion of the clouds caused by the meeting of the opposite currents of air when the change took place, and probably also of the sea, raising it in columns of spray. Pliny, in describing the effects of sudden blasts, says that they cause a vortex, which is called 'typhoon;'[2] and Gellius, in his account of a storm at sea, notices 'frequent whirlwinds,'

[1] Captain J. Stewart, R.N., in his remarks on the Archipelago, observes, 'It is always safe to anchor under the lee of an island with a northerly wind, as it dies away gradually; but it would be extremely dangerous with *southerly winds, as they almost invariably shift to a violent northerly wind*.'

See also the note at p. 100. So also Messrs. Tennent and Brown, when they landed to examine Port Phenice, their vessel being becalmed with light airs from the south and south-east, before they could reach the bay, saw a heavy squall from the north blowing out of it; this blew the yacht, a large powerful vessel of about 200 tons, out to sea, and left the visitors on shore for the night. (See Appendix No. 1.)

[2] Lib. ii. c. xlviii. De Repentinis Flatibus: 'Vortic m faciunt qui Typhon vocatur.'

'. . . . and the dreadful appearances in the clouds which they call typhoons.'[1]

St. Luke therefore by the single word 'typhonic' expresses the nature and violence of the gale, and by another, its direction. In the subjoined Dissertation on the wind Euroclydon I have stated my reasons for preferring the reading of the most ancient manuscripts and versions, Euro-aquilo, which must be between Eurus and Aquilo, or E.N.E.[2]

I now proceed to inquire into the effects it produced upon the ship. Nothing more is said in the narrative than that it defeated their object of reaching Port Phenice, and forced them to run under the lee (*ὑποδραμόντες*[3]) of Claude. It will, however, be found

16 Νησίον δέ τι ὑποδραμόντες, καλούμενον Καῦδα, ἰσχύσαμεν μόλις περικρατεῖς γενέσθαι τῆς σκάφης,	16 And having run under a certain island, which is called Cauda, we had much work to come by the boat,

[1] Lib. xix. c. i.: 'Turbines etiam crebriores . . . et figuræ quædam nubium metuendæ quas *τυφῶνας* vocabant.' Hesychius merely calls it the 'great wind,' *τυφῶν ὁ μέγας ἄνεμος.*

[2] This is another question in Biblical criticism set at rest by recent discovery. Since that of the Codex Sinaiticus, no critic, who knows how to weigh evidence, will sanction the word Euroclydon, or suppose that St. Luke could have written the passage *ἄνεμος τυφωνικὸς ὁ καλούμενος εὐροκλύδων*, 'a typhonic wind which is called an eastern wave'! Canon Wordsworth, Dr. Tregelles, Bornemann, and Lachmann, in their critical editions adopt the reading *εὐρακύλων*, and my friends Dean Alford and Dr. Howson, although they at first adhered to the received reading, have also given up Euroclydon. (See Dissertation 1, 'On the wind Euroclydon.')

[3] *Ὑποδραμόντες*, 'having *run* under the lee of.' St. Luke exhibits here, as on every other occasion, the most perfect command of nautical terms, and gives the utmost precision to his language by selecting the

that the ship must have strained and suffered severely in her hull, and that the leaks she then sprang were gradually gaining upon the crew, and that if they had not providentially made the land, and been thereby enabled to save their lives by running the ship on shore, she must have foundered at sea, and all on board perished.

As the knowledge of this fact can only be gained by circumstantial evidence, and as it throws a clear light upon the subsequent proceedings, it is necessary to state the proofs at some length; but before I do so, I would observe that such a result of a typhoon, not unfrequent in modern times, seems to have been almost inevitable in ancient times. Pliny calls the typhoon—

> 'The chief pest of seamen, destructive not only to the spars but to the hull itself.' [1]

In the accounts of shipwrecks which have come down to us from ancient times, the loss of the ship must, in a great number of instances, be ascribed to this cause. Josephus tells us that on his voyage to Italy the ship sank in the midst of the Adriatic Sea.[2] He and some of his companions saved themselves by swimming; the ship, therefore, did not go down during the gale, but in consequence of the damage she sustained during its continuance. One of St.

most appropriate; they ran before the wind to leeward of Clauda, hence it is ὑποδραμόντες: they sailed with a side wind to leeward of Cyprus and Crete; hence it is ὑπεπλεύσαμεν.

[1] 'Præcipua navigantium pestis non antennas modo verum ipsa navigia contorta frangens.' (Lib. ii. cap. xlviii.)

[2] Βαπτισθέντος γὰρ ἡμῶν τοῦ πλοίου κατὰ μέσον τὸν 'Αδρίαν. (*Vita*, c. iii.)

Paul's shipwrecks must have taken place under the same circumstances; for he tells us, 'a day and a night I have been in the deep,' supported, no doubt, on spars or fragments of the wreck, or it may be in boats. In Virgil's description of the casualties of the ships of Æneas, some are driven on rocks, others on quicksands; but,

> 'Laxis laterum compagibus *omnes*
> Accipiunt inimicum imbrem, rimisque fatiscunt.'

The fact, that the ships of the ancients were provided with hypozomata, or cables ready fitted for undergirding, as a necessary part of their stores, proves how liable they were to such casualties; and I may add as another proof the frequent notice of lightening ships we meet with in ancient authors. In the present narrative they occur not less than three times. In the ship of Jonah it is stated that 'they cast forth the wares that were in the ship into the sea to lighten it' (i. 5); and Juvenal, in describing the dangers encountered by Catullus, not only uses similar language, but assigns the reason—

> 'Cum plenus fluctu medius foret alveus, ...
> . . . . . .
> . . . . decidere jactu.' (*Sat.* xii. 30.)

It is easy to account for the comparative immunity of modern ships from such casualties. The most obvious cause is the improvement in naval architecture; but another, and I suspect a more efficient one, is the manner in which they were rigged. In modern times the strain is spread over three masts, with small sails which can be quickly taken in; but the ancient ships had to sustain the leverage of a single mast, with a ponderous yard at the upper end. We can scarcely suppose that St. Paul's ship escaped uninjured. The circumstances mentioned, of her being undergirded, lightened, and finally run ashore, afford conclusive evidence that she did not.

Keeping this in view, we may form some idea of the hardships the ship's company endured. St. Luke shared them all; but he never mentions them, except on one occasion, and that was to illustrate a passage in the life of St. Paul.

At the time the ship was caught in the gale, she must have been near a small group of islands, called the Paximades, in the Gulf of Messara. The island of Clauda lay about twenty-three miles to leeward, and thither they were driven, as the expression *ἐπιδόντες ἐφερόμεθα* (ver. 15) [1] implies, before the gale. Upon reaching it they availed themselves of the smooth water under its lee, to prepare the ship to resist the fury of the storm. Their first care was to secure the boat, by hoisting it on board. This had not been done at first, because the weather was moderate, and the distance they had to go short. Under such circumstances it is not usual to hoist the boats on board, but it had now become necessary. In running down upon Clauda it could not be done, on account of the ship's way through the water. To enable them to do it, the ship must have been

[1] Rightly rendered by Canon Wordsworth, 'We gave the ship to the gale and scudded before it,' ad ἐπιδόντες supplendum τὸ πλοῖον quod præcessit. Heliod. *Æthiop.* i. 3, τοῦ κυβερνήτου ἐνδόντος (scil. τὸ πλοῖον) τῷ ἀνέμῳ . . . Herod. iii. 30, ἐφέροντο κατὰ κῦμα καὶ ἄνεμον. (Note on the passage.)

rounded to, with her head to the wind, and her sails if she had any set at the time trimmed, so that she might have no head way, or progressive movement.

> 'The boats then hoisted in are fix'd on board
> And on the deck with fastening gripes secured.'
> ('Shipwreck,' canto ii.)

In this position the ship would drift bodily to leeward. I conclude that they passed round the east end of the island; not only because it was nearest, but because there are dangers at the opposite end.[1] In this case the ship would be brought to on the starboard tack,—that is, with the right side to windward.[2] This must be kept in mind, because it throws light upon a subsequent passage. St. Luke tells us that they had much difficulty in securing the boat (v. 16). He does not say why; but independently of the gale which was raging at the time, the boat had been

17 Ἣν ἄραντες βοηθείαις ἐχρῶντο ὑποζωννύντες τὸ πλοῖον·

17 Which when they had taken up, they used helps, undergirding the ship;

---

[1] 'An extensive reef, with numerous rocks, extends from Gozo to the N.W., which renders the passage between the two isles very dangerous.' (*Sailing Directions* p. 207.) 'On peut passer entre Gozo et Gozo Pulo; il faut de la pratique, et nous ne voyons pas la nécessité de s'engager dans un passage dangereux.' (*Manuel de Pilotage*, p. 412.)

[2] 'I consider the ship to have drifted with her starboard side towards the wind, or on the starboard tack, as a sailor expresses it. When the south wind blew softly, the ship was slowly sailing along the coast of Crete with her starboard side towards the land, or towards the north . . . The storm came on her starboard side, and in this manner . . . . she drifted.' (Admiral Penrose's observations; Conybeare and Howson, vol. ii. p. 339.)

towed between twenty and thirty miles after the gale sprung up, and could scarcely fail to be filled with water. Having accomplished this necessary task, their next care was to undergird the ship, which the state in which she was had rendered imperative. This expedient is so rarely had recourse to in modern times, that I have only met with one naval officer who had seen it put in practice, although almost all of my nautical friends whom I have consulted, could furnish me with instances in which they had heard of its being done. The officer to whom I allude, Mr. Henry Smartley, who was master of the Royal Sovereign, was employed in 1815, to pilot the Russian fleet from England to the Baltic. One of the ships (the Jupiter) was frapped round the middle by three or four turns of a stream cable. Mr. Smartley is father to the talented marine painter, Mr. Smartley of Jersey; and it was under his direction that the undergirding is represented in the view which I have given of the ship anchored by the stern.

The mode in which ships are undergirded is thus described by Falconer, in his 'Marine Dictionary:'—

> 'To frap a ship (*ceintrer un vaisseau*) is to pass four or five turns of a large cable-laid rope round the hull or frame of a ship, to support her in a great storm, or otherwise, when it is apprehended that she is not strong enough to resist the violent efforts of the sea; this expedient, however, is rarely put in practice.'

It would not be difficult to multiply instances where this mode of strengthening ships has been put in practice in modern times;[1] I content myself with

[1] The *Albion*, 74, encountered a hurricane on her voyage from India, and was under the necessity of frapping her hull together, in

the latest I can find. Captain (now Sir George) Back, on his perilous return from his Arctic voyage, in 1837, was forced, in consequence of the shattered and leaky condition of his ship, to undergird her. It was thus done :—

'A length of the stream chain-cable was passed under the bottom of the ship four feet before the mizen mast, hove tight by the capstan, and finally immovably fixed to six ring-bolts on the quarter-deck. The effect was at once manifested by a great diminution in the working of the parts already mentioned ; and in a less agreeable way, by impeding her rate of sailing ; a trifling consideration, however when compared with the benefit received.' [1]

We are told, that subsequent to this they met with a gale :—

'The water rushed in violently below, more especially about the stern-post and heel-hook, and oozing through different parts higher up, fell like a cascade into the bread-room and run . . . While apprehensive that further injury had been sustained about the keel, another length of chain was passed under the bottom and set well tight to a part of itself, across the after part of the quarter-deck.' (P. 438.) [2]

We are next told by St. Luke, 'that being apprehensive of being driven towards the Syrtis, they lowered the gear.' It is not easy to imagine a more

order to prevent her sinking. (*United Service Mag.* May 1846.) The *Queen* came home from Jamaica frapped or undergirded ; and the *Blenheim,* in which Sir Thomas Troubridge was lost, left India frapped. See other instances in Conybeare and Howson's *Life of St. Paul*, vol. ii. p. 337, note.

[1] *Voyage*, p. 433.

[2] See details of undergirding in Dissertation on Ancient Ships.

erroneous translation than that of our authorised version :—

'Fearing lest they should fall into the quicksands, strake sail, and so were driven.' (Ver. 17.)

It is in fact equivalent to saying that, fearing a certain danger, they deprived themselves of the only possible means of avoiding it.[1] It is not by striking mast or sail that such dangers are to be avoided.

I have already shown that the same wind which drove them, 'when yielding to it' (ἐπιδόντες), to Clauda, would, if they had continued to scud, have driven them directly towards the Syrtis. Under the circumstances in which they were now placed, they had but one course to pursue in order to avoid the apprehended danger, which was to turn the ship's head off shore, and to set such sail as the violence of

Φοβούμενοί τε μὴ εἰς τὴν Σύρτιν ἐκπέσωσιν, χαλάσαντες τὸ σκεῦος, οὕτως ἐφέροντο.	And, fearing lest they should fall into the quicksands, lowered the gear, and so were driven.

[1] Of course, if any sail were set it could not be the mast which was lowered, as many commentators suppose ; indeed, it is not possible to suppose that the main-masts of large sailing ships were made to strike, like those of a Thames barge, although no doubt those of the row-galleys were :—

Ἐν δὲ καὶ αὐτὸν
Ἱστὸν ἄφαρ χαλάσαντο.

(Apollonius Rhodius, ii. 1267.)

Juvenal tells us that the mast of the ship of Catullus was '*cut* away' (*Sat.* xii. 54), and recommends his friends to provide themselves with hatchets before going to sea :

Adspice sumendas in tempestate secures.' (*Sat.* xii. 61.)

the gale would permit them to carry. As they did avoid the danger, we may be certain, notwithstanding the silence of the historian, that this was the course which was adopted. I have already assigned my reasons for supposing that the ship must have been laid to on the starboard tack under the lee of Clauda, for it was only on this tack that it was possible to avoid being driven on the African coast; when, therefore, they had taken every precaution against foundering which prudence or skilful seamanship could dictate, all that was required was to fill their storm sail, probably already set, and to stand on.

The question remains to be answered, What is the meaning of the expression 'lowering the gear,' '*χαλάσαντες τὸ σκεῦος*'? *Σκεῦος*, which I have translated 'gear,'[1] when applied to a ship, means appurtenances of every kind, such as spars, sails, rigging, anchors and cables, &c. Now, every ship situated as this one was, when preparing for a storm, sends down upon deck the 'top-hamper,' or gear connected with the fair-weather sails, such as the *suppara*, or top-sails. A modern ship sends down top-gallant masts and yards;[2] a cutter strikes her topmast, when preparing for a gale. The author here, as elsewhere, states the fact, but gives no details; a seaman could scarcely

[1] Rightly translated by Böckh, 'Geräthe;' Scoticè, 'Graith.' 'There I beheld a galeasse *gaily graithit for the weyr*, lyand fast at ane ankir' (*Complaynte of Scotland*), i.e. 'Gallantly furnished for the war.' M. Jal, whose courage as a translator is more conspicuous than his caution, amusingly renders it—'Qui virait gaiement sur l'ancre.'

[2] Gower in his *Treatise on Seamanship*, gives the following instructions for preparing for a gale:—'Let the top-gallant yards and masts, mizen-topsail yard, mizen yard, and cross-jack yard, be got down on deck, that the ship may be made as snug as possible.' (P. 54.)

have avoided doing so, if he had mentioned the circumstance at all. It is unnecessary to multiply instances which are so common as to occur in almost every account of a storm at sea; I content myself, therefore, by giving a parallel case with the present, namely that of one who was not a seaman, but was perfectly cognisant of nautical matters, Donald Campbell of Barbreck.[1] On his passage from Goa to Madras he was shipwrecked on the coast of Malabar. Many of the events bear a striking resemblance to those recorded by St. Luke in his account. 'Lowering the gear' is mentioned in the following terms:—

> 'Such exertions were made that, before morning, every stick that could possibly be struck was down upon the deck.

The only plausible conjecture I have met with respecting what was lowered, is that of Pricæus, who supposes it was 'not the mast, but the yard with the sail attached to it.'[2] This, indeed, is but a conjecture, but it is a probable one. We know, from the representations on coins and marbles, that the ancients were in the habit of furling their sails aloft; and unless the main-yard was lowered when the ship was running before the wind, which we are not told was the case, it must have been done now. This, however, is but conjecture; and, in such an inquiry as the present, it is necessary to distinguish between conjecture and inference. At all events, we may conclude with perfect certainty, that their object in 'lowering the gear' was to enable them to avoid the Syrtis; because we are, in effect, told that it was so,

[1] *Journey to India*, pt. iii. p. 16.

[2] 'Non malum, sed cum appenso velo antennam.' (*Pricæus in loq.*)

—'fearing lest they should be driven to the Syrtis, they lowered the gear.' This alone, however, was not sufficient to have kept the ship off a lee shore. There were but two ways by which that could have been effected. She might have been anchored,[1] or her head might have been turned off shore, and such sail set as the violence of the gale would permit her to carry. We know that the first of the alternatives was not adopted; we must therefore conclude that the last was, for by no other way could she have avoided the apprehended danger.

A ship at sea, in a gale, must either scud or lie-to. In the present case, to have adopted the former alternative would have been to have rushed on certain destruction. Falconer, in his notes on the shipwreck, observes:—

'The movement of scudding is never attempted in a contrary wind unless, as in the present instance, the condition of the ship rendered her incapable of any longer sustaining on her side the mutual effort of the wind and waves. The principal hazards incident to scudding are generally a *pooping* sea; the difficulty of steering, which exposes the vessel perpetually to the risk of broaching-to; and the want of sufficient sea-room. A sea striking the ship violently on the stern may dash it inwards, by which she must inevitably founder; in broaching-to suddenly, she is threatened with being immediately over-set; and for want of sea-room she is endangered with shipwreck on a lea-shore, a circumstance too dreadful to require explanation.'

This last must have been the inevitable consequence,

[1] There is an anchorage at Clauda; but it is open to the E.N.E., and therefore would have afforded no shelter in the present case.

had the ship been allowed to be driven at the mercy of the winds, as is generally supposed.

The only question which now remains to be answered is, Which tack was the ship laid-to upon? The answer is not difficult: if it had been on the port tack, that is, with her left side to the wind, she must have inevitably drifted upon the coast of Africa, with the wind at E.N.E., as we have proved it to have been,[1] and would, moreover, have been driven completely out of her course.

We are thus forced to the conclusion, when we are told that 'they were thus borne along,' *οὕτως ἐφέροντο*, that it was not only with the ship undergirded and made snug, but that she had storm sails set,[2] and was on the starboard tack, which was the only course by which she could avoid falling into the Syrtis. With this notice concludes the first eventful day.

On the following day (*τῇ ἑξῆς*, ver. 18), the gale continuing unabated, they lightened the ship.[3] Every

---

18 Σφοδρῶς δὲ χειμαζομένων ἡμῶν τῇ ἑξῆς ἐκβολὴν ἐποιοῦντο,

18 And we being exceedingly tossed with a tempest, the next *day* they lightened the ship.

---

[1] See Dissertation on Euroclydon.

[2] 'In a storm with a contrary wind or on a lee-shore, a ship is obliged to lie-to under a very low sail; some sail is absolutely necessary to keep the ship steady, otherwise she would pitch about like a cork, and roll so deep as to strain and work herself to pieces.' (*Encyc. Brit.* art. 'Seamanship.')

[3] The technical terms for taking cargo out of a ship, given by Julius Pollux, are, *ἐκθέσθαι, ἀποφορτίσασθαι, κουφίσαι τὴν ναῦν, ἐπελάφρυναι, ἐκβολὴν ποιήσασθαι τῶν φορτίων.* So that both here and afterwards in the 38th verse, when St. Luke says, *ἐκούφιζον τὸ πλοῖον,* he uses appropriate technical phrases.

step hitherto taken indicates skilful seamanship. In an old French work on maritime law,[1] I find every one of these precautions pointed out as proper to be taken by able mariners under similar circumstances.

1st. With regard to undergirding, the author observes :—

'Il y a des mariniers habiles, lesquels prévoyant les tourmentes, plongent en l'eau, ceignent ou rident par bas tout le corps du navire avec des guerlins nommez en Levant *gomenes*, c'est à dire, grosses cordes, ce qui l'*assiste* et le rend plus puissant à résister aux secousses.' (P. 528.)

2nd. 'Lowering the gear :'—

'*Abaisser* les mâts de hune ou *mâtereaux*.'

3rd. 'Laying the ship to :'—

'Dans le péril convient caposer ou mettre le navire à la cape, c'est à dire, amarrer le gouvernail bien ferme et immobile pour suivre l'abandon du vent ; trousser toutes les voiles sauf le pafi (mainsail, old French), qu'on laisse boursoufler, d'autant que le vent s'enfermant en iceluy pousse en haut le vaisseau, le soulagent beaucoup au hurt et à la tombée.'

4th. 'Lightening the ship :'—

'Pour prévenir le malheur en ces occurrences et pour se conserver, le jet est nécessaire, "echason á la mar de lo qui viene en la nave para salvarla."'

On the third day they threw overboard 'the tackling of the ship' (ver. 19). From the expression

[1] *Us et Coutumes de la Mer.* Rouen, 1672.

'with our[1] own hands,' *αὐτόχειρες*, I suppose the main-yard is meant; an immense spar, probably as long as the ship, which would require the united efforts of passengers and crew to launch overboard. The relief which a ship would experience by this, would be of the same kind as in a modern ship when the guns are thrown overboard.

A dreary interval of eleven days succeeds; the gale continues with unabated fury (*σφοδρῶς δὲ χειμαζομένων*); neither sun nor stars can be observed; and at length we are told that 'all hope of being saved was taken away.' But why was all hope taken away? An ancient ship, without a compass and without celestial observation, had no means of keeping a

---

19 Καὶ τῇ τρίτῃ αὐτόχειρες τὴν σκευὴν τοῦ πλοίου ἔριψαν.	19 And the third *day* they cast out with their own hands the tackling of the ship.
20 Μήτε δὲ ἡλίου μήτε ἄστρων ἐπιφαινόντων ἐπὶ πλείονας ἡμέρας, χειμῶνός τε οὐκ ὀλίγου ἐπικειμένου, λοιπὸν περιῃρεῖτο ἐλπὶς πᾶσα τοῦ σώζεσθαι ἡμᾶς.	20 And when neither sun nor stars in many days appeared, and no small tempest lay on *us*, all hope that we should be saved was then taken away.
21 Πολλῆς τε ἀσιτίας ὑπαρχούσης τότε σταθεὶς ὁ Παῦλος ἐν μέσῳ αὐτῶν εἶπεν	21 But after long abstinence Paul stood forth in the midst of them, and said,

---

[1] [The MS. authority (A, B, ℵ, C, &c.) is conclusive for *ἔριψαν*, '*they* threw overboard,' instead of the received *ἐρρίψαμεν*, 'we threw.' *τὴν σκευὴν*, which Alford explains 'the *furniture* of the ship—beds, movables of all kinds, cooking utensils, and the spare rigging,' is probably distinct from *τὸ σκεῦος* in ver. 17.]

reckoning. This was no doubt a situation of danger, but not one of despair, for she might have been driven into safety. The true explanation, I apprehend, is this: their exertions to subdue the leak had been unavailing; they could not tell which way to make for the nearest land, in order to run their ship ashore, the only resource for a sinking ship; but unless they did make the land, they must founder at sea. Their apprehensions therefore were not so much caused by the fury of the tempest, as by the state of the ship.

We are now told that after much abstinence Paul addressed them; but before we hear his address the question occurs, what caused the abstinence? A ship with nearly three hundred people on board, on a voyage of some length, must have had more than a fortnight's provisions; in point of fact the ship was loaded with wheat, as we learn afterwards; and it is not enough to say that, 'worn out with their labours and fears, they did not think of eating.'[1] Now, although the connection between heavy gales and 'much abstinence' is by no means obvious, yet we find it is one of their most frequent concomitants. The impossibility of cooking, or the destruction of provisions from leakage, are the principal causes which produce it. Breydenbach, the dean of Mentz, in his pilgrimage to the Holy Land, experienced two gales of wind,[2] and very feelingly records the absti-

[1] 'Continui labores et metus a periculis effecerant ut de cibo capiendo non cogitarent.' (Kuinoel.)

[2] Mentz, 1486. See account of this curious work in Dibdin's *Ædes Althorpianæ*, and the *Journal of the Geographical Society*, vol. ix. p. 311; as it is not paged, I count the leaves from the end.

nence that ensued on each occasion. In one case a sea struck their vessel, and 'destroyed their caboose or cooking-place, and broke everything within it;[1] in the other he tells us 'there was no thought of eating or drinking, because the cooking-place was altogether under water.'[2]

John Newton, the celebrated vicar of Olney, in his interesting autobiography, relates a circumstance which occurred in his own experience of sea life; on a voyage from Cape Lopez a sea struck his ship, and strained her so much that she nearly foundered:—

> 'We found that the water having floated all our movables in the hold, all the casks of provisions had been beaten in pieces by the violent motion of the ship. On the other hand, our live stock, such as pigs, sheep, and poultry, had been washed overboard in the storm; in effect, all the provisions we saved . . . would have subsisted us but a week, at a scanty allowance.' (Omicron's 'Letters,' letter vii.)

In the case of the 'Guipuscoa,' the Spanish ship mentioned in Anson's Voyage, those who could work

[1] 'Porro tempestate illa durante cum naves ab invicem longius essent separatæ, una vi ventorum acta ad latus nostræ galeæ grandi impetu impegit vehementer barcamque collateralem dirupit penitus, et destruxit nostram vero coquinam fregit earum et omnia quæ in ea erant.' — 19th leaf from the end. On the same leaf will be found the following invocation by the mariners to the Virgin, which I have not met with elsewhere:—

'Salve, Splendor Firmamenti!
Tu caliginosæ menti
Desuper irradia.
Placa mare, Maris Stella!
Ne involvat nos procella
Et tempestas obvia.'

[2] 'Nec fuit memoria cibi aut potus hac tempestate, quia coquina era in aquis tota.' (*Ib.* 17th fol. from end.)

at the pumps were reduced to an ounce and a half of biscuit per diem ; those who could not were allowed an ounce of wheat. To some such cause the abstinence mentioned by St. Luke may doubtless be ascribed.

The hardships which the crew endured during a gale of such continuance, and their exhaustion from labour at the pumps and hunger, may be imagined, but are not described. Under these circumstances St. Paul encourages them by the assurance that their lives would be spared. He thus addresses them :—

'Sirs, ye should have hearkened unto me, and not have loosed from Crete, and to have gained this harm and loss. And now I exhort you to be of good cheer ; for there shall be no loss of *any man's* life among you, but of the ship. For there stood by me this night, an angel of God, whose I am, and whom I serve, saying, Fear not, Paul ; thou must be brought before Cæsar : and, lo, God hath given thee all them that sail with thee. Wherefore, sirs, be of good cheer ; for I believe God, that it shall be even as it was told me. Howbeit we must be cast upon a certain island.'

Ἔδει μέν, ὦ ἄνδρες, πειθαρχήσαντάς μοι μὴ ἀνάγεσθαι ἀπὸ τῆς Κρήτης κερδῆσαί τε τὴν ὕβριν ταύτην καὶ τὴν ζημίαν.	Sirs, ye should have hearkened unto me, and not have loosed from Crete, and to have gained this harm and loss.
22 Καὶ τὰ νῦν παραινῶ ὑμᾶς εὐθυμεῖν, ἀποβολὴ γὰρ ψυχῆς οὐδεμία ἔσται ἐξ ὑμῶν πλὴν τοῦ πλοίου.	22. And now I exhort you to be of good cheer : for there shall be no loss of *any man's* life among you, but of the ship.
23 Παρέστη γάρ μοι ταύτῃ τῇ νυκτὶ τοῦ Θεοῦ οὗ εἰμί, ᾧ καὶ λατρεύω, ἄγγελος,	23 For there stood by me this night an angel of God, whose I am, and whom I serve,

At length, on the fourteenth night of their being 'driven through' (*διαφερομένων*) the sea of Adria, towards midnight the seamen suspected (*ὑπενόουν*) that land was near (*προσάγειν αὐτοῖς*, literally, was nearing them [1]). St. Luke does not tell us what the indications were ; and the only conjecture I have seen is that of Calmet, that they became aware of it by the sense of smell. He says :—

'Ils soupçonnèrent l'approche de la terre, non par la vue, parce que c'était à minuit et qu'ils étaient dans des profondes ténèbres, mais apparemment par l'odeur de la terre, ou par la fraîcheur, ou par les vents.'

---

24 Λέγων Μὴ φοβοῦ, Παῦλε· Καίσαρί σε δεῖ παραστῆναι, καὶ ἰδοὺ κεχάρισταί σοι ὁ Θεὸς πάντας τοὺς πλέοντας μετὰ σοῦ.

25 Διὸ εὐθυμεῖτε, ἄνδρες· πιστεύω γὰρ τῷ Θεῷ ὅτι οὕτως ἔσται καθ' ὃν τρόπον λελάληταί μοι.

26 Εἰς νῆσον δέ τινα δεῖ ἡμᾶς ἐκπεσεῖν.

27 Ὡς δὲ τεσσαρεσκαιδεκάτη νὺξ ἐγένετο διαφερομένων ἡμῶν ἐν τῷ Ἀδρίᾳ, κατὰ μέσον τῆς νυκτὸς ὑπενόουν οἱ ναῦται προσάγειν τινὰ αὐτοῖς χώραν.

24 Saying, Fear not, Paul ; thou must be brought before Cæsar : and, lo, God hath given thee all them that sail with thee.

25 Wherefore, sirs, be of good cheer : for I believe God, that it shall be even as it was told me.

26 Howbeit we must be cast upon a certain island.

27 But when the fourteenth night was come, as we were driven up and down in Adria, about midnight the shipmen deemed that they drew near to some country ;

---

[1] St. Luke here uses the graphic language of seamen, to whom the ship is the principal object, whilst the land rises and sinks, nears and recedes—

'Terræque urbesque recedunt.'

The word *χώραν* evidently means the land as distinguished from the sea.

But all these conjectures require off-shore winds. A storm on the face of a lee shore is not the time when—

> 'Gentle gales,
> Fanning their odoriferous wings, dispense
> Native perfumes, and whisper whence they stole
> Their balmy spoils.'

The only other conjecture is that they saw or heard the breakers on a rocky coast.

Such are the usual premonitory warnings to ships unexpectedly falling in with the land at night.

If we assume that St. Paul's Bay, in Malta, is the actual scene of the shipwreck, we can have no difficulty in explaining what these indications must have been. No ship can enter it from the east without passing within a quarter of a mile of the point of Koura; but before reaching it the land is too low, and too far from the track of a ship driven from the eastward, to be seen in a dark night. When she does come within this distance, it is impossible to avoid observing the breakers; for with north-easterly gales the sea breaks upon it with such violence, that Admiral Smyth, in his view of the headland, has made the breakers its distinctive character, realising Campbell's line—

> 'The white wave foaming to the distant sky.'

By a singular chance I can establish an important link in the chain of evidence respecting the identity of this locality, namely that the distance at which the breakers could be seen here is about a quarter of a mile, and that they are seen at this distance when the land itself is not seen.

On one of those rare occasions when there was no ground-swell and a boat could land on the point of Koura, I landed with my friend the Rev. Mr. Robertson of Saline, and was engaged in demonstrating to him upon the spot, how rigidly every one of the conditions required to make it agree with the narrative was here fulfilled. To the east lay the low and receding shores of Malta, nowhere 'approaching' within a mile of the track of a ship coming from Clauda, and which therefore could not be seen on a night such as that described in the narrative. In the opposite direction the shore, begirt with mural precipices (*τραχεῖς τόπους*), where a ship would be dashed to pieces, but with 'creeks with shores,' into which she might be thrust; and on the rocks where we stood, not more than twenty feet above the surface of the sea, and totally destitute of vegetation, lay huge fragments of rock, forcibly torn up by the waves, and lodged at least twelve feet above the level of a tideless sea, affording no doubtful evidence of what must have been the force of the breakers in a gale from the Greco Levante E.N.E. (Euro-aquilo), the point at which it is most exposed. One of our boatmen, who was listening attentively, said he knew what I was speaking about, and could point out the spot of the shipwreck; that he was a boy when it happened, and had gone to see the ship next day. This produced an explanation. He told us that thirty or forty years ago, the 'Lively' frigate fell in unexpectedly with the point, in a dark night, and, missing stays, had run ashore at a spot which he showed us, and that, a gale coming on, she had gone to pieces.

Struck with the coincidence, on my return to England I applied at the Admiralty, and examined the proceedings of the court-martial held on the officers of the ship, from which it appears that on August 10, 1810, the 'Lively' frigate, coming from the westward with a fair wind, made the land of Gozo and the west end of Malta before it was dark. The weather, however, afterwards turned thick, and the land was lost sight of. When the captain (M'Kinlay) went below, he left orders with the master to heave the ship to at a certain hour, to get her put in order, before running into the harbour of Valetta next morning. This was accordingly done; but the ship was, unfortunately, and against the opinion of the Lieutenant of the watch (Lieutenant, now Admiral Lord Fitzhardinge), brought to with her head in-shore. Soon afterward the quartermaster on the look-out gave the alarm of rocks to leeward.[1] He states, in his evidence, that he did not see the land, but 'the curl of the sea' upon the rocks, at the distance of about a quarter of a mile. This was upon the point of Koura, the very spot where a ship driving from the east into St. Paul's Bay must

[1] In reporting to the master, the quartermaster said there was neither room to tack nor wear, but 'if all was thrown aback the ship might back out stern foremost.' There can be no doubt but that if this plan had been adopted, the ship would have drifted clear of the point; but the officers could not know how far the rocks extended, and there was no reason to fear that the frigate, *if properly* handled, would 'miss stays;' this was evidently the opinion of the court, who put repeated questions as to the cause of the ship's not coming round: one of the witnesses attributed it to the confusion caused by the captain's coming suddenly on deck, another to a brace being let go too soon. The master was reduced in rank for bringing the ship to with her head in-shore.

have seen and heard the breakers, and the only spot where she could have done so. Upon perceiving the danger, the order 'ready about and *clear the anchor*' was immediately given by Lieutenant Berkeley; and as they were bracing round the maintop-sail to fill upon the ship, the man at the lead *sounded, and found twenty-five fathoms.* Before, however, she had sufficient way upon her, the helm was put down; but the ship missed stays, that is they could not get her head round on the opposite tack. *The anchor was then let go;*[1] but before the ship brought up, she fell off broadside on the rocks, and a gale coming on she went to pieces.

Before proceeding to compare the notices in the narrative with the peculiarities of the supposed site, let us stop to inquire whether the data with which this inquiry has furnished us will not enable us to ascertain, within certain limits, by *à priori* reasoning, whereabouts the ship was, that is her longitude and latitude, when the 'shipmen deemed that she drew near to some country.'

I have already shown, from three independent sources, that the wind must have been E.N.E. ¼ N. to the nearest quarter of a point; and that the ship must have been on the starboard tack, that is with her head to the north, in order to avoid the Syrtis. The first question which presents itself is, what was the direction of the drift mentioned in the seventeenth verse, 'so were driven' (*οὕτως ἐφέροντο*). The answer depends on the angle the ship's head makes

[1] This does not appear from the proceedings of the court; but one of our boatmen told us he assisted in sweeping for it, and that it was found many years afterwards.

with the wind and the lee-way. But an ancient ship could probably not lie nearer the wind than seven points, which added to six points of lee-way, makes thirteen points, as the angle which such a ship would probably make with the wind.[1] E.N.E. $\frac{1}{4}$ N. is $2\frac{1}{4}$ points to the north of east: if we add thirteen to this, it makes the azimuth of the ship's course from Clauda W. $\frac{3}{4}$ N., or W. 8° N., *which is the bearing of Malta to the nearest degree.*

The next point to be ascertained is, how far would she have driven from Clauda about midnight 'when the fourteenth night was come.' The knowledge of this depends upon the rate of drift and the time consumed. The result which the calculations founded upon these data gives us is so very striking, that I feel called upon to state the elements on which it is founded at some length, lest I should be accused of 'cooking' them—that is of selecting those only which answered my purpose, and rejecting those which did not.

In order to ascertain what might be supposed to be the mean rate of drift of a ship circumstanced as that of St. Paul was, I consulted two nautical friends, both of them at the time commanding ships in Valetta harbour, and both of them familiar with the navigation of the Levant. To the first of these officers whom I met with (the late Captain W.

[1] I arrive at these results thus: ancient ships could sail on opposite tacks, 'in contrariam' (Pliny, ii. 48), hence they could lie with eight points of the wind, but they certainly could not lie so near the wind as modern ships, say six points; the mean, therefore, is seven points. The lee-way of a ship in a gale varies from $5\frac{1}{2}$ to $6\frac{1}{2}$ points (see Falconer's *Marine Dictionary*, article 'Lee-way'); the mean of which is six points.

M'Lean, R.N.), I put the question, 'What would you say would be the probable rate of drift of a ship laid to in a gale of wind?' His answer was, 'That depends on the force of the gale and the size of the ship.' Upon explaining that I considered it a large ship, even as compared with modern merchantmen, and that the gale might be reckoned as one of mean intensity, he said, after considering the matter, that speaking in round numbers forty miles in twenty-four hours might be reckoned a fair allowance. I put the same question to Captain Graves, R.N., who replied, 'From three-quarters of a mile an hour to two miles an hour.' The mean of these extremes is thirty-three miles in twenty-four hours, and the mean of both estimates is thirty-six and a half miles in twenty-four hours.[1]

I come now to the time elapsed. It is quite clear from the narrative that St. Luke counts the time from the day the ship left Fair Havens. We hear of the 'third day' (ver. 19); the preceding is termed 'next day,' which brings us to the first day both of the gale and the voyage. It is also clear that the events of that day must have occupied a large portion of it. The time consumed in driving through the Sea of Adria, from the time they left the island of Clauda till they became aware of the vicinity of land at midnight of the fourteenth day, is therefore thirteen days complete and a small fraction. But the distance from Clauda to the point of Koura, where I suppose

[1] When Captain Graves said from three-quarters of a mile to two miles an hour, I replied, 'Very well, I may suppose a mile and a half an hour about a mean rate,' to which he assented, agreeing exactly with Admiral Penrose's estimate of the probable rate of drift.

that this happened, is 476·6 miles, which, at the rate as deduced from the information of Captains M'Lean and Graves, would take exactly thirteen days, one hour, and twenty-one minutes.[1]

The coincidence of the actual bearing of St. Paul's Bay from Clauda, and the direction in which a ship must have driven in order to avoid the Syrtis, is if possible still more striking than that of the time actually consumed, and the calculated time.

The direction of the ship's course is inferred from that of the wind, from the angle of the ship's head with the wind, and from the lee-way. I have shown (see p. 101) that the mean direction of the wind, as deduced from the notices in the narrative, was E. 26° 15′ N. In the Dissertation on Ancient Ships I have assigned reasons for supposing seven points as the angle a ship's head would make with the wind, which, added to six points for lee-way, makes an angle of 146° 15′, which, added to the angle of the wind, makes the azimuth of the ship's course, as

[1] This distance is deduced from the position of the places by the following formula :—

	Lat. N.			Lon. E.
Point of Koura,	35° 56′	mer. parts	2313	14° 25′
Clauda,	34 52	mer. parts	2235	24 2
Dif. . .	1° 4′ = 64′	Diff.	78	Diff. 9° 37′ = 577′

As mer. diff. of lat. 78 . log.	1·892095	As rad.	10·000000
is to rad. . .	10·000000	is to diff. lat. 64° . .	1·806180
so is diff., lon. 577	2·761176	so is sec. course 82° 17′.	12·872007
	12·761176		12·678187
	1·892395		10·000000
to tang. course 82° 17′ . .	10·869081	to distance 476·6 . .	2·678187

drawn from these data, E. 172° 30′ N., or N. 82° 30′ W., which agrees with the bearing of St. Paul's Bay, 82° 17′, as drawn from the foregoing calculation to 13′, which at the distance between Clauda and Malta is equivalent about two miles and a half.

Hence according to these calculations, a ship starting late in the evening from Clauda would, by midnight on the 14th, be less than three miles from the entrance of St. Paul's Bay. I admit that a coincidence so very close as this, is to a certain extent accidental, but it is an accident which could not have happened had there been any inaccuracy on the part of the author of the narrative with regard to the numerous incidents upon which the calculations are founded, or had the ship been wrecked anywhere but at Malta, for there is no other place agreeing, either in name or description, within the limits to which we are tied down by calculations founded upon the narrative.

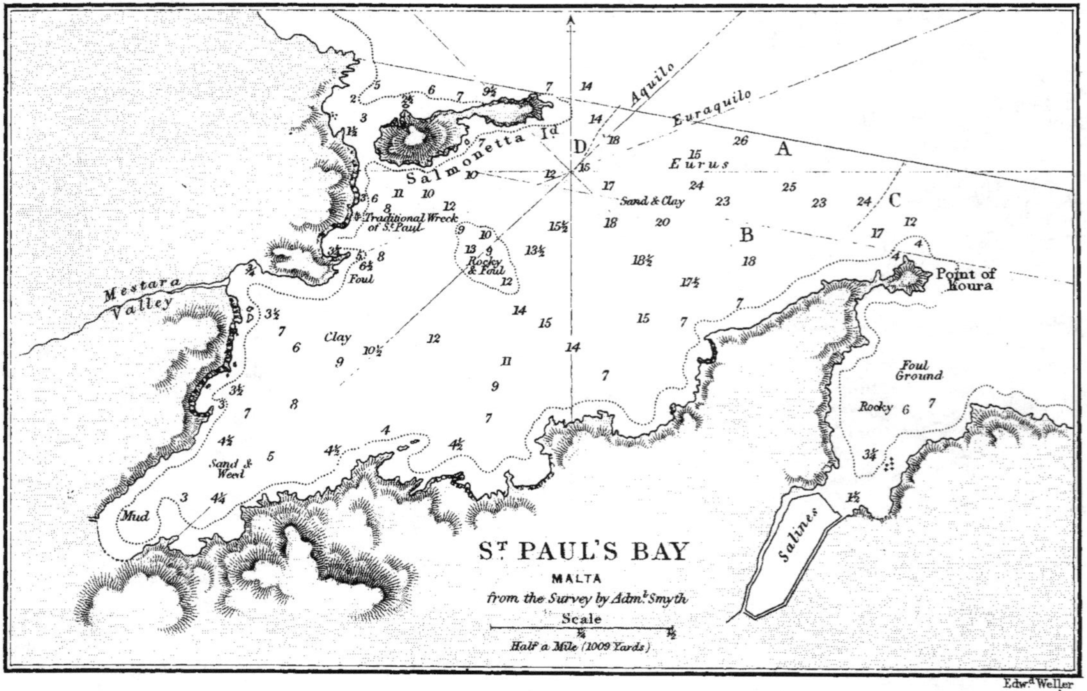

London: Longman & Co.

CHAPTER IV.

THE SHIPWRECK.

THE ship now approaches the termination of her disastrous voyage. Land is not indeed in sight, but to the watchful senses of the 'shipmen' the sound or appearance of breakers tells them that it is near, or in the nautical language of St. Luke, that it is approaching. Such indications are the usual harbingers of destruction ; here they call forth a display of presence of mind, promptitude and seamanship, which could not be surpassed in the present day, and by which, under Providence, the lives of all on board were saved.

However appalling the alarm of breakers may be to a ship unexpectedly falling in with the land on an unknown coast, and in a dark and stormy night, it afforded in the present case a chance at least of safety. The hope which was taken away is restored. They can now adopt the last resource for a sinking ship, and run her ashore ; but to do so before it was day would have been to have rushed on certain destruction. They must bring the ship, if it be possible, to anchor, and hold on till day-break, when they may perhaps discover some 'creek with a shore,' into which they may be able to 'thrust the ship.'

The progress of the narrative has brought us to the question, Whether the traditional locality is in reality that of the shipwreck? Now, if we attend minutely to the narrative, it will be seen that the number of conditions required to be fulfilled, in order to make any locality agree with it, are so numerous as to render it morally impossible to suppose that the agreement which we find here can be the effect of chance.

The first circumstance mentioned is that at midnight the shipmen suspected the vicinity of land evidently without seeing it. The ship was driving from Clauda; her previous track must have been at such a distance from the land, and the land itself must be so low, as to prevent its being seen. Now, upon laying down the track of a ship driving in that direction to St. Paul's Bay, on Admiral Smyth's chart of Malta, I find that the land, which in that part of the island is very low, nowhere approaches within a mile of it,[1] but that it is impossible to enter the bay without passing within a quarter of a mile of a low rocky point, which juts out and forms its eastern entrance (the point of Koura). When the 'Lively' frigate unexpectedly fell in with this very point, the quartermaster on the look-out, who first observed it, states in his evidence at the court-martial, that at the distance of a quarter of a mile the land could not be seen, but that he saw the surf on the shore. Here then we establish the explanation of a hitherto unexplained passage of Scripture, by the oath of a competent

[1] Off Valetta the distance of the track of a ship from Clauda to St. Paul's Bay is three miles; it gradually diminishes to one mile,

POINT OF KOURA.

witness. Till the ship arrived at the entrance of the bay they could not be aware of the vicinity of land; when they did come to it they could not avoid becoming aware of it. When they did so, they sounded, and found twenty fathoms.[1] But a ship coming from the eastward must, immediately after passing the point, pass over this depth.[2] It is quite true that every ship in approaching the land must pass over twenty fathoms and fifteen fathoms; but here not only must the twenty-fathom depth be close to the spot where they had the indications of land, but it must bear E. by S. from the fifteen-fathom depth, and at such a distance as would allow of preparation for anchoring, with four anchors from the stern; for we are not to suppose that ships from sea, unexpectedly falling in with land, can be prepared to anchor in an unusual manner on the instant. Now, about half an hour farther, estimating the ship's rate of progression by the time which had been hitherto consumed, we find the depth to be fifteen fathoms.

---

28 Καὶ βολίσαντες εὗρον ὀργυιὰς εἴκοσι, βραχὺ δὲ διαστήσαντες καὶ πάλιν βολίσαντες εὗρον ὀργυιὰς δεκαπέντε·

28 And sounded, and found it twenty fathoms, and when they had gone a little further, they sounded again, and found it fifteen fathoms.

---

[1] The ancient fathom (ὀργυιά) so nearly agrees with the English fathom, that the difference may be neglected. According to Hesychius, it is ἡ τῶν ἀμφοτέρων χειρῶν ἔκτασις, the space between both hands extended.

[2] See chart of St. Paul's Bay to the west of the point of Koura. I have given the soundings as they are laid down in Admiral Smyth's chart. Although the depth of twenty fathoms is not marked, we know it must be between seventeen and twenty-four.

Here we are told that fearing lest they should have fallen upon rocks,[1] they cast four anchors out of the stern. This implies that there were rocks to leeward, on which, if they had not anchored, they must have fallen, but the fifteen-fathom depth is as nearly as possible a quarter of a mile from the shore, which is here girt with mural precipices, and upon which the sea must have been breaking with great violence. Upon the former alarm the ship weathered the point; here it was impossible. From the position of the ship's head, the breakers must have been seen over the lee bow. Their only chance of safety, therefore, was to anchor; but to do so successfully in a gale of wind, on a lee shore, requires not only time for preparation, but holding ground of extraordinary tenacity. In St. Paul's Bay the anchorage is thus described in the sailing directions:—

'The harbour of St. Paul is open to easterly and north-east winds. It is, notwithstanding, safe for small ships, the ground, generally, being very good; and while the cables hold there is no danger, *as the anchors will never start.* (P. 161.)

---

29 Φοβούμενοί τε μή που κατὰ τραχεῖς τόπους ἐκπέσωμεν ἐκ πρύμνης ῥίψαντες ἀγκύρας τεσσάρας, ηὔχοντο ἡμέραν γενέσθαι.	29 And fearing lest we should have fallen upon rocks, they cast four anchors out of the stern and wished for day.

---

[1] **Τραχύς** is mentioned as a hydrographic term by Julius Pollux, and classed with the words *δύσορμος*, *ἀλίμενος*, &c., lib. i. 101. When Ulysses is wrecked on the coast of Phæacia,—

> Τόφρα δέ μιν μέγα κῦμα φέρε τ ρ η χ ε ῖ α ν ἐπ' ἀκτήν.
> Ἔνθα κ' ἀπὸ ῥινοὺς δρύφθη, σὺν δ' ὀστέ' ἀράχθη,
> Εἰ μή, κ.τ.λ. (*Od.* v. 425.)

ST. PAUL'S BAY, MALTA, FROM THE SOUTH.

The proximate cause of anchoring was no doubt that assigned by St. Luke, namely the fear of falling on the rocks to leeward; but they had also an ulterior object in view, which was to run the ship ashore as soon as daylight enabled them to select a spot where it could be done with a prospect of safety; for this purpose the very best position in which an ancient ship could be, was to be anchored by the stern.

We have no occasion, therefore, to account for this proceeding, by showing that a certain class of vessels in the eastern seas anchor in this manner. To explain away the difficulty, is much the same as if the biographer of Lord Nelson were to explain away the well-known manœuvre of anchoring by the stern at the battle of the Nile,[1] by attempting to prove that this was a common practice with English ships. That of the ancients was the same as the moderns; except under particular circumstances, they anchored by the bow,—'Anchora de prora jacitur.' The reasons for doing so are obvious; it is much easier to arrest a ship's way by the bow than by the stern.

It is proper, however, to observe, that from the very necessity of the case the ancient navigators were forced to depend much more upon their ground-tackle

[1] Appian ascribes the success of a former naval victory on the coast of Africa to the manœuvre of anchoring by the stern, and for the same reasons as Lord Nelson's—it obviated the necessity of exposing the weak points of the ships to the enemy in turning round. The ships of the Carthaginians were anchored along-shore, like the French fleet. The Romans attacked them from the sea, in the usual manner, but in turning round to repeat their blows, they received those of the enemy on their sides, till at last they let go their anchors by the stern, and with a long scope of cable hauled out their ships, κατὰ πρύμναν, by the stern. (*De Bell. Pun.*, edit. Stephani, p. 76.)

than the moderns. Ships constructed and rigged like theirs could not, when caught in a gale, work off a lee shore, they must of necessity anchor; hence they must have been very amply provided with anchors and cables, and habituated to the use of them in every possible contingency. I may also add that as both ends of their ships were alike, there was nothing in their form to prevent this mode of anchoring from being put in practice.

There is still one difficulty to be obviated, which I am indebted to a naval friend for starting. Upon pointing out to Captain M'Lean, R.N., whose authority I have already cited, the advantageous position in which it placed the ship for the purpose of running her ashore, he replied, 'Very true; but were the ships of the ancients fitted to anchor by the stern? had they hawse-holes aft? because, if they were, we are only coming back to old practices.'

This is the difficulty of a seaman, who immediately thinks of how the thing is to be done. I must admit myself too much of a landsman to have thought of it, otherwise I should have been able to have answered it, which I was not at the time; for I had copied from the 'Antichità di Ercolano' the figure of the ship, in the picture of Theseus deserting Ariadne, which contains details showing, not only that they were so fitted, but the manner in which it was done; and that too in a ship so strictly contemporaneous with that of St. Paul, that there is nothing impossible in the supposition, that the artist had taken his subject from that very ship, on loosing from the pier of Puteoli. A hawser is seen towing astern,—it passes through the rudder-port, and within board it is seen coiled round an upright beam or capstan, in front of the break of the poop-deck.

We see, therefore, that ships of the ancients were fitted to anchor by the stern ; and in the present instance that mode of anchoring was attended with most important advantages.

If St. Luke had been a seaman, we can scarcely suppose that he would have omitted to have men-

tioned the reasons for this particular mode of anchoring, or the precautions which were necessary in order to insure its being done with success ; but as usual he is contented with a bare statement of facts, without assigning reasons or offering explanations. One most essential precaution in such a case, and probably under the circumstances a difficult one, was to lift the rudders out of the water, and secure them by lashings ; we are not expressly told that this precaution was taken, but we learn afterwards indirectly that it was. Perhaps also the main-mast was cut away. Falconer, a seaman, contemplates the possibility of saving the ship by doing so,—

> 'The hull dismasted there awhile may ride,
> With lengthened cables on the raging tide.'
> ('Shipwreck,' canto ii.)

The circumstance of the artemon having been hoisted[1] when they ran the ship ashore, lends probability to the conjecture, and nothing can be inferred from the author's silence, but it is nothing more than a conjecture; and I have not ventured, in the view of the ship anchored by the stern, to represent it so. (See Frontispiece.)

The advantages of being anchored in this manner are, that by cutting away the anchors (*τὰς ἀγκύρας περιελόντες*), loosing the bands of the rudder (*ἀνέντες τὰς ζευκτηρίας τῶν πηδαλίων*), and hoisting the artemon (*ἐπάραντες τὸν ἀρτέμωνα*), all of which could be, as they were in effect, done simultaneously, the ship was immediately under command, and could be directed with precision to any part of the shore which offered a prospect of safety. Whereas, if anchored in the usual mode, she might have taken 'the wrong cast,' or drifted on the rocks before she was under command.

The number of anchors which were let go shows that the able commander (*κυβερνήτης*) left nothing to

[1] In the ship of Catullus, when the mast is cut away, they hoist the artemon,—'velo prora suo,' which the scholiast explains 'artemone solo velificaverunt.' (Juv. *Sat.* xii. 69.) See Dissertation on Ships, for proof that the artemon was the foresail.

chance. The ship is now in a situation where escape is possible, but not certainly one in which it is probable. From the state of the ship she may go down at her anchors, or the coast to leeward may be iron-bound, affording no beach (*αἰγιαλός*) upon which they can land in safety. Hence their anxious longing for day; hence also the ungenerous but natural attempt of the seamen to save their own lives, by taking to the boat; an attempt not peculiar to ancient times.[1] They lower the boat under pretence of laying out anchors from the bow.[2] The design is penetrated and defeated by St. Paul. He tells the centurion, that unless they remain in the ship they cannot be saved. The soldiers cut the boat's hawsers, and allow her to go adrift.

---

30 Τῶν δὲ ναυτῶν ζητούντων φυγεῖν ἐκ τοῦ πλοίου καὶ χαλασάντων τὴν σκάφην εἰς τὴν θάλασσαν προφάσει ὡς ἐκ πρῴρης ἀγκύρας μελλόντων ἐκτείνειν,	30 And as the shipmen were about to flee out of the ship, when they had let down the boat into the sea, under colour as though they would have cast anchors out of the foreship,

---

[1] When the *Athénienne*, 64, was lost on the Skerki rocks, near Sicily, in 1806, two boats' crews deserted her. There were no officers in the boats. (See *United Service Magazine*, February 1845, p. 229.)

[2] We hear of anchors being laid out from both ends of a ship (ἑκατέρωθεν). (Appian.)

It is to be observed, that casting anchors out of the foreship could have been of no possible advantage in the circumstances, and that as the pretext could not deceive a seaman, we must infer that the officers of the ship were parties to the unworthy attempt, which was perhaps detected by the nautical skill of St. Luke, and communicated by him to St. Paul.

During the interval which remained till day, St. Paul exhorted them to take food, saying,—

'This is the fourteenth day[1] that ye have tarried and continued fasting, having taken nothing, wherefore I pray you to take some food, for this is for your health, for there shall not an hair fall from the head of any of you.'

They were now to eat in the ship for the last time, and needed no longer to stint themselves to

---

31 Εἶπεν ὁ Παῦλος τῷ ἑκατοντάρχῃ καὶ τοῖς στρατιώταις Ἐὰν μὴ οὗτοι μείνωσιν ἐν τῷ πλοίῳ, ὑμεῖς σωθῆναι οὐ δύνασθε.	31 Paul said to the centurion and to the soldiers, Except these abide in the ship, ye cannot be saved.
32 Τότε ἀπέκοψαν οἱ στρατιῶται τὰ σχοινία τῆς σκάφης, καὶ εἴασαν αὐτὴν ἐκπεσεῖν.	32 Then the soldiers cut off the ropes of the boat, and let her fall off.
33 Ἄχρι δὲ οὗ ἡμέρα ἤμελλεν γίνεσθαι, παρεκάλει ὁ Παῦλος ἅπαντας μεταλαβεῖν τροφῆς λέγων Τεσσαρεσκαιδεκάτην σήμερον ἡμέραν προσδοκῶντες ἄσιτοι διατελεῖτε, μηθὲν προσλαβόμενοι·	33 And while the day was coming on, Paul besought them all to take meat, saying, This day is the fourteenth day that ye have tarried, and continued fasting, [literally, 'that ye wait for and continue fasting'] having taken nothing.

---

[1] Granville Penn thinks the reading ought to be 'τεσσάρας, καὶ δὲ καὶ τὴν σήμερον ἡμέραν, four, days even this very day,' supposing that the apostle meant that they had literally taken nothing for so many days; but surely there is no difficulty in the case. St. Luke, when he speaks as a historian, terms their fasting 'much abstinence' (πολλῆς ἀσιτίας, ver. 21). St. Paul uses the strong but common language, of calling taking very little taking nothing. It could not be mistaken by those to whom it was addressed.

an allowance; the apostle sets the example, and giving thanks to God takes a piece of bread, and breaking it, begins to eat; inspirited by this, all of them partake a full meal, the first since the commencement of the gale; and with renewed strength make a last effort to lighten the ship,[1] not only by pumping, but by throwing the wheat[2] into the sea.

34 Διὸ παρακαλῶ ὑμᾶς μεταλαβεῖν τροφῆς, τοῦτο γὰρ πρὸς τῆς ὑμετέρας σωτηρίας ὑπάρχει· οὐδενὸς γὰρ ὑμῶν θρὶξ ἀπὸ τῆς κεφαλῆς ἀπολεῖται.	34 Wherefore I pray you to take some meat, for this is for your health: for there shall not an hair fall from the head of any of you.
35 Εἴπας δὲ ταῦτα καὶ λαβὼν ἄρτον εὐχαρίστησεν τῷ Θεῷ ἐνώπιον πάντων καὶ κλάσας ἤρξατο ἐσθίειν.	35 And when he had thus spoken, he took bread, and gave thanks to God in presence of them all, and when he had broken it, he began to eat.
36 Εὔθυμοι δὲ γενόμενοι πάντες καὶ αὐτοὶ προσελάβοντο τροφῆς.	36 Then were they all of good cheer, and they also took some meat.
37 Ἤμεθα δὲ αἱ πᾶσαι ψυχαὶ ἐν τῷ πλοίῳ διακόσιαι[3] ἑβδομήκοντα ἕξ.	37 And we were in all in the ship two hundred three score and sixteen souls.

[1] Ἐκούφιζον τὸ πλοῖον, they lightened the ship. Amongst the nautical terms of Julius Pollux we find κουφίσαι τὴν ναῦν. (See note to verse 18.) The Septuagint has κουφισθῆναι (Jonah, i. 5).

[2] Some suppose that by τὸν σῖτον the remainder of the ship's provisions is meant; but to suppose that they had remaining such a quantity as would lighten the ship is quite inconsistent with the previous abstinence; and besides wheat was the staple commodity imported from Alexandria to Italy.

[3] [Westcott and Hort read ὡς ἑβδομήκοντα ἕξ (about seventy-six), διακόσιαι in margin.]

When day broke they did not know the land;[1] but it had certain peculiarities, and unless we can show that the shore to the west of the ship's supposed position possesses the same peculiarities, it will not agree with that mentioned in the text. The first of these is, 'rocky places' (*τραχεῖς τόπους*); the fear of falling upon which at night had caused them to come to anchor. Now the shore here is skirted with precipices, against which the ship must have been dashed in pieces, had she not been anchored. The next is, a 'creek with a sandy beach' (*κόλπον ἔχοντα αἰγιαλόν*);[2] and the third is, 'a place of two

38 Κορεσθέντες δὲ τροφῆς ἐκούφιζον τὸ πλοῖον ἐκβαλλόμενοι τὸν σῖτον εἰς τὴν θάλασσαν.	38 And when they had eaten enough, they lightened the ship, and cast out the wheat into the sea.

[1] It has been asked, if Malta was the island, how came it not to be known to some of the crew, for it is not to be supposed that Alexandrian seamen could be ignorant of that island? Major Rennel, with his usual candour, says: 'It must be admitted, that, on a supposition that it was the island of Malta (as the author certainly concludes), it might appear extraordinary that it should not have been recognised by some of the crew of the ship, which belonged to Alexandria (chap. xxvii.), as it may be supposed that Malta was well known to the navigators of that port. This, however, I cannot pretend to account for.' *Archæologia*, xxi. 103.) But St. Paul's Bay is remote from the great harbour, and possesses no marked features by which it could be recognized.

[2] 'A creek with a shore.' Commentators tell us that every creek has a shore, and that it should be 'a shore with a creek' (*vide* Kuinoel ad loc.); but *αἰγιαλός*, although it sometimes means the shore in general, in a restricted sense means a sandy beach, in contradistinction to a rocky coast. St. Luke here uses the correct hydrographical term. Arrian uses it frequently in this sense. Thus, in describing the shores of the Red Sea, he talks of a great and small beach, *αἰγιαλὸς καὶ μικρὸς καὶ μέγας* (*Perip. Mar. Eryth.* p. 9); and in the *Periplus* of Nearchus,

Painted by H. Smartly, Jersey

Engraved by H. Adlard

The situation of the ship on the fifteenth morning.

London: Longmans & Co.

seas' (τόπον διθάλασσον). It will be seen how perfectly these features still distinguish the coast.

Having observed from the ship a creek, such as we have described, they determined if it were possible to thrust the ship into it; they now cut their cables,[1] and left the anchors in the sea; and loosing (ἀνέντες) the lashings of the rudders,[2] and hoisting up the artemon,[3] or foresail (ἀρτέμωνα), they made for the creek, which they had previously selected for the purpose.

---

39 Ὅτε δὲ ἡμέρα ἐγένετο, τὴν γῆν οὐκ ἐπεγίνωσκον, κόλπον δέ τινα κατενόουν ἔχοντα αἰγιαλὸν εἰς ὃν ἐβουλεύοντο

39 And when it was day they knew not the land, but they discovered a certain creek with a shore, into the

---

we are told that the fleet was moved from one sandy beach to another, which was named Neoptana. Ἀλλὰ ἔπλεον γὰρ ἀπὸ τοῦ αἰγιαλοῦ, ἄραντες, τῇ γῇ προσεχέες, καὶ πλεύσαντες σταδίους ὡς ἑπτακοσίους ἐν ἄλλῳ αἰγιαλῷ ὡρμισάντο. Νεόπτανα ὄνομα τῷ αἰγιαλῷ. (P. 23.)

[1] The marginal translation in our version is certainly the correct one: literally, cutting off the anchors and leaving them in the sea.

[2] Ancient ships were steered by two large paddles, one on each quarter. When anchored by the stern in a gale, it would be necessary to lift them out of the water and secure them by lashings or rudder-bands, and to loose the rudder-bands when the ship was again got under way.

[3] The artemon was certainly the foresail, not the mainsail, as in authorized version. (See Dissertation on Ancient Ships.) A sailor will at once see that the foresail was the best possible sail that could be set under the circumstances. In the gale in the Crimea, in November 1854, the captain of the ship the *Lord Raglan* states that he cut away the main and mizen masts, but adds, '*I held on the foremast in case of her parting, to carry her end on.*' . . . 'There was nothing left for us but to beach; accordingly we ran before it, trying to avoid running foul of the other ships on shore, which we fortunately managed. The foresail was blown adrift, which helped her on. On striking, the sea swept over her,' &c. (*Times*, December 5, 1854.)

The ship must have been driven to the west side of the bay, which is rocky, but has two creeks. One of these, Mestara Valley, has a beach. (See chart.) I am, however, inclined to think that the point of appulse was in the other creek, which has no longer a sandy beach, but which must have had one formerly, although now worn away by the wasting action of the sea; it is near the spot marked in the chart of St. Paul's Bay, as the traditional scene of the wreck. My chief reason for supposing that it was hereabouts that the ship was run ashore, is its proximity to what St. Luke calls 'a place of two seas' (*τόπον διθάλασσον*),[1] or as our authorised version renders it by a

---

εἰ δύναιντο, ἐξῶσαι τὸ πλοῖον.

which they were minded, if it were possible, to thrust [2] in the ship.

40 *Καὶ τὰς ἀγκύρας περιελόντες εἴων εἰς τὴν θάλασσαν, ἅμα ἀνέντες τὰς ζευκτηρίας τῶν πηδαλίων, καὶ ἐπάραντες τὸν ἀρτέμωνα τῇ πνεούσῃ κατεῖχον εἰς τὸν αἰγιαλόν.*

40 And when they had cut the anchors, they left them in the sea (marginal translation), and loosed the rudder bands, and hoised up the foresail to the wind, and made toward shore.

---

[1] *Εἰς τόπον διθάλασσον*, in locum bimarem. It is generally supposed to mean an isthmus, which is no doubt dithalassic; but the interposition of land between the two seas is not necessary. Strabo calls the Bosphorus dithalassic.—*Πέλαγος δ' καλοῦσι Προποντίδα· κᾀκεῖνο εἰς ἀλλο τὸ Εὔξεινον προσαγορευόμενον πόντον, ἔστι δὲ διθάλαττος τρόπον τινα οὗτος.* (Lib. ii. cap. 5, 22, Oxford fol. vol. i. p. 164.) The narrow sound between the island and the main in St. Paul's Bay is a Bosphorus in miniature.

[2] [The ordinary reading *ἐξῶσαι* (which is adopted by Tregelles) means *to run the ship aground.* Westcott and Hort read *ἐκσῶσαι*, which would mean *to save the ship*; but *ἐξῶσαι* in the margin.]

happy conjecture, 'a place where two seas met.' From the entrance of the bay, where the ship must have been anchored, they could not possibly have suspected that at the bottom of it there should be a communication with the sea outside ; this unexpected circumstance naturally attracted the attention of the author, and served to mark the spot where the ship was wrecked. Selmoon Island, which separated the bay from the sea on the outside, is formed by a long rocky ridge, separated from the mainland by a channel of not more than a hundred yards in breadth.

Near this channel, which a glance at the chart will show must be where a ship from the eastward would be driven, they ran the ship ashore (*ἐπέκειλαν τὴν ναῦν*) ;[1] the fore part stuck fast (*ἐρείσασα*), and remained entire, but the stern was dashed to pieces by the force of the waves. This is a remarkable circumstance, which, but for the peculiar nature of the bottom of St. Paul's Bay, it would be difficult to account for.

---

41 Περιπεσόντες δὲ εἰς τόπον διθάλασσον ἐπέκειλαν τὴν ναῦν, καὶ ἡ μὲν πρῷρα ἐρείσασα ἔμεινεν ἀσάλευτος, ἡ δὲ πρύμνα ἐλύετο ὑπὸ τῆς βίας [τῶν κυμάτων.]

41 And falling into a place where two seas met, they ran the ship aground, and the forepart stuck fast, and remained unmoveable, but the hinder part was being broken by the violence [of the waves.]

---

[1] Julius Pollux has ὤκειλεν ἡ ναῦς, προσώκειλεν, ἐξώκειλεν. The word is used in the same sense as in the text by Arrian, Xenophon, Polybius, &c.

The rocks of Malta disintegrate into extremely minute particles of sand and clay, which, when acted upon by the currents or by surface agitation, form a deposit of tenacious clay; whilst in still water where these causes do not act, mud is formed; but it is only in the creeks where there are no currents, and at such a depth as to be undisturbed by the waves, that the mud occurs. In Admiral Smyth's chart of the bay, the nearest soundings to the mud indicate a depth of about three fathoms, which is about what a large ship will draw. A ship, therefore, impelled by the force of a gale into a creek with a bottom such as that laid down in the chart, would strike a bottom of mud graduating into tenacious clay, into which the fore part would fix itself and be held fast, whilst the stern was exposed to the force of the waves.

The ship has now reached the shore; but, before relating the escape of the passengers and crew, I shall endeavour to give the reader some idea of what must have been their privations and sufferings, and to supply what is wanting, or merely hinted at, in St. Luke's account, by citing examples of ships circumstanced as theirs was. I take the outline from the ancient voyage, and fill up the details with 'modern instances,' limiting myself to two cases, that of a crazy ship (Captain Back's) undergirded, and struggling with a gale; the other of the India Company's ship 'Bridgewater' caught in a typhoon.[1]

I have already shown that the inevitable result of such a storm must have been to have strained the hull severely, and rendered the ship leaky to an

[1] From the *United Service Magazine*, 1831, part ii. p. The ship encountered the typhoon, March 4, 1829.

alarming degree; and that the knowledge of this fact, which we only arrive at by inference, gives us a key which explains all the subsequent incidental notices which drop from the author. Such was the case both with the 'Terror' and the 'Bridgewater.' The leaks in the former ship were partly, no doubt, caused by the ice; in the latter case they were the effects of a typhonic gale. The officer who describes it says, they 'found the ship had suffered severely in the hull.'

After undergirding St. Paul's ship,—

Ver. 17. 'They lowered the gear.'

'Got our top-gallant masts and yards on deck.' (Bridgewater.)

Ver. 18. 'Exceedingly tossed by a tempest.'

'The unabated fury of the gale, strengthened by squalls, raised a long breaking sea, in which she plunged so heavily, that it was often unusually long before she recovered herself. It was evident she was getting more water-logged, and the straining and creaking of her whole frame, the working of the bulk-heads, which actually raised the officers' bed-places, the rickety twisting occasioned by the fore and aft motion, and the prolonged dull roll to windward, to say nothing of the cascade-like rushing of the water within; all these were certain indications of a consummation which no exertions of ours would probably be sufficient long to defer.' ('Voyage of Terror,' p. 438.)

'Next day they lightened the ship.'

'It was determined that the guns should be thrown overboard, as well as part of the cargo.' (Bridgewater.)

Ver. 19. 'Cast out . . . the tackling of the ship.'

'Cut away the sheet and stream anchors.' (Bridgewater.)

Ver. 20. 'All hope that we should be saved was then taken away.'

'I confess that all hope of ultimate preservation entirely left me.' (Bridgewater.)

Ver. 21. 'After long abstinence.'

'To aggravate our disasters, the ship too laboured so as to make it impossible to light a fire, and thus deprived us of the nourishment essential to the restoration of our exhausted energies.' ('Terror,' p. 440.)

'With the exception of a biscuit and a glass of spirits occasionally, not a man in the ship had throughout three days either sustenance or sleep. Owing to this, together with the great exertions required of them at the pumps, they had become completely exhausted and dispirited.' (Bridgewater.)

Ver. 29. 'They anchor the ship.'

'Near midnight anchored safely in Loch Swilly.' ('Terror,' p. 441.)

Ver. 39. 'They discovered a certain creek with a shore (beach), into which they were minded, if it were possible, to thrust in the ship.'

'Finding that their united efforts were unable to keep her afloat, it was determined to run her ashore on a small sandy beach, selected for the purpose.' ('Terror,' p. 442.)

I offer these extracts, not as curious coincidences, but that the reader may see from parallel cases what was the state of the ship, and the cause of their running her ashore.

They have now escaped the dangers of the sea; but other dangers await them: the guard, in conformity with the stern behests of Roman law, proposed to kill the prisoners, in order to prevent their escape. 'But the centurion, willing to save Paul, kept them from their purpose; and commanded that they which could swim should cast themselves first into the sea, and get to land, and the rest, some on boards, and some on broken pieces of the ship. And so it came to pass that they escaped all safe to land.'

---

42 Τῶν δὲ στρατιωτῶν βουλὴ ἐγένετο ἵνα τοὺς δεσμώτας ἀποκτείνωσιν, μή τις ἐκκολυμβήσας διαφύγῃ·

43 Ὁ δὲ ἑκατοντάρχης, βουλόμενος διασῶσαι τὸν Παῦλον ἐκώλυσεν αὐτοὺς τοῦ βουλήματος, ἐκέλευσέν τε τοὺς δυναμένους κολυμβᾷν, ἀπορίψαντας πρώτους ἐπὶ τὴν γῆν ἐξιέναι,

44 Καὶ τοὺς λοιποὺς οὓς μὲν ἐπὶ σανίσιν οὓς δὲ ἐπί τινων τῶν ἀπὸ τοῦ πλοίου· καὶ οὕτως ἐγένετο πάντας διασωθῆναι ἐπὶ τὴν γῆν.

42 And the soldiers' counsel was to kill the prisoners, lest any of them should swim out and escape.

43 But the centurion, willing to save Paul, kept them from their purpose, and commanded that they which could swim should cast *themselves* first into the sea, and get to land,

44 And the rest, some on boards, and some on broken pieces of the ship: and so it came to pass that they escaped all safe to land.

CHAPTER V.

MELITA TO ITALY.

(Chap. xxviii. 1.)

AFTER reaching the shore, they learnt, for the first time, that the name of the island was Melita. Their previous ignorance of this has been adduced as an argument[1] that this could not be a place so well known as the African Melita, now Malta. Major Rennel, with his usual candour, states the difficulty, and admits that he cannot remove it. This circumstance, however, will not be felt as a difficulty by any one acquainted with the locality; the sailors were probably little acquainted with any part of the island, except the great harbour (of Valetta) and the coast near it; the scene of the shipwreck lies remote from it, and is out of the usual track of ships approaching the harbour; and there is no marked feature in the configuration of the land which could make it known even to a native, if he came unexpectedly upon it.[2]

1 *Καὶ διασωθέντες τότε ἐπέγνωμεν ὅτι Μελίτη*[3] *ἡ νῆσος καλεῖται.*	1 And when we were escaped then we knew that the island was called Melita.

[1] *Georgi*, p. 191. See note at p. 140.

[2] Admiral Smyth makes use of Selmoon palace, the university tower, and *the breakers on the point of Koura*, as landmarks.

[3] Westcott and Hort read Μελιτήνη.

The natives[1] received the unfortunate voyagers with kindness, and kindled a fire, because of the rain, and because of the cold.

These meteorological remarks prove that the wind was to the north of east, for if it had been a Sirocco wind (S.E.), as Bryant and others contend, it would have been hot and sultry, for such is the character of that wind in the Mediterranean even so late as the month of November. I may add, that the Sirocco seldom or never lasts more than three days.[2]

---

2 Οἵ τε βάρβαροι παρεῖχαν οὐ τὴν τυχοῦσαν φιλανθρωπίαν ἡμῖν, ἅψαντες γὰρ πυρὰν προσελάβοντο πάντας ἡμᾶς διὰ τὸν ὑετὸν τὸν ἐφεστῶτα καὶ διὰ τὸ ψῦχος.

2 And the barbarous people showed us no little kindness, for they kindled a fire, and received us every one, because of the present rain, and because of the cold.

---

[1] In the Dissertation on the Island of Melita, I have answered the arguments of Bryant, founded on the term βάρβαροι, applied by St. Luke to the natives.

[2] Gales, in other directions, are of much longer continuance. Mr. Greswell cites a case which agrees in a remarkable manner with that of St. Paul. Aristides (the orator) encounters a gale in the Ægean Sea, and is driven through it for fourteen days and nights. Τέτταρες πάλιν αὗται πρὸς ταῖς δέκα ἡμέραι καὶ νύκτες, χειμῶνος κύκλῳ διὰ παντὸς τοῦ πελάγους φερομένων. (*Dissertations*, vol. iv. p. 197.) Professor Newman met with a continuous easterly gale on the coast of Cyprus, in December 1830. He writes: 'We were bound for Latakia in Syria, the course almost due east; but were driven back and forced to take refuge in the port of Famagousta, the ancient Salamis. Here we lay wind-bound for days. Owing to our frequent remonstrances, the captain three times sailed out, . . . but was always driven back, and once after encountering very heavy seas and no small danger. It was finally the first of January when we reached the Syrian coast.'

A circumstance now occurs which has given rise to much discussion :—

'When Paul had gathered a bundle of sticks, and laid them on the fire, there came a viper out of the heat and fastened on his hand ; and when the natives saw the venomous beast hang upon his hand, they said among themselves, No doubt this man is a murderer, whom, though he hath escaped the sea, yet vengeance suffereth not to live. He, however, shook off the beast into the fire, and felt no harm. But they expected that he would have swollen, or

---

3 *Συστρέψαντος δὲ τοῦ Παύλου φρυγάνων τι πλῆθος καὶ ἐπιθέντος ἐπὶ τὴν πυράν, ἔχιδνα ἀπὸ τῆς θέρμης ἐξελθοῦσα καθῆψε τῆς χειρὸς αὐτοῦ.*	3 And when Paul had gathered a bundle of sticks, and laid them on the fire, there came a viper out of the heat and fastened on his hand.
4 *Ὡς δὲ εἶδαν οἱ βάρβαροι κρεμάμενον τὸ θηρίον ἐκ τῆς χειρὸς αὐτοῦ, πρὸς ἀλλήλους ἔλεγον Πάντως φονεύς ἐστιν ὁ ἄνθρωπος οὗτος ὃν διασωθέντα ἐκ τῆς θαλάσσης ἡ δίκη ζῆν οὐκ εἴασεν.*	4 And when the barbarians saw the venomous beast hang on his hand, they said among themselves, No doubt this man is a murderer, whom though he hath escaped to sea, yet vengeance suffereth not to live.
5 *Ὁ μὲν οὖν ἀποτινάξας τὸ θηρίον εἰς τὸ πῦρ ἔπαθεν οὐδὲν κακόν·*	5 And he shook off the beast into the fire, and felt no harm.
6 *Οἱ δὲ προσεδόκων αὐτὸν μέλλειν πίμπρασθαι ἢ καταπίπτειν ἄφνω νεκρόν. ἐπὶ πολὺ δὲ αὐτῶν προσδοκώντων καὶ θεωρούντων μηδὲν ἄτοπον εἰς αὐτὸν γινόμενον, μεταβαλόμενοι ἔλεγον αὐτὸν εἶναι θεόν.*	6 Howbeit, they looked when he should have swollen, or fallen down dead suddenly : but after they had looked a great while, and saw no harm come to him, they changed their minds, and said that he was a God.

fallen down dead suddenly ; but after they had looked a great while, and saw no harm come to him, they changed their minds and said that he was a God.'

The difficulty here is that although there are serpents in Malta, they are not venomous, as the term ἔχιδνα (viper) implies. Upon this point I would merely observe that no person who has studied the changes which the operations of man have produced on the Fauna (animals) of any country, will be surprised that a particular species of reptiles should have disappeared from that of Malta. My lamented friend, the late Rev. Dr. Landsborough, in his interesting excursions in Arran, has repeatedly noticed the gradual disappearance of the viper from that island since it has become more frequented.

In the statistical account of the parish of Urr, the writer informs us that 'The small deadly coluber, said to be found in Galloway, has very probably existence ; though this animal be rare. This probability is admitted not only from numerous traditions, but because the writer of this account has once or twice met with a copper-coloured worm or little serpent, differing greatly from both the viper and the common blindworm (*Anguis fragilis*).' (*Stat. Acc.* vol. xi. p. 67.) The reasoning is not conclusive ; but it proves that there is a tradition of the former existence of vipers in Galloway, although now unknown.

Mr. Lyell, in quoting the travels of Spix and Martius in Brazil, observes :—

'They speak of the dangers to which they were exposed from the jaguar, *the poisonous serpents*, crocodiles, scorpions, centipedes, and spiders. But with the increasing population and cultivation of the country, say these naturalists, these evils will gradually diminish; when the inhabitants have cut down the woods, drained the marshes, made roads in all directions, and founded villages and towns, man will by degrees triumph over the rank vegetation and the noxious animals.'[1]

Perhaps there is nowhere a surface of equal extent in so artificial a state as that of Malta is at the present day, and nowhere has the aboriginal forest been more completely cleared; but it by no means follows that this was the case when St. Luke wrote. Indeed, there are traditions and other indications of former woods in the island. We need not, therefore, be surprised that with the disappearance of the woods, the noxious reptiles which infested them should also have disappeared.

We are now told, that 'In the same quarters were the possessions of the chief man of the island, whose name was Publius, who received us and lodged us three days courteously.'

---

7 Ἐν δὲ τοῖς περὶ τὸν τόπον ἐκεῖνον ὑπῆρχεν χωρία τῷ πρώτῳ τῆς νήσου, ὀνόματι Ποπλίῳ, ὃς ἀναδεξάμενος ἡμᾶς ἡμέρας τρεῖς φιλοφρόνως ἐξένισεν.

7 In the same quarters were possessions of the chief man of the island, whose name was Publius, who received us and lodged us three days courteously.

---

[1] *Principles of Geology*, 10th edit. vol. ii. p. 454. The evidence of Pliny has been adduced to show that when he wrote there were no noxious animals in the African islands. The passage is as follows:—'Mox Gaulos (Gozo) et Galata, cujus terra scorpionem dirum animal Africæ necat.' (Lib. v. c. 7.) Answer: Melita is not mentioned; scorpions are not vipers; there are scorpions both in Gozo and Malta.

The term πρῶτος τῆς νήσου, 'the chief or first of the island,' may mean either that Publius was the principal person in the island, as our translators have understood it; or it may be an official title. There are several reasons for supposing that it is in the latter sense that St. Luke uses it. The word in the plural, οἱ πρῶτοι, is elsewhere appropriately used to designate the principal men of a place: Mark vi. 21, Acts xiii. 50, xxviii. 17; but it is nowhere in the New Testament used in this sense in the singular, and it is difficult to suppose that in a populous island there was any one who, independently of official rank, was so prominent as to be mentioned, by his position, even in preference to his name. It is also to be observed that the father of Publius was alive, and it is unlikely that, except by official rank, the son should have been so emphatically styled the chief man of the island, in his lifetime.

But we have nearly conclusive proof that πρῶτος was an official designation, in two inscriptions, one in Greek and the other in Latin, still, or lately,[1] in

[1] These interesting and important inscriptions were certainly seen and carefully copied by Ciantar, from whose work I give the Greek inscription, as being probably the most correct copy. He says,—'Questo marmo si trova oggi posto alla pila d'un fonte che scaturische nel fosso sotto la mura e alla porta della Città Notabile (Città Vecchia).' (T. i. p. 515.) The inscription is as follows:—

A. K. . . . ΚΙΟΣ ΚΥΡ ΠΡΟΥΔΙΝΣ ΙΠΠΕΥΣ ΡΩΜ ΠΡΩΤΟΣ ΜΕΛΙΤΑΙΩΝ ΚΑΙ ΠΑΤΡΩΝ ΑΡΞΑΣ ΚΑΙ ΑΜΦΙΠΟΛΕΥΣ Α Σ ΘΕΩ ΑΥΤΟΥ . . . . ΣΤΩ . . . ΕΣΚ . . . . Ν . . Ε . . Ι . . ΝΕ.

which has been restored conjecturally thus,—

Α(υλος) Κ(αστρι)κιος Κυρ. Προυδινς ιππευς Ρωμ Πρωτος Μελιταιων και Πατρων αρξας και αμφιπολευς Α(υγουστῳ) Σ(εβαστῳ) Θεῳ αυτου (Σεβα)-στῳ . . κ.τ.λ.

Malta. In the former, a certain Roman knight, A.K . . . *κιος*, is styled by the same title as Publius, chief of the Melitans (*πρῶτος Μελιταίων*); and in the Latin inscription subsequently discovered, the same title occurs, MEL. PRIMUS.

I conclude, therefore, that *πρῶτος* here is an official title.[1]

We come now to the miraculous cure of the father of Publius. His disease is mentioned in the accurate and professional language which distinguishes the writings of St. Luke: it is stated that he lay, seized with, or labouring under (*συνεχόμενον*),[2] fevers and dysentery (*πυρετοῖς καὶ δυσεντερίῳ*).

---

8 Ἐγένετο δὲ τὸν πατέρα τοῦ Ποπλίου πυρετοῖς καὶ δυσεντερίῳ συνεχόμενον κατακεῖσθαι, πρὸς ὃν ὁ Παῦλος εἰσελθὼν καὶ προσευξάμενος ἐπιθεὶς τὰς χεῖρας αὐτῷ ἰάσατο αὐτόν.	8 And it came to pass, that the father of Publius lay sick of a fever and of a bloody flux: to whom Paul entered in, and prayed, and laid his hands n him, and healed him.

It is supposed to form a votive inscription by a Roman knight, named Aulus Castricius, chief of the Melitans (Πρῶτος Μελιταίων), to the emperor. The Latin inscription was discovered at Città Vecchia, in excavating the foundation of the Casa del Magistrato, in 1747; it is incribed on the pedestal of a column, and is said by Ciantar to be preserved in the hall of that building.

I was unable to find either of these inscriptions. It is to be hoped that they will be brought to light, and preserved in the valuable collection of Maltese antiquities, in the Knights' Library.

[1] Schaeffer, in his *Dissertatio de Publio* Πρώτῳ *Melitensium* (4to. Jena, 1755), arrives at the same conclusion. His labour, however, is chiefly bestowed upon the attempt to prove that Publius was of a Roman family.

[2] 'In speaking of Simon's wife's mother, who was taken with a great fever, he uses the term *συνεχομένη* in the same sense that the

'To whom Paul entered in and prayed, and laid his hands on him and healed him. So when this was done, the others also which had diseases in the island came and were healed.'

Here we have the evidence of a medical man distinguished for his caution, upon a point upon which he could not be mistaken, and where he was an eye-witness.

But this was not the only miraculous cure wrought by the apostle; for 'the others also, which had diseases in the island, came and were healed, who also honoured us with many honours: and when we were departing, they laded us with such things as were necessary.

---

9 Τούτου δὲ γενομένου [καὶ] οἱ λοιποὶ οἱ ἐν τῇ νήσῳ ἔχοντες ἀσθενείας προσήρχοντο καὶ ἐθεραπεύοντο,

10 Οἳ καὶ πολλαῖς τιμαῖς ἐτίμησαν ἡμᾶς καὶ ἀναγομένοις ἐπέθεντο τὰ πρὸς τὰς χρείας.

11 Μετὰ δὲ τρεῖς μῆνας ἀνήχθημεν ἐν πλοίῳ παρακεχειμακότι ἐν τῇ νήσῳ Ἀλεξανδρινῷ, παρασήμῳ Διοσκούροις.

9 So when this was done, the others also, which had diseases in the island, came and were healed:

10 Who also honoured us with many honours, and when we departed they laded us with such things as were necessary.

11 And after three months, we departed in a ship of Alexandria, which had wintered in the isle, whose sign was Castor and Pollux.

Greek (medical) writers do.' (Walker *On the Medical Language of St. Luke*; *Gent. Mag.* June 1841.) And Hippocrates uses the term πυρετοί (fevers) in the plural. (*Epid.* iii.)

'And after three months we departed in a ship of Alexandria, which had wintered in the isle, whose sign was Castor and Pollux.

'And landing at Syracuse, we tarried there three days.'

After leaving this port, which is not more than a day's sail from Melita, they proceeded circuitously (περιελθόντες) towards Rhegium. The meaning of the expression is not very clear. I am inclined to suppose that the wind was north-west, and that they worked to windward, availing themselves of the sinuosities of the coast; but with this wind they could not proceed through the Straits of Messina, from the tendency which the wind always has to blow parallel to the direction of narrow channels; they were therefore obliged to put into Rhegium, at the entrance of the strait. But after one day the wind became fair (from the south); and on the following they arrived at Puteoli, having accomplished a

12 Καὶ καταχθέντες εἰς Συρακούσας, ἐπεμείναμεν ἡμέρας τρεῖς,	12 And, landing at Syracuse, we tarried there three days.
13 Ὅθεν περιελθόντες[1] κατηντήσαμεν εἰς Ῥήγιον. Καὶ μετὰ μίαν ἡμέραν ἐπιγενομένου νότου δευτεραῖοι ἤλθομεν εἰς Ποτιόλους.	13 And from thence we fetched a compass, and came to Rhegium; and after one day the south wind blew, and we came the next day to Puteoli.

[1] [Westcott and Hort read περιελόντες, i.e. 'having cast loose,' cf. xxvii. 40. But there the meaning seems to be that they cut the cables, which would be quite unsuitable here. They read περιτεθόντες in the margin.]

distance of about 180 nautical miles in less than two days.[1]

Puteoli was then, as it is now, the most sheltered part of the Bay of Naples. It was the principal port of southern Italy, and, in particular, it was the great emporium for the Alexandrian wheat-ships. Seneca, in one of his epistles, gives an interesting and graphic account of the arrival of the Alexandrian fleet.[2] All ships entering the bay were obliged to strike their topsails (*suppara*), except wheat-ships, which were allowed to carry theirs. They could therefore be distinguished whenever they hove in sight. It was the practice to send forward fast-sailing vessels (*tabellariæ*), to announce the speedy arrival of the fleet; and the circumstance of their carrying topsails, made them distinguishable in a crowd of vessels. The supparum, therefore, was the distinguishing signal of the Alexandrian ships.

The further proceedings of the apostle, till his

[1] See remarks on the rate of sailing of ancient ships, in the Dissertation on the Ships, &c. of the Ancients.

[2] 'Subito nobis hodie Alexandrinæ naves apparuerunt, quæ præmitti solent et nuntiare secuturæ classis adventum. Tabellarias vocant. Gratus illarum adspectus Campaniæ est. Omnis in pilis Puteolorum turba consistit, et ex ipso genere velorum, Alexandrinas quamvis in magna turba navium intelligit, solis enim licet supparum intendere, quod in alto omnes habent naves. Nulla enim res æque adjuvat cursum, quam summa pars veli; illinc maxime navis urgetur. Itaque quoties ventus increbuit majorque est quam expedit, antenna submittitur, minus habet virium flatus ex humili; cum intrare Capreas et promontorium ex quo

Alto procellas speculatur vertice Pallas—

cæteræ velo jubentur esse contentæ, supparum Alexandrinarum insigne est.' (*Epist.* 77.)

arrival at Rome, I give in the words of our Authorised Translation. At Puteoli, St. Luke says (v. 14),—

'We found brethren, and were desired to tarry with them seven days; and so we went toward Rome; and from thence, when the brethren heard of us, they came to meet us as far as Appii Forum and the Three Taverns, whom when Paul saw, he thanked God and took courage. And when we came to Rome, the centurion delivered the prisoners to the captain of the guard; but Paul was suffered to dwell by himself, with a soldier that kept him.'

We learn, in the thirtieth verse, that St. Paul hired a house, and dwelt in it for at least two years. During this period, St. Luke wrote the Acts of the Apostles. This must have been in the third year of the governorship of Festus, the Roman procurator of Judea, an important date, for it establishes the still earlier date of his Gospel.

This work, in its turn, proves the previous existence of written accounts of the transactions of our Saviour, by eye-witnesses and ministers of the word.[1]

[1] See Dissertation on the Life of St. Luke.

DISSERTATION I.

ON THE WIND EUROCLYDON.

IN the former editions I gave Bryant's arguments in favour of the reading 'Euroclydon' at full length, with my answers; but since then, the discovery of the Sinaitic manuscript, which for reasons elsewhere assigned I consider the earliest existing evidence for the text of the New Testament, and the determination of the true reading of the Vatican manuscript by such competent observers as Dr. Tregelles and Dean Alford, have established, as I think, beyond dispute, the conclusion long ago arrived at by Bentley, Grotius, and others, that the true reading of the term employed by St. Luke was *εὐρακύλων*. When Bryant wrote the only manuscript authority which he had to contend with was the Alexandrian; to this we have now to add the Sinaitic, and, as I shall now show by an extract of a letter from Dr. Tregelles in answer to my inquiries on the subject, the Vatican. Referring to a former letter, he says:—

'I suppose that I wrote to you about the original reading in Acts xxvii. 14. In consequence of the incorrect manner in which the correction of B is given by Mai and Vercellone, I examined the point carefully myself when I was at Rome, so as to be *sure* that ΕΥΡΑΚΥΛΩΝ is the original reading. Several, as you are aware, have thought that the word was originally made to end in ΔΩΝ, not ΛΩΝ, but I am sure that the Δ was at first Λ. I was glad to find that Alford also examined this passage himself. For your satisfaction I give you his words :—

'"Acts xxvii. 14. 1. m. decidedly wrote ευρακυλων : 2. m. placed υ over the α, and λ between the κ and the υ, and altered Λ to Δ, but in so doing, he has left the right foot of the Λ of 1. m. visible beyond the corner of his own Δ."

'As our examinations were quite independent, and as they both confirm the collation of Birch, I hope that the united testimony will be thought satisfactory.'

Hence the three most ancient and authoritative Greek MSS. A, B, א, concur in the reading ευρακυλων. In the only others which rank with them in antiquity or authority, C and D, the passage is wanting ; and there are no manuscripts entitled to the name of ancient,—that is, according to Dr. Tregelles, anterior to the seventh century,—which have any other reading. The same may be said of the ancient versions, especially the Vulgate, which contains what may be called St. Jerome's critical decision on the subject.

We have thus the unanimous testimony of *ancient* MSS. in favour of the reading in question ; for in the only others which rank with the foregoing, the Codices Bezæ and Ephraemi, the account of the voyage is wanting ; hence the ancient documentary authority is unanimous in favour of the reading Euro-aquilo ; but this is a case in which the antiquity of a reading is all-important, for it is not only a word of rare occurrence,—indeed, so far as our knowledge goes, it is unique,—but is in a different language from the rest of the narrative, and every person who has had to correct the press, must know how apt such terms are to be blundered. St. Luke, writing in Greek, makes use of the Latin term *Euro-aquilo*, for *eurus* is the Latin for east, and *aquilo* for north-east, adding, it was 'called so' (ὁ καλούμενος), doubtless by the crew of the ship. I have elsewhere stated that an east-north-east wind accounted exactly for every event subsequently narrated, which in itself is a conclusive proof that it must be the true reading.

I now proceed to show the grounds upon which the earliest printers of the New Testament were induced to adopt the reading 'Euroclydon;' and here again I have to avail myself of the kind assistance of Dr. Tregelles, and give his statement in his own words:—

> 'In reply to your question, the only known uncial MSS. which contain the reading ευροκλυδων in Acts xxvii. 14, are the Codex Mutinensis (H) and Codex Passionei (G or L).
>
> 'In H, which is supposed to be of the ninth century, the part from xxvii. 4 to the end has been supplied by a hand apparently of the eleventh century, *but still in uncial letters.*
>
> 'In L, of the ninth century, it has the rough breathing εὐροκλυδων.
>
> 'The margin of the Harcleian Syriac (of the beginning of the seventh century) has ευρακλυδον in Greek letters, and this is the oldest Greek authority, I believe, for anything of the kind.'

In the later manuscripts the errors, as might have been expected, multiplied. Dr. Tregelles, in his critical edition, enumerates no less than ten ways of spelling the word: one of these happened to be the first which was printed. Such is the ground upon which the term Euroclydon rests.

DISSERTATION II.

ON THE ISLAND MELITA.

I NOW proceed to notice the arguments brought forward by Bryant and others in support of the opinion that it was the Illyrian, and not the African, Melita upon which St. Paul was shipwrecked.

Bryant, after concluding his remarks on the wind Euroclydon, proceeds thus :—

> 'Having thus despatched, and I hope satisfactorily, what I first premised to take in hand, I come now to the second part, which was to ascertain the particular island upon which the Apostle Paul was shipwrecked. This, one would imagine, could be attended with no difficulty; for it is very plainly expressed that, after being tossed for some time in the Adria, they were at last cast upon the island Melite. The only question is, which is the sea called Adria, and what island can be found *in that sea* mentioned by such a name?' (P. 23.)

This is not a fair statement of the question; the author of the narrative does not say that Melita was in Adria, but only that the ship was *driven through* Adria (διαφερομένων), after leaving Clauda, before she reached Melita. The real question is this—Was the sea which is interposed between Crete and Malta termed Adria when the narrative was written? for it is not denied by Bryant that this sea was known by the name of Adria afterwards. It is only necessary to cast a glance at the map of the Mediterranean to see that this part of it forms a natural geographical division. Major Rennel terms it, with much propriety, 'the middle basin of the Mediterranean.'[1] Now, this sea, as well as the gulf at present known by the same name, was then known as the Adriatic. The proof of this is very easily established. Ptolemy, who flourished immediately after St. Luke, describes this sea so often and so particularly by this name, as to leave the point without a shadow of doubt. With the accuracy of a geographer, he distinguishes the *Gulf* of Adria from the *Sea* of Adria; thus, in enumerating the boundaries of Italy, he tells us that it is bounded on one side by the shores of the Gulf of Adria, and on the south by the shores of the Adria[2] (lib. iii. c. 1),

[1] Humboldt calls it the Syrtic Basin. 'More to the west we have the Ionian Sea, or the Syrtic Basin, in which Malta is situated.' (*Kosmos*, Sabine's translation, ii. 118.) Procopius calls this basin the Adriatic Sea, and places Gaulos and Melita (Gozo and Malta) upon the verge of it, making them the boundary between it and the Tyrrhenian Sea on the west: Ἀράμενοί τε κατὰ τάχος τὰ ἱστία, Γαύλῳ τε καὶ Μελίτῃ ταῖς νήσοις πρόσεσχον αἳ τό τε Ἀδριατικὸν καὶ Τυῤῥηνικὸν πέλαγος διορίζουσιν. (*Bel. Vand.* i. 14.) Commentators gravely tell us that because Ptolemy calls Melita an African island it cannot be in the Adriatic Sea.

[2] The only perplexing circumstance connected with Bryant's speculations on this subject is the fact, that he should have succeeded in persuading himself that St. Paul's ship was driven into the Gulf of Venice, as I believe he did. That he should have persuaded others by an array of one-sided evidence is not wonderful. Macknight, who has adopted his views, assigns this as his reason: he says, 'In support of his opinion, Bryant cites ancient authors, who, in enumerating the Adriatic islands, mention Melite very particularly.' (Note, p. 128.) Mason, the poet, thus accounts for his self-deception: 'He had been much engaged in antiquities, and consequently had imbibed too much of the spirit of a professed antiquary. Now we know from a thousand instances that no set of men are more willingly duped than these, especially by anything that comes to them under the fascinating form of a

ἀπὸ δὲ μεσημβρίας τῇ τε τοῦ Ἀδρίου παραλίῳ; and that Sicily is bounded on the east by the sea of Adria (Ib. c. 4), *ἀπὸ δὲ ἀνατολῶν ὑπὸ τοῦ Ἀδρίου πελάγους*. He further informs us that Italy is bounded on the south by the Adriatic Sea (Ib. c. 14), that the Peloponnesus is bounded on the west and south by the Adriatic Sea (Ib. c. 16), and that Crete is bounded on the west by the Adriatic Sea (Ib. c. 17).

Here, then, we have the bounds of this sea, which Ptolemy sometimes calls Adria, sometimes the Sea of Adria, and sometimes the Adriatic Sea, laid down with such precision, that it is difficult to understand how it could be made a question; and those who have not read Bryant's work must be puzzled to guess how he disposes of such proofs. The answer is that, although he adduces the authority of Ptolemy often enough when it answers his purpose, he passes over those parts of the work which bear directly on the question in total silence! I will, as in the case of his observations on Euroclydon, allow Bryant to state his own case:—

'The grand difficulty, and, indeed, an insurmountable one, lies here; that, as *St. Paul says* expressly that the island he was cast upon was in the *Adria*, *Malta*, to be proved the place spoken of, must be made an *Adriatic* island. To effect this the learned *Bochart* labours hard. He shows that the sea we are speaking of encroached upon

---

new discovery.' The patronising manner in which Bryant excuses the erroneous views, as he holds them to be, of such writers as Bentley, Grotius, Beza, Bochart, Grotius, Beza, Bochart, Cluverius, is amusing: the field they were conversant in was so ample, that 'a person of the most extensive knowledge might sometimes be bewildered and lost' 65). It is to be hoped that the school of antiquarians to which he belonged has now passed away.

the *Ionian*,—that it extended itself to the *Sinus Corinthiacus*; then, in order, it engrossed the Sicilian sea and the Cretan: and thus, advancing step by step, he includes Malta within its verge; makes the coast of Africa washed by its waves, and would persuade you that Leptis, in Agro Tripolitano, was situated upon the Adriatic coast. All this he does upon the authority of the poets and a few later historians.

'As for the poets, their evidence is not worth taking notice of; they make everything subservient to measure. Yet, even of these, nothing he quotes comes up to his purpose. The learned writer makes use of their trespasses, merely to prepare the reader for what is to come, that he may not be too much shocked by the violence of the after-evidence. What Ovid and Tibullus say is only preparative. Philostratus and Pausanias come but halfway; those that speak to the purpose are Procopius, Orosius, and Æthicus. These are they that advance the Adriatic to the confines of Barca; and by the same proceedings might make Carthage itself, if they pleased, an appendage to Ragusa.

'But we ought to inquire of what rank and of what age the writers are whose authority he appeals to; . . . doubtless writers of some eminence in their several times, so let them have their due; who lived, however, many centuries after the fact we are determining; so that all you can learn from their evidence in respect to St. Paul and his shipwreck, is how things were called four or five hundred years afterwards; this is the utmost it will amount to. (P. 26.)

It would be difficult to string together a greater tissue of blunders even from Bryant's writings. Yet, with the exception of those mentioned in the foregoing paragraphs, he has not noticed one of the authorities adduced by Bochart,[1] whom he undertakes to refute.

[1] See Bochart's observations on this subject, Appendix No. v. [See also Appendix No. vi. by the editor of this edition.]

Let us examine his statement in detail. It begins with the double blunder of supposing St. Paul the author of the Acts, and that it is expressly said in the narrative 'that the island he was cast upon was in the Adria;' the next assertion is that Bochart confines his authorities to the poets and a few later historians. The poets are easily disposed of, 'they make everything subservient to measure.' Let us, therefore, pass to the later historians. He says in one place that they are not to be believed because they 'lived four or five hundred years,' in another 'many centuries,' after the fact.

The first question to be determined here is the date of the fact, When did St. Luke write the account of the shipwreck? Without entering very minutely into the inquiry as to its date, I think it probable that it was written A.D. 63. Now two of Bochart's authorities, Ptolemy and Pausanias,[1] were contemporaries of Adrian, who was born A.D. 76. We do not know the dates of their births, but the chances are two to one against the supposition that they were both younger than the emperor. One of these authors,

[1] Ptolemy has recorded an eclipse observed by him in the eighth of Adrian (A.D. 125), (*Almagest*, lib. iv. c. 9); and Pausanias speaks of that emperor as living when he wrote. He relates the legend of the fountain of Arethusa, which is said to be the river Alpheus, which flows under the Adria from Greece to Ortygia (Syracuse), ἔμελλε δὲ ἄρα μηδὲ Ἀδρίας ἐπισχήσειν αὐτὸν τοῦ πρόσω, 'Nor would the Adria restrain its flowing on' (*Arcadica*, lib. viii.), and speaks of the Straits of Messina as communicating with the Adriatic and Tyrrhenian seas (*Eliaca*, lib. v.). Solinus does the same; he says, 'Sunt et alteri montes duo (in Sicilia), Nebrodes et Neptunus; e Neptuno specula est in pelagus Tuscum et Adriaticum' (*Polyhistor*, 6, xi.). Camertinus thinks that this author was a contemporary of Pliny, whom he abridged: 'Suspicor vivente adhuc Plinio opusculum hoc suum scripsisse' (*Vita Solini*).

and it is immaterial which, was probably born about the time when St. Luke wrote, or very soon afterwards.[1] The supposition that either of them invented the name does not require notice. But in point of fact there is ample evidence that this name was given to the lower sea, between Crete and Malta, long before either of them wrote. Like the seas in modern times, this sea had different names. It was called the Ionian, the Sicilian, and the Adriatic. Bryant is at pains to extract passages from ancient authors, who used other names than the Adriatic, and, as might have been expected from such a line of argument, proves a great deal too much. If his arguments be good for anything, there was no such sea at all as the Adria. This he admits in a note, apparently unconscious that it destroys his own case. The note is as follows :—

'The truth is, Appian calls the whole sinus the Ionian Gulf : and not only Appian, but Dio, in lib. 41, and Herodian do the same ; so far from extending the Adriatic to Sicily or Malta, they do not seem to allow that such a sea existed.' (Note, p. 33.)

I proceed to Bryant's next argument, which I will state in his own words :—

'It is observable, that in speaking of the natives, the sacred writer never calls them Μελιταῖοι or Νησιῶται, but

---

[1] [Mr. T. Falconer points out justly (p. 75) that there is here a mistake. There is sufficient reason for believing that Ptolemy was alive A.D. 161, and Pausanias mentions a battle which appears to have taken place A.D. 174. Thus Ptolemy was alive 98 years and Pausanias 111 years after the probable date of the Acts (A.D. 63).]

βάρβαροι. The ancient Greeks called all nations that were not of Grecian origin indiscriminately *barbarians.* This continued for a long time; but after they had been conquered by the Romans, and, as it were, beat into manners, they by degrees laid aside their saucy distinction, and were more complaisant to their neighbours. Hence we find that Polybius, Diodorus, and others, who wrote after the decline of the Grecian power, seldom made use of the distinction, unless the people they treat of are notorious for their ferity or rudeness. But supposing a Grecian writer might continue this partial distinction, and look upon every country but his own as barbarous, yet St. Paul cannot be supposed to have acted so. He was no *Greek*, but a *Jew* of *Tarsus*, and in the same predicament as those that are spoken of.

'Whenever the Apostle calls a people barbarous, you may be sure it was the real character of the nation.' (P. 39.)

We have here again the blunder of supposing St. Paul the author of the Acts, and the still greater one of supposing that St. Paul would only have applied the term barbarian to people 'notorious for ferity and rudeness.' St. Paul repeatedly uses the word; but upon no occasion does he use it in the sense which Bryant supposes he would, or in a sense inapplicable to the ancient inhabitants of Malta in contradistinction to the Greeks. The Melitans were not Greeks, therefore they were barbarians. (Rom. i. 14.) If they did not understand the language of him who addressed them, then each party would be barbarous to the other. (1 Cor. xiv. 11.) The natives would not understand their visitors, therefore they were barbarians.

Bryant is at great pains to contrast the civilisation of the ancient inhabitants with that of the Illyrian

Melitans. He tells us that according to Diodorus Siculus and others,

> '*Melite Africana* was first a colony of *Phœnicians*, and was afterwards inhabited successively by Carthaginians, Greeks, and Romans. Who will be so hardy as to denominate any of these nations barbarous?'

The answer to this question is not difficult; nobody called the Greeks barbarians, but Scylax calls the Phœnicians barbarous,[1] and Polybius makes one of his speakers, a Greek, call both the Carthaginians and Romans barbarians.[2]

In his anxiety to vindicate the ancient Maltese from the charge of barbarism, he actually quotes the Acts to show that the term did not even apply to the lower orders—again unconscious that he was overturning his own argument, by admitting that it was the Maltese who received them hospitably.

> 'But it is said that some of the lower sort might still be rude and savage, though the people of rank were otherwise. But St. Paul experienced nothing but civility from the lower sort, nay, οὐ τὴν τυχοῦσαν φιλανθρωπίαν, uncommon civility, as *he himself witnesses.* Therefore, if the common people are civil and humane, and their superiors polite and ingenious, a general imputation of barbarism can never square with that nation. In short, take them separately or collectively, this stain is incompatible with the natives of Malta.' (P. 42.)

---

[1] Scylax places the Phœnicians amongst the inhabitants of Sicily, who are barbarians. Ἐν δὲ Σικελίᾳ ἔθνη βάρβαρα τάδε ἐστίν, Ἐδυνοί, Σικανοί, Σικελοί, Φοίνικες, Τρῶες. (*Periplus*, p. 4.)

[2] Agalaus of Naupactus advises the Greeks not to fight with each other, but unite to resist the barbarians (the Romans and Carthaginians). (*Hist.* lib. v. 104.)

The next argument is, that there are no vipers in Malta; but St. Luke mentions that one fixed itself on St. Paul's hand (ver. 3). Bryant does not dwell much upon this, but Giorgi lays considerable stress upon it, and Dr. Falconer[1] does the same. Both of these writers attribute the presence of these animals in Meleda to the moisture of the climate, caused by its woods, 'densissimas habet silvas' (Giorgi),[2] and their absence from Malta to its aridity. I am not disposed to call this in question.

At present Malta is entirely clear of wood, and its surface is in the most artificial state; but when St. Paul visited the island this was not the case, for there are still a few ancient carouba trees—evidently the remains of former woods. We have therefore sufficient cause for such a change in the Fauna as will account for the disappearance of this species of reptiles, as already noticed in the account of the voyage.

Bochart says that as the ship in which St. Paul sailed from Melita was on her voyage from Egypt to Puteoli, we cannot suppose she would winter at the Illyrian Melita; if she did, she must have gone much out of her way, 'toto salo aberrasse.' Bryant meets

[1] 'The circumstance of the viper or poisonous snake that fastened on St. Paul's hand merits consideration. Father Giorgi, an ecclesiastic of Melita Adriatica, who has written upon that subject, suggests very properly that as there are now no serpents in Malta, and, as it should seem, were none in the time of Pliny, that there never were any there: the country being dry and rocky, and not affording shelter or proper nourishment for animals of that description. But Meleda abounds with these reptiles, being woody and damp, and favourable to their way of life and propagation.' (Falconer.)

[2] Giorgi consulted Vallisneri, a celebrated naturalist, who proved by experiment, that the earth of Malta was no protection against the bite of a viper.

this with the case of Lucian's ship, which was driven to Athens. He says :—

'Upon Bochart's principle one might argue that this ship coming to Attica and the Piræus must be a mistake, for it was certainly Malta that it arrived at, because Attica is quite out of the way for any ship to touch at that is bound from the Nile to the Tiber,—"Toto cœlo et toto salo errant,' &c. But ships that lose their passage cannot always choose their retreat : they are at the will of the winds, and are sped in all directions.' (8vo. ed. p. 412.)

But there is no parallelism whatever in the cases : ships crossing the Ægean, as this ship was, may meet with a southerly gale and be driven to the north. Every reader of Falconer's 'Shipwreck' must be familiar with such a case ; the ship was driven from Crete towards Athens :—

'Now, through the parting waves, impetuous bore,
The scudding vessel stemmed the Athenian shore ;'

but, less fortunate than that of Lucian, was wrecked on the coast of Attica. But if we are to believe that Adria means the Gulf of Venice, then we must suppose that by some means or other almost every ship coming from the Levant to the west side of Italy, found its way into it. We hear of four cases of ships in this predicament all about the same time, possibly in the same year :—1st. St. Paul's ship. 2nd. The 'Castor and Pollux.' 3rd. The ship of Josephus, which sank in Adria. 4th. The ship of Cyrene which picked him up and carried him to Puteoli.[1]

[1] *Josephi Vita*, edit. Hudsoni, p. 905.

The only other argument against the supposition that Malta was the scene of the shipwreck which remains unanswered, is brought forward by Dr. Falconer; he says—

'The disease with which the father of Publius was affected (dysentery combined with fever) affords a presumptive evidence of the nature of the island. Such a place as Melita Africana (Malta), dry and rocky, and remarkably healthy, was not likely to produce a disease which is almost peculiar to moist situations.' (P. 21.)

It is obvious that the answer to the former argument applies also to this one; but in point of fact, Dr. Galland, of Valetta, informs me that the disease is by no means uncommon in Malta.

L'Avocat,[1] a French writer, merely repeats without adding anything to the arguments of Giorgi. He does not, however, as Bryant and Falconer have done, pass over the unequivocal testimony of Ptolemy in silence; he says—

'Ptolémée, qui n'a vécu que plus de 80 ans après St. Luc, est le premier qui a donné plus d'étendue à la Mer d'Adriatique au Golfe de Venise.' (P. 40.)

The answer to this is, that we do not know that Ptolemy lived even one year after St. Luke; neither was he the first who used it. I have already noticed his contemporary Pausanias, who also used it, and as Major Rennel observes, 'changes of names in geography take place very gradually, and almost imper-

[1] '*Dissertation Historique et Critique sur le Naufrage de St. Paul, dans laquelle on examine si c'est dans l'île de Meleda qu'il fut mordu d'une vipère, et qu'il guérit miraculeusement le père de Publius.*' (1745.)

ceptibly.'[1] But Josephus, who made the same voyage, and probably in the same year, if not the year before, tells us in his life that his ship sank in the Adria,[2] and that he and others were picked up by a ship of Cyrene and carried to Puteoli. The events related by Josephus could not have happened in the Gulf. Ovid repeatedly calls this sea Adria,[3] and Horace places Actium on Adria.[4]

There is another modern writer who takes the same side of the question, who is entitled at least to the merit of originality. In a modern French work, entitled 'L'Univers,' M. La Croix, the author of the account of Malta, tells us—

'Qu'on remarque bien qu'il avait fait halte dans un port de la côte *septentrionale* de Candie :'

---

[1] Father Giorgi admits that after the time of Ptolemy the name of Adria was almost universally adopted ; he answers the question, 'Cur autem, si universi antea geographi secus docuerant, nova hæc atque insolens opinio non per gradus sed quasi uno impetu deinceps apud scriptores invaluerit ?' by attributing it to the celebrity of Ptolemy.

[2] Dr. Gray supposes that Josephus was in St. Paul's ship ! (*Connection of Sacred and Profane Literature*, i. 362.)

[3] 'Adriacumque patens late bimaremque Corinthum.'
(*Fasti*, lib. iv. 501.)

'Aut hanc me, gelidi tremerem cum mense Decembris,
Scribentem mediis Adria vidit aquis ;
Aut, postquam bimarem cursu superavimus Isthmon,
Alteraque est nostræ sumta carina fugæ.'
(*Trist.* lib. i. Eleg. 12.)

[The above seem to be the only passages in Ovid which have any bearing on the question.]

[4] 'Actia pugna,
Te duce, per pueros hostili more refertur ;
Adversarius est frater ; lacus, Adria.'
(*Epist.* lib. i. ep. xviii. 61.

that the wind Euroclydon is—

'suivant Pline, Vitruve, Aristote, et Strabon, un vent qui tient le milieu entre le midi et le levant ; c'était donc, pour parler le langage moderne, un vent de sud-est, ou ce qu'on nomme dans la Méditerranée le sirocco. Sur ce point il ne peut y avoir une ombre de doute.'

He then asks,

'Dira-t-on que l'Ecriture Sainte a pu confondre la mer de Sicile, où est située Malte, avec la Mer Adriatique? Une telle supposition est inadmissible. D'abord, Malte est très-éloignée de la Mer Adriatique ; ensuite cette mer n'a jamais eu d'autres bornes que celles que les géographes lui assignent aujourd'hui ; elle a toujours été deux cents lieues de longueur sur quarante dans sa plus grande largeur ; dimensions sur lesquelles s'accordent Pline, Strabon, et Thucydide.'

The information that Fair Havens is on the *north side* of Crete ; that Pliny, Vitruvius, Aristotle, and Strabo tell us the direction of Euroclydon ; and that Pliny, Strabo, and Thucydides tell us that the Adriatic never had any other boundaries than its present, requires confirmation. M. La Croix cannot understand how, if Malta had been the island, St. Paul could have been delayed three months. The island, wherever it was, he says, must have been 'bien peu fréquentée par les navigateurs, ce qui n'a jamais été vrai pour Malte ;' he should have added, not even in winter. It would be a waste of words to answer such arguments.

Since the above was written, a new defender of the Dalmatian hypothesis has started up, in the Rev.

J. M. Neale, who has actually visited Dalmatia, and comes back with the *certainty*, as he assures us, 'that Meleda is Melita.' This conclusion, however, does not rest upon any observations of his own, for although he passed that side of the island of Meleda on which he tells us there is a creek called St. Paul's Bay, which exactly answers the description, he passed it at night, his authorities being those put into his hands by the Dalmatian monks. Admiral Sir Charles Penrose, as quoted by Dr. Howson, had stated the distance of Meleda from Clauda as 780 miles, and that no ship could reach it without making a curve. Now it happens that there are two islands of nearly the same name in the Adriatic—Melada and Meleda. Admiral Penrose understood that Bryant meant the former, which is 780 miles from Clauda; but he became aware of the mistake, and remarks in a supplement to his MS., 'I never saw Bryant's work, but I have seen an extract which makes me think he meant the southernmost of the Melitas in the Adriatic. This makes no difference in my argument, but it does in the distance, as the southern isle is 150 miles nearer Crete than the other.' This is a sufficient answer to a very immaterial mistake, and neither distance can be reconciled to the facts stated in the narrative. Mr. Neale assumes, as plain facts, the objections of Coleridge and others; I have noticed them already, and need not repeat my answers here. Mr. Neale has, however, a theory of his own, which requires to be considered; he admits that the wind was E.N.E., and carried the ship to long. 22° in lat. 35°; this course would have led to Malta; but at this point he supposes the wind to have shifted to E.S.E., *as it often does.* The italics are the author's own; the meaning is that a northerly levanter often changes to a southern levanter; but this is entirely contrary to the observed wind-phenomena of the Mediterranean. Captain Stewart, R.N., in his sailing directions, states that it is always safe to anchor under the lea of an island with northerly winds, *as they die away gradually.* No such event took place in St. Paul's voyage; but let us suppose that it did, and attend to the consequences. According to this author, there was not one *single* island to pass: this can only mean to pass within sight, for the Ionian Islands, Zante, Cephalonia, Corfu, &c. were passed on the right. This hypothesis of the ship's track—for it is no more—is meant to show the possibility of the ship's making the land at Meleda without seeing it; otherwise it would not agree with St. Luke's narrative, which precludes the possibility of their having seen the land till after they were in 20 fathoms soundings. If, then, it can be shown that a ship could not sail from Clauda to Meleda without seeing the land before she was in 20 fathoms soundings, then Meleda cannot be the Melita on which St. Paul was wrecked. Now the supposed track of the ship when abreast of Cephalonia is less than half a degree of longitude distant from that island, or about twenty-four geographical miles; but Cephalonia, which is 5,300 feet high, can be seen at the distance of eighty miles. Before losing sight of it, the ship must have come within sight of the mountains of Corfu and the Acroceraunian range, followed by the high land on both sides of the Strait of Otranto, on the left by the mountains of Calabria, and on the right by those of Albania, till they came in sight of the mountain-range of the island of Meleda, seen according to Lithgow in his *Travels* from the entrance of the Gulf of Cattaro (p. 53),—a distance of forty miles.

Lady Strangford, who visited Dalmatia since Mr. Neale, remarks on his work, 'It appears to me impossible to imagine for an instant, that the ship (of St. Paul) could have passed up the narrow way between the coast of Otranto and the Acroceraunian mountains without seeing land.' (*The Eastern Shores of the Adriatic*, p. 215.) On the south side of Meleda is a range of mountains sloping down to the water's edge, with deep water close to the land: they must have been in sight directly in front of the ship's course for more than one whole day. Nothing will account for the facts recorded by St. Luke, but a low flat island distant from any mountainous region, insular or continental.

With regard to the Meledan St. Paul's Bay—the creek so 'exactly answering the description.' It could not possibly be the first land they would make; no ship from the south ever reached Meleda without making the high land on each side of the Adriatic below and above the straits of Otranto. It will not do to say it was at midnight, for the mountains of Meleda must have been seen right ahead on the two preceding days. I presume the monks of Dalmatia must have given the name to some creek in the island, but I have not been able to discover it, although I have searched both in the Hydrographic department in the Admiralty, and the map-room of the Geographical Society. As to its answering the description, I have the Admiralty chart of the island before me, and I can neither find the name nor any creek which ingenuity could make to agree with the narrative ; for we must have a twenty-fathom depth and a fifteen-fathom depth, with such a distance between them as to allow their standing on, *διαστήσαντες*, till they had time to prepare for anchoring with four anchors from the stern. They must moreover, at this depth, have had good holding-ground, with a creek having a sandy beech to leeward of their anchorage, and this creek must have been in a place where two seas met (*τόπον διθάλασσον*). We are told by this author—on the authority of course of his informers—not only that there is a creek 'exactly answering this description' in Meleda, but 'there is no creek in Malta such as described ; the Maltese hypothesis makes the sailors take the Salmonetta Strait for a creek.' I never heard of such an hypothesis, although I believe I have read nearly all that has been written on the subject. I call it a place where two seas meet (*τόπον διθάλασσον*), the term which Strabo[1] applies to the Bosporus, which divides the Euxine from the Propontis ; and the strait in question is a Bosporus in miniature. At the inside entrance of the strait Admiral Smyth has placed the traditional wreck of St. Paul's ship,[2] in exactly the spot where a ship would be driven, and where the unexpected circumstance of a connection with the sea on the outside would naturally arrest the attention of the spectator. I admit this is no longer a creek having a shore or beach on which a ship could run ashore (*κόλπον ἔχοντα αἰγιαλόν*) ; but every

[1] Lib. ii. cap. 5.   [2] See chart of St. Paul's Bay (p. 129).

geologist must know that it must have had one, and that at a period, geologically speaking, from the dip of the beds, by no means remote. It may almost be said to be in the act of falling, for a fissure runs parallel to the verge of the mural precipice which here forms the shore, and which threatens ere long the fall of a prodigious mass of the rock. There is another creek, only separated from the above by a point, which still has a beach, namely the opening of the Mestara Valley. A ship anchored at the fifteen-fathom depth might run for either of these creeks, and from both of them the unexpected opening to the sea outside could not fail to arrest the attention of the crew.

The monks of Dalmatia, like their Maltese rivals, make it a point of honour to uphold the claims of their own island; and the Austrian proclivities of the reverend author, which he displays by emblazoning the vowels in letters of gold on the outside of his book, signifying 'Austriæ Est Imperare Orbi Universo,' has led him, unconsciously no doubt, to give credit to reasoning resting on no foundation of fact.

It is always an advantage to the cause of truth that both sides of a question like the present should be carefully and fully investigated. Our author endeavours to show that a ship may have made the land of Meleda in the manner described by St. Luke, that is without seeing it till after she was in twenty fathoms of water; but as this is impossible, it is impossible that the Dalmatian Melita can have been the scene of the shipwreck.

*** The Admiralty chart above referred to is of Austrian as well as British authority. It is entitled, 'Adriatic Sea—Sheet 5.' The Dalmatian Islands, from Slozella to Ragusa Vecchia. From the Austrian, English, and Neapolitan co-operations, directed by Colonels Campana and Visconti, and Captain W. H. Smyth, R.N., K.S.F.

DISSERTATION III.

ON THE SHIPS OF THE ANCIENTS.

THERE are few branches of classical antiquity of which so little is known as that which relates to ships, navigation and seamanship; no work written expressly on those subjects by any ancient author has come down to us,[1] and the scattered notices which we meet with in historians and poets often tend to mislead. The representations of ancient ships are in a great measure confined to coins and marbles, where we cannot expect to find accuracy of detail, except in detached parts, such as the aplustra or head and stern ornaments, rudders, anchors, &c.

There are, however, two circumstances to which we are indebted for much valuable information respecting the very class of ships with which we are at present chiefly concerned.

The Emperor Commodus during a season of scarcity imported grain from Africa: in commemoration of which a series of coins (great and middle brass) was struck, bearing upon the reverse figures of ships under sail; and one of the Alexandrian wheat ships was driven by stress of weather into the

[1] The Emperor Leo, in his *Tactics*, in treating περὶ ναυμαχίας, makes the same complaint. He says he could find nothing written on the subject by the ancients.

Piræus. The extraordinary size of this vessel excited much curiosity on the part of the Athenians; and Lucian, who visited her, lays the scene of his dialogue entitled 'The Ship or Wishes' (Πλοῖον ἢ Εὐχαί) on board of her; in the course of which we learn incidentally many interesting circumstances regarding the ship, her voyage, and management.

The marbles and paintings of Herculaneum and Pompeii also afford valuable details, and have the advantage of synchronising perfectly with the voyage of St. Paul; the catastrophe to which they owe their preservation having happened less than twenty years after his shipwreck.

As all these authorities agree very well with each other, we can derive from them what we may consider a tolerably correct idea of a merchant ship of the period.

The forepart of the hull below the upper works differed but little in form from that of the ships of modern times; and as both ends were alike, if we suppose a full-built merchant ship of the present day cut in two, and the stern half replaced by one exactly the same as that of the bow, we shall have a pretty accurate notion of what these ships were. The sheer or contour of the top of the sides was nearly straight in the middle, but curving upwards at each end, the stem and stern posts rising to a considerable height, and terminated by ornaments, which were very commonly the head and neck of a water-fowl bent backwards. This was called the cheniscus (χηνίσκος). It forms the stern ornament of the ship on the tomb of Nævoleia Tyche at Pompeii (p. 206), the stern post of which terminates with the head of Minerva. Lucian, in describing the Alexandrian ship, mentions that the stern rose gradually in a curve surmounted by a golden cheniscus, and that the prow was elevated in a similar manner. In the coins of Commodus we find the cheniscus in some instances at the head, and in others at the stern.

The bulwarks round the deck appear to have generally been open rails. There were projecting galleries at the bow and stern. The stern gallery is often covered with an awning, as in the ship on the tomb of Nævoleia. The galleries at the bow served, as it would appear from Lucian's description, as places where to stow the anchors and also the *στροφεῖα* and *περιαγωγεῖς*. The exact meaning of these terms is not clear. Some think they meant instruments for heaving up the anchors, others for helping the ship round. I think it is not improbable that both were meant. The *στροφεῖα*, 'winders,' were probably windlasses or capstans. We have evidence that both were used by the ancients, for in the ship of Theseus represented in one of the paintings found at Herculaneum, we see a capstan with a hawser coiled round it;[1] and in a figure of the ship of Ulysses, said to be taken from an ancient marble, in the edition of Virgil (3 vols. fol., Rome, 1765), we see the cable coiled round a windlass. The *περιαγωγεῖς*, 'drive-abouts,' were probably paddles, for the purpose of helping the ship round when 'slack in the stays.'

The ancient ships were not steered, as those in modern times are, by rudders hinged to the stern-post, but by two great oars or paddles (*πηδάλια*), one

[1] See figure of this ship, p. 207.

on each side of the stern: hence the mention of them in the plural number by St. Luke; a circumstance which has caused, as Dr. Bloomfield observes, 'no little perplexity to commentators.'[1] But no sea-going vessel has less than two rudders, although small boats and river craft, such as those on the Nile,

[1] Note to Acts xxvii. 40. This is scarcely to be wondered at, at least by those who have had recourse to the most obvious sources of information—the writers de re navali antiquâ. Berghaus, the most voluminous, and I believe the most laborious writer on the subject, has given a restoration of the after-part, *Hintertheile*, of St. Paul's ship, with a square stern, a single hinged rudder with the tiller pointing aft, and with rudder bands with dead eyes spliced into the ends!—about as like an ancient ship as a Chinese junk is to an English yacht. The work of this author, which is entitled *Geschichte der Schiffartskunde der Vornehmsten des Alterthums* (8vo. Leipzic, 1792), is in three ponderous volumes (1670 pp.), scarcely a page of which is not fortified by an array of authorities, all of which, he tells us, he has verified ('habe ich meines Wissens kein Citatum von andern auf Treu und Glauben unternommen, ohne von der Richtigkeit desselben überzeugt zu seyn,' Vorrede, xxiv.). As may be supposed, he has carefully preserved all the blunders of his predecessors; his anchors have no stocks, and the artemon is set at the mast-head. This author is fairly outdone in absurdity by M. Le Roy, author of *Mémoires sur la Marine des Anciens*, Hist. de l'Acad. des Inscript., tom. xxxvii.; of *Nouvelles Recherches sur les Navires des Anciens*, Mém. de l'Institut, tom. i.; and of *Les Navires des Anciens considérés par rapport à leurs Voiles*. 8vo. Par. 1783. M. Le Roy has undertaken to explain the difficulties attending the description of the ship of Ptolemy Philopator, given by Athenæus; amongst others we are told by that author that she took twelve hypozomes (undergirders) with her (ὑποζώματα δὲ ἐλάμβανε δώδεκα); this he renders, 'Il avoit douze ponts ou étages,' twelve decks or platforms! but the most amusingly absurd part of his writings is his work on the sails of ancient ships: a full-rigged ship, according to him, had a lateen sail at the bow (le dolon); the main-sail (l'acatian) is, in his representation, triangular with the apex below; further aft than this was another lateen sail (l'artimon), and at the stern another lateen sail (l'épidrome). M. Le Roy had a boat rigged in this manner, and found she could both tack and turn to windward. Probatum est.

were sometimes steered by one. Dr. Bloomfield is at the very unnecessary trouble of quoting a passage from Orpheus to prove, what was in fact the universal practice, that large ships had two rudders, and that it is—

'Probable they were regularly taken off when the ship was in port and laid in dock. But the question is, *how* and *where* were they fixed on? Many (as Alberto, Bishop Pearce, and Kuinoel) think that the rudders were one at the stern and the other at the bow of the ship; while others suppose both to have been at the stern. I know not, however, of the numerous passages cited by the above commentators, any one that *determines* this point; but that which I have adduced from Orpheus undoubtedly does—namely, as we have seen, that they were both at the stern.'

Writers are not in the habit of telling what every one knows. I question if I could prove by a quotation that the rudders in English ships are at the stern; but every representation—and they are numerous—shows us that those of the ancients were there. Commentators who suppose that the two rudders in sailing ships were, one at the head and one at the stern ('unum in prora, alterum in puppi,' Kuinoel), have been misled by a passage in Tacitus (*An.* ii. 6), who is not describing sailing vessels, but flat-bottomed boats on the Rhine, which were to be moved by the current, and had a rudder at each end, just as river boats of the same description have at the present day, in which the ancient paddle rudders are retained. With regard to the question how they were fixed, the answer is that they were not fixed any more than other oars are. In small vessels they rested in a notch or rowlock in the upper gunwale, and were secured by a tropoter or leathern thong, or by an iron clamp. Instances of both modes of retaining the rudder in its place may be seen on Trajan's Column. In those vessels which had projecting gangways, or stern galleries, the rudders were often passed through them.[1] Some larger vessels had a rudder case fixed on the outside, on each quarter. In others the wales of the ship projected far enough from the side at the stern to allow space for the rudder to pass through them. This may be observed in the ship on the Tomb of Nævoleia Tyche at Pompeii;[2] but the most common way was to have rudder ports at each quarter, as in the ship of Theseus (see figure at page 135). These also served for hawseholes, when the ship was anchored by the stern.

This mode of steering was retained till a comparatively late period. In a bas-relief over the doorway of the leaning tower of Pisa, built in the twelfth century, ships are represented with the paddle rudders, as are those in the Bayeux tapestry, representing the Norman invasion. They must have been in use till after the middle of the thirteenth century, for in the contracts to supply Louis IX. with ships, the contractors are bound to furnish them with two

[1] There is a bronze model of a ship under sail in the Grand-Ducal gallery at Florence, with the rudders fitted in this manner. See also the figures of galleys on the coins of Adrian, pp. 228, 229.

[2] In the *Peregrinatio ad Terram Sanctam* of Breydenbach, Mentz, 1486, in which the details of the figures of ships are extremely correct, we have the figure of a ship in the transition state, in respect to her rudders. She has a hinged rudder, but she has also a paddle rudder slung at her side, passing through the wales, as in the above example. See view of Modon.

rudders (*duos timones*).[1] This may no doubt mean a spare one; but we learn from Joinville that the king's ship had rudders, expressed in the plural, 'gouvernaus' (ch. 78).

By the middle of the following century we find the hinged rudders on the gold noble of Edward III. The change in the mode of steering must therefore have taken place about the end of the thirteenth, or early in the fourteenth century.

With regard to the dimensions of the ships of the ancients, some of them must have been quite equal to the largest merchantmen of the present day. The ship of St. Paul had, in passengers and crew, 276 persons on board, besides her cargo of wheat; and as they were carried on by another ship of the same class, she must also have been of great size. The ship in which Josephus was wrecked contained 600 people. But the best account we have of the size of some of these ships is that which I have already alluded to as given by Lucian, on the authority of the carpenter (*ναυπηγός*) of the Isis, the Alexandrian wheat ship, which was driven by contrary winds to Athens. Both Bryant[2] and Dr. Falconer adduce this ship as an example of the great size of vessels of the class to which she belonged; but both of them exaggerate her dimensions to an absurd degree. Bryant compares her with the Royal George, which was at that time probably the largest ship in the British navy, the dimensions of which he gives; but, with his usual inaccuracy, he makes the breadth of the ancient ship one-third, in place of one-fourth of her length, or nine feet broader,

[1] *Archéologie Navale*, ii. 388.

[2] Bryant's *Observations*, p. 16.

instead of six feet narrower, than the Royal George. Dr. Falconer corrects this error, but falls into one nearly as great; for in calculating her tonnage, he multiplies by the length given by Lucian, which is evidently the extreme, instead of by the length of the keel, which was till lately the rule, and is the only one applicable in cases where the only dimensions given are length and breadth. The consequence of calculating in this manner is that he increases her tonnage by at least one-half, making it more than 1,900 tons, whereas it must have been less than 1,300. The rule by which the tonnage of the Royal George was computed, was to multiply the length of keel[1] by the extreme breadth, and the product by half the breadth for depth, and divide the whole by 94. Dr. Falconer has made the ship of Lucian to measure 1,938 tons. Her length, according to Lucian, was 120 cubits, which, at a foot and a half each, is 180 feet; her breadth one-fourth, or 45 feet. Now, it is evident that Dr. Falconer has calculated in the manner I suppose: for if we take the extreme length, 180 feet, as the multiplier, the tonnage is exactly what he makes it, $\frac{180 \times 45 \times 22\cdot5}{94} = 1,938$ tons.

Although we have no means of knowing the length of this ship's keel, we may from the dimensions given by Lucian form an estimate of her relative size, as compared with any other ship the dimensions of which are known. I take the Royal George, as the ship these authors compare her with, and the dimen-

[1] As the fore-part of the keel joins the stem-post in a curve, in order to obviate uncertainty it was measured as far as the perpendicular of the length on deck, and three-fifths of the breadth of beam deducted for the fore-rake.

sions of that ship as given by Bryant, which appear to be correct; but as the height is given in one case to the taffrail, and in the other to the upper deck, I take one-half of the breadth for the depth, which is the usual rule for computation, in both cases. Hence,

Royal George, $212{\cdot}75 \times 51 \times 25 = 276681$
Isis, Lucian's ship, $180 \times 45 \times 22{\cdot}5 = 182250$

This is in the ratio of 2,000 tons to 1,320; if, therefore, the keel of the ancient ship was as long in proportion to her extreme length as that of the Royal George, she would measure upwards of 1,300 tons; but we know that the ancient ships had projections at each end, much greater than in modern ships, and as they are not included in the measurement for tonnage, they must be deducted; that at the prow of the one in question is distinctly mentioned by Lucian. In the Navicella at Rome the keel is only about half the extreme length.

Perhaps an early-built English ship, when the ancient 'beak-head,' or projection forward, was still retained, will give the most correct idea of her proportions. We have a very particular account of the Royal Sovereign,[1] or, as she was called during the Commonwealth, 'The Sovereign of the Seas.' Her

[1] See account of her, bearing the title, 'The Commonwealth's great ship, commonly called the *Sovereign of the Seas*, built in the year 1637, with a true and exact account of her bulk and burden, and those decorements which beautify and adorn her, with the carving work, figures, and mottoes upon them. She is, besides her tonnage, 1,637 tons in burden; she beareth five lanthorns, the biggest of which will hold ten persons to stand upright, without shouldering or pressing on one another, with the names of all the ropes, masts, sails, and cordage that belong unto a ship.' 4to. Lon. 1653.

length is stated to be, 'a prora ad puppim, 232 foote,' the length of the keel 120 feet.

If the keel of the ancient ship bore the same proportion to her length 'a prora ad puppim,' which this one did, it would be only 99 feet; and the tonnage, calculated by its length, instead of the extreme length, would be 1,015 tons. Taking the mean of the two results, it is probable that the ship of Lucian would measure between eleven and twelve hundred tons. Although, therefore, her dimensions are not so wonderful as former calculations make them, they were equal to those of a large modern merchant-vessel. We need not therefore be surprised at the numbers we sometimes hear of as being carried in ancient ships.

From every representation which has come down to us, as well as from every notice in authors, they appear to have been rigged with extreme simplicity. They depended for progression upon a single square sail, all the other sails which we hear of being subsidiary. It is evident that this was the case in Lucian's ship, notwithstanding her unusual size. We hear of his friends looking up with wonder on the magnitude of the mast and yard; the sail therefore must have been furled aloft. We hear indeed in another part of the same dialogue, of ships with three sails (*τριάρμενα*[1]), but we are not told whether they were set upon

[1] Lucian has mentioned a circumstance which has perplexed commentators, and which I do not pretend to explain: he speaks of 'looking up and counting the piles of hides' (*ἀναβλέποντες ἀριθμοῦντες τῶν βύρσων τὰς ἐπιβολάς*), or rather the rows of hides placed above each other. Scheffer supposes that by hides the author means sails, which, he says, 'ex corio pellibusque primum facta videntur. Nomen indicare potest, est enim velum a vellere, id est pelle, ut Varro docet' (p.

separate masts, or one above another. From the manner in which they are mentioned, it is obvious that these three-sailed ships were of the largest size; we must conclude therefore, that it was not a common circumstance to have so many as three principal sails. What may be considered, therefore, as the plain sails of an ancient ship consisted of one great square sail, with a small one at the bow.

The following figure, taken from the 'Archéologie Navale' of M. Jal, from a marble in the Borghese col-

lection at Rome, appears to give a good idea of the relative size and position of the sails, except that the mainmast is evidently placed too near the bow.

141). He translates the above passage 'sursum spectantes numerantes vela alia aliis imposita,' adding the following criticism on the Latin translation: 'interpres ibi coria scripsit, quod nullum habet sensum.'

Captain Spratt R.N. supposes with Scheffer that sails are meant: he writes me, 'That passage of Lucian, "looking up and counting the hides," may be explained by supposing the sails to have been sometimes made of light hides sewn together . . . . The thin flexible goat-skins now tanned in the Levant would form excellent sails.'

We hear of other sails, but from the manner in which they are mentioned by Pliny,[1] we must suppose that they were considered as extra sails. Julius Pollux calls 'the great and proper mast' (ὁ μέγας καὶ γνήσιος ἱστός) the acatian; he adds, however, that some give that name to the smallest. Xenophon,[2] on the other hand, calls the principal sails 'the great sails,' τὰ μεγάλα ἱστία, and the small ones 'acatia.' The propriety of Xenophon's terms is confirmed by the Attic Tables, which speak of the acatia, in contradistinction to the great sails.

The name of the small sail at the bow of the vessel, or the fore-sail, has very generally been supposed to be the dolon. I believe, however, that this is a mistake, and that the name of this sail was the 'artemon.' As this is the name of the sail stated by St. Luke to have been hoisted when the ship was run ashore, and as lexicographers and translators differ as

[1] 'Jam nec vela satis esse majora navigiis. Sed quamvis amplitudini antemnarum singulæ arbores sufficiant, super eas tamen addi velorum alia vela præterque alia in proris et alia in puppibus, ac toto modio provocari mortem.' (*Proœm.* in lib. xix.) This is surely a *non sequitur*; it could be no good reason for not setting more sail that single spars were sufficient for the size of the yards. Instead of 'quamvis,' the reading 'cum vix' has been suggested. I am, however, satisfied that the word 'non' has been dropped out, and that it ought to be read, 'singulæ arbores *non* sufficiant.' In point of fact, single spars are *not* sufficient for the great yards of the single-masted Mediterranean vessels of the present day; and we find, wherever the details are correctly given, that the same was the case in the Middle Ages and in ancient times. See the views in Breydenbach, and the ship on the tomb at Pompeii. Pliny's dislike of additional sails does not say much for his seamanship, although he died in command of a fleet; it proves however, that they were only occasionally used.

[2] Xenophon, in the *Hellenica* (lib. vi.), speaking of the manner in which Iphicrates exercised his crews, says, he left 'the great sails,' τὰ μεγάλα ἱστία, and took the small ones, ἀκάτια.

to the meaning of the word, I shall endeavour to ascertain what is its true meaning, by adducing all the evidence I have been able to discover on the subject.

The word artemon (*ἀρτέμων*) does not occur in any ancient Greek author, except in St. Luke's account of St. Paul's voyage; neither does it occur in any mediæval Greek author. It is, however, still used in the French nautical vocabulary, to designate the sail at the stern (the mizen, or in modern language, the mizen-trysail). Hence the French translators, by using the word 'artimon,' give it that meaning. In our authorised version it is rendered 'mainsail.' In Wyclif's it is 'a litil sail.' Dr. Bloomfield considers it to be 'the foresail.' It is, however, most commonly supposed to be the same as the *supparum*, or topsail.[1] Böckh supposes it to be the highest of all the sails, equivalent to the modern top-gallant-sail. He says, 'There was also, above the upper sail (*obern Segel*), a third smaller sail, which is doubtless the artemon.'[2] Alciati supposes it 'the bonnet,' or addition to a sail, which can be removed. Papias Vocabulista makes it a storm-sail,[3] &c. It has also been supposed to mean the mast, the yard, the rudder, the vane at the mast-head, the main block, &c.; but it is unnecessary to takes these latter suppositions into consideration, as they are manifestly untenable. We learn from Isidore of Seville that the artemon was a sail; and the

[1] 'Ἀρτέμων, Supparum, das ober am Mast hing.' (Berghaus.) See also *Schneider*, ad verb.; *Scheffer*, p. 140, &c.

[2] 'Ausser den untern und obern Segeln der beiden Masten liess sich gewiss auch ein drittes kleineres anbringen; und dieses ist ohne Zweifel der Artemon.' (p. 140.)

[3] 'Artemon, velum navis breve, quod quia melius levari potest in summo periculo extendit malus et antenna.'

question is, which sail was it? I shall endeavour, in the first place, to point out what sails it was not.

Professor Böckh says very decidedly (*ohne Zweifel*) that it was the highest sail of all, but does not give his reasons, as being foreign to his object, the artemon not being mentioned in the Attic Tables (p. 140). I presume, however, he derives them from the following passage in Scheffer:—'Nomina eorum (velorum) ex Polluce hæc sunt: . . . artemon, quod in fuso supra antemnam suspenditur.' ('Milit. Naval.' p. 140.)

Now, there can be no doubt but that if the artemon be suspended from the spindle at the mast-head, it must be the highest sail. Scheffer gives Pollux as his authority; but, upon turning to Pollux, we find that it is the *vane* (ἐπισείων) at the mast-head he is speaking of, and not the artemon. Scheffer had looked at the Latin translation, which is, 'Et quod supra antemnam est fusus nominatur, a qua parte *artemonem* suspendunt,' and not at the original, which is τὸν ἐπισείοντα, the streamer or vane, so called from its fluttering motion. The translator, ignorant of the meaning both of this word and artemon, has chosen to translate the one by the other, and Scheffer has adopted his blunder, and from him it has become traditional, and has been adopted by every succeeding writer 'de re navali.' Scheffer himself, however, became aware of his blunder, and explains it away ingeniously, if not ingenuously, in the Addenda to his work. He says—

> ''Επισείων, id est tænia, seu velum ludens in aere; . . . forte hoc est quod Artemona Isidorus ait, quia ἀπαρτῶσι τοῦ ἀτράκτου, ut Pollux loquitur, dirigit sane navem quia ex ejus situ gubernatores ventum cognoscunt!'

Which is as much as to say that because the vane or streamer shows the direction of the wind, it must be synonymous with the artemon, which Isidore says was principally useful in directing ships. We may very safely reject this explanation of the word, which takes its rise in a blunder.

I come now to those who translate it the mizen, or sail at the poop. The cause of this is obvious enough : the word *artimon* still exists in the French nautical vocabulary, and translators, not competent to determine whether it retains its original signification or not, have very naturally left the word unchanged. They have committed the same error which an English translator would do who should render the French word ' misaine,' the foresail, into ' mizen,' for there can be no doubt but that, in this case also, the words in both languages are originally the same, coming from the Italian ' mezzana,'[1] middle size, in contradistinction to ' vela grande,' although the ' mât de misaine ' has changed its place as well as the ' mât d'artimon.' Before I show that such a change has taken place, I shall consider our English translation where it is rendered mainsail, because the evidence which clears up this mistranslation explains the other also.

The English translators naturally consulted Bayfius, or De Baif, the earliest of the modern writers ' de re navali,' and probably the only one when the translation was made ; he thus explains the word :

> ' Est autem artemon velum majus navis, ut in Actis Apost. xxvii. ; . . . etenim etiam nunc nomen Veneti vulgo retinent et *Artemon* vocant.' (P. 121.)

[1] In Italian the mast at the stern (mizen) is ' álbero di mezzana.

It appears, therefore, that when this author wrote, in the middle of the sixteenth century, the word was still in use at Venice as a marine term, and that it meant the 'velum majus,' or *largest sail* in the ship. De Baif is good authority, because it appears that he had spent the three years preceding the publication of his work at Venice. But the largest sail of the Venetian vessels of the time was the *foresail.* The error, therefore, does not lie with him, but with the translation of 'velum majus' into *mainsail.* The mainsail was at first, no doubt, the largest sail; but, in very many vessels, it has ceased to be so. In modern ships, it is smaller than the maintop-sail, and in many two-masted vessels it is smaller than the foresail. Dr. Bloomfield, in his Note on the subject, states that 'Bayfius, Junius, Alberti and Wolf explain it as the large sail of the poop, answering to our mizen-sail, and even yet called by the Venetians artemon.' (Note on v. 40.) This, however, is a mistake: it was the largest sail in two-masted vessels of the period; but, instead of being at the poop, it was at the prow; it was in reality the *foresail.* The word, although formerly an Italian nautical term, has now become obsolete in that language. The 'Vocabolario della Crusca' calls it 'la maggior vela che abbia la nave,' and quotes Dante[1] and Ariosto[2] as authorities.

[1] 'Chi ribatte da proda, e chi da poppa;
Altri fa remi, ed altri volge sarte;
Chi terzeruolo, ed artimon rintoppa.'
(*Inferno*, canto xxi. st. 5.)

[2] 'Di cui per men travaglio avea il padrone
Fatto l' arbor tagliar dell' artimone.'
(*Orlando Furioso*, c. xix. st. 48.)

There is nothing in Dante but a mere enumeration of terms; but in the Commentary of Landino upon that author, printed at Venice in 1493, we find the following remark on the passage: 'La minore, terzeruolo, et una in mezzo delle due lequale si chiama la mezza.' This at least shows that it was not in the middle of the vessel, or the mainsail, but at one end. The terzeruolo is said to be the smallest sail; in the modern Italian nautical nomenclature, it means 'a reef,' or the part of a sail tied up to reduce it. It is clear then that if the artemon was neither the sail in the middle nor the smallest sail, it must have been the foresail, which was the largest sail in the vessel when Landino wrote.

Ariosto, in the passage quoted in the 'Vocabolario,' says the artemon was cut away:—

'Il padrone
Fatto l'arbor tagliar dell' artimone.'

He says afterwards that, when the storm subsided,

'La disiata luce di Sant' Ermo,
Ch' *in prua* s' una cocchina a por si venne;
Che più non v' erano arbori nè antenne.' (xix. 50.)

'Saint Ermo's light
Low settling *on the prow* with ray serene
It shone, for masts or sails no more were seen.' (Hoole.)

The artemon was therefore, according to Ariosto, the mast of the prow, for it was that mast which had been cut away.

The latest authority which I can find for the meaning of this word in Italian is in the 'Dizionario di Marina,' Venice, 1769. It does not occur in the dictionary itself; but in the index the reader is referred to 'Trinchetta' as its synonym. Now the trinchetta, in modern Italian, is the foresail; in the dictionary it is described as 'vela triangulare che in alcuni bastimenti si pone nel davanti o a prua.' I think this passage explains the reason why the French term 'artimon' is applied to the sail at the stern. The foresail, anciently, was very often a triangular or lateen sail.[1] Latterly, and up till the end of the eighteenth century, the mizen was a triangular sail; when, therefore, the triangular sail was placed at the stern by the French, it retained the name which had been given to the triangular sail when placed at the bow. From the dimensions of the sails taken from the contracts of the Genoese with Louis IX. of France, to be afterwards quoted, it will be seen that the artemon, although placed at the bow, was in fact the largest sail. This is confirmed by one of the figures in the views of Breydenbach.[2] The ship in question is a two-masted vessel, with the sails furled on the yards, the foremast being the largest. De Baif was therefore correct in saying that the artemon was the largest sail in the ship.

I come now to the ships of the middle ages, and avail myself of the documents published by M. Jal in his Archéologie Navale. From the Capitulaire Nautique, 1255, we have the following list of sails of ships of certain dimensions:—

[1] 'Artimon, c'est une voile latine, ou faite en tiers pointe à la différence des autres voiles, qui sont quarées.' (Aubin, *Dict. de Marine*, 1702.)

[2] This ship is figured in Creuze's article on Ship-building, *Encyc. Brit.* 4th edit. See also another ship taken from the same view in Dibdin's *Ædes Althorpianæ*, vol. iii. p. 222.

'Navis de milliariis CCC usque DC in proda ita sit contata in velis, habeat artimonem terzarolem et dolonum, unum de fustagno vel de bombasio, et parpaglonem unum de canaveza. In medio habet majorem et dolonum de bombassio.' (T. ii. p. 434.)

Here we find the artemon at the prow (*proda*). The dolon is not, as generally supposed, confined to the prow, as we find one 'in medio,' on the middle or mainmast.

This is confirmed by certain contracts, entered into by the Genoese, to provide ships for Louïs IX. In one of these, given by Jal (ii. 388), they are bound to supply two ships, each to have—

'Arborem unam de prorra (*sic*) longitudinis cubitorum quinquaginta unius, grossitudinis palmorum tredecim minus quarta; . . . item arborem unam de medio longitudinis cubitorum quadraginta septem. . . . Item debet habere vela sex cotoni infra scriptarum mensurarum, videlicet, *pro artimono* cubitorum sexaginta sex; . . . item velum unum de medio cubitorum quinquaginta octo.'

Here the artemon is the largest sail, and belongs to the largest mast, which is the *foremast*, 'arbor de prora.'

According to Wetstein, there is in the 'Versio Syra Posterior,' on the margin, 'artemon est stipes in capite,' *i.e.* the mast at the head of the vessel; and in the ancient Scholia on Juvenal, in the passage in the 12th Satire, where he describes the disabled state of the ship of Catullus,

'Vestibus extentis, et quod superaverat unum,
Velo prora suo,'

the scholiast observes, 'Artemone solo velificaverunt.' The artemon is not mentioned by Julius Pollux.

There is a passage in Isidore of Seville which would seem to imply that the name of the sail at the prow was dolon ; and we are told by many writers that Pliny and Pollux gave this sail the same name ; but Pliny does not mention the dolon at all, and Pollux merely says that it is the smallest sail (ὁ δὲ ἐλάττων δόλων, i. 91). The meaning of the passage in Isidore depends on the punctuation. It is as follows:—'Dolon est minimum velum et ad proram defixum. Artemo dirigendæ potius navis causa commendatum quam celeritate.' (*Origines*, xix. 3.) As it is pointed, this means that 'the dolon is the smallest sail, and placed at the bow. The artemon rather for the purpose of directing the ship than for speed.' I suspect, however, that it should be read thus—'The dolon is the smallest sail ; and, placed at the bow, the artemon rather for directing the ship than for speed :' and that the authority of Isidore may be added to the others, to show that it is the foresail. It is, at all events, not contradictory to that of the authors I have quoted. Isidore is, however, by no means high authority on such a subject.

According to etymologists,[1] the word is derived from ἀρτάω, appendere, or ἄρτημα, an appendage. Now, knowing as we do, that the ancients depended for speed upon one principal sail, an appendage or additional sail at the bow of the ship was required for the purpose of directing the vessel when in the act of putting about ; for, although there could be no diffi-

[1] See Calepenius, ad verb.

culty in bringing the ship's head to the wind with the great sail alone, a small sail at the bow would be indispensable for making her 'pay off,' that is, bringing her head round; otherwise she would acquire sternway,[1] and thereby endanger the rudders, if not the ship itself.

The annexed figure of an African corn-ship, from the reverse of a coin of the Emperor Commodus,[2] appears to give a good idea of the relative size and position of the two principal sails.

I am inclined to think that the etymology is a correct one, as Vitruvius uses the word to denote the 'leading block' in a system of pulleys. But this block forms no part of the purchase, but is a mere appendage used for the purpose of changing the direction of the force.

The sails were strengthened by bands of rope sewed across them ; so that if one part were rent, the injury would be confined to one compartment. This mode of strengthening sails appears to have been continued till a late period, as we find it in one of the figures in Breydenbach.[3]

[1] If any of my readers have tried to heave a cutter to, with her square-sail set and kept aback, they will understand this ;—haud inexpertus loquor.

[2] Taken from a coin in the Museum at Avignon, by the author.

[3] The modern practice of using canvas bands is, perhaps, no improvement on the ancient practice of using rope bands. A correspondent of the *Nautical Magazine* (1834, p. 87), who signs himself Master of a British Merchant Ship, states that in a long voyage his stock of

In one of the coins of the Emperor Commodus, representing a wheat-ship, we have this mode of strengthening the sails clearly expressed.[1]

The sail at the stern (ὁ κατόπιν) is called by Pollux, ‘epidromus’ (ἐπίδρομος); and by Hesychius, ‘pharos,

and the smallest’ (φάρον καὶ ἔλασσον, art. ἐπίδρομον). Pliny also mentions that there was a sail at the stern, and we frequently see a mast there, as in the above figure; but I have seen no representation of one with a sail set upon it.

The next class of sails are the Suppara, or top-sails. Isidore describes them as having only one

spare canvas was expended, and he was forced to employ rope bands instead. This he found to answer perfectly well, and thinks it an improvement.

[1] Admiral Smyth observes with regard to this coin, that it ‘was struck A.D. 186, and it testifies the care of Commodus in the frumentarian supply. He established a company of merchants, and a fleet for conveying corn from Africa to Rome, to guard against any misfortunes that might befall the ships which transported it from Egypt. As this was a good act, his inflated vanity on the occasion shall pass uncensured.’ (No. 294 of *Admiral Smyth's Collection*, p. 161 of his Catalogue.)

sheet,[1] *i.e.* the rope which extends the foot of the sail, and which is named in Latin 'pes veli' (Gr. πούς).[2] This would imply that the sail was triangular, attached to a yard with the apex undermost. This seems so strange a mode of setting a triangular sail as to be almost incredible. It would appear, however, that in the middle ages such topsails were actually in use; for in an old collection of views in the Knights' Library at Malta, printed about the beginning of the sixteenth century, there is one of 'La Città di Trepani,' with a topsail agreeing with the description of Isidore. I have not, however, seen any which belong to the classical period. There are, indeed, triangular topsails upon the ships in some of the coins of the Emperor Commodus; but the apex, instead of being the foot of the sail (pes veli), is the head, whilst the

[1] 'Siparum, genus veli unum pedem habens, quo juvari navigia solent in navigatione quoties vis venti languescit; de quo Lucanus:—

"Summaque pandens
Suppara velorum, perituras colligit auras."'
(*Origines*, lib. xix. c. iii.)

[2] Commentators and translators have no difficulty as to the meaning of πούς or 'pes veli,' the rope which extends the lower corner of the sail to the side of the ship, Anglicè 'the sheet;' but they are puzzled with πρόπους, or 'propes.' Böckh supposes it the lower end of the rope, or that which was fastened to the ship's side: 'Untern Ende der Schote, und wurden am Schiffe befestigt.' (*Urkunde*, p. 154.) I can see no difficulty in the matter; all large square sails must have two ropes at each lower corner of the sail, one to draw it aft, and the other to draw it forward; the former is called the *sheet*, the latter the *tack*. Now πρόπους, or 'propes,' is obviously the *tack*, it would naturally be called the fore-sheet, but that is appropriated to the sheet of the foresail: with the ancients, both ropes were called ποδές, 'sheets;' thus Aristotle, describing the shifting of a sail, says, τὸ δὲ πρὸς τὴν πρῷραν ποδιαῖον ποιησάμενοι ἐφιᾶσιν (*Mechan.* 8), hence what the ancients called the fore-sheet is now called the tack.

base of the triangle is extended on the main-yard. This, at least, is a shipshape way of setting a sail, as no additional spars are required for it.

When we read of at least three tiers of sails above each other, we must be certain that they had topsail-yards. Montfaucon has given a figure of a coin of Nero, representing the port of Ostium (vol. iv. pl. 143), in which one of the ships has top and top-gallant yards across: but the details of his figures, at least those from coins, are not to be depended upon. I have a sulphur impression from the same type, from a coin in the British Museum, in fine condition, in which there is no appearance of yards above the great sail. But in one of the ancient paintings which illustrate a MS. of Homer, supposed of the fifth century, preserved in the Ambrosian Library, which was published at Rome, 1835, the ships are represented with topsail-yards across, with the sails furled on them (pl. 32).

In addition to the three lower sails, and the suppara or topsails, we hear of 'acatia' and 'dolones.' The meaning of both terms has hitherto been misunderstood,—the acatium is not the mainsail, nor is the dolon the foresail. It is not, however, so easy to say what they were, as what they were not. We have sufficient proof that both the acatia and dolones were small sails. Now, small sails may be either set in addition to large sails in fine weather, or substituted for them in bad weather,—*i.e.* 'storm sails.' It would appear from the passage from Xenophon (cited at p. 192), that the former were substituted for the great sails: all we can learn with regard to the dolones is, that they were the small masts or sails in ships (οἱ μικροὶ ἱστοὶ ἐν τοῖς πλοίοις, Hesych.; τὰ μικρὰ ἱστία, Suidas). Suidas quotes a passage from Procopius, which shows that they also were occasionally substituted for the great sails: χαλάσαντες τὰ μεγάλα ἄρμενα, τοῖς μικροῖς ἃ δὴ δόλωνας καλοῦσιν, ἕπεσθαι. I must say, therefore, with Dindorf, 'manemus igitur incerti.' In one of the paintings from Herculaneum, representing a galley under sail, two triangular sails are seen attached to the main-yard, with the apices below.[1] I suspect that in stormy weather the great sail was furled, and triangular sails substituted; two of these would reduce the sail to one-half, and one to one-fourth: by bringing down the fore-yard-arm to the deck, and leading aft the sheet, we have the modern lateen sail.

The spars and wooden gear (σκεύη ξύλινα) are, with the exception of the hinged rudder, precisely the same as we see in the coasting craft in the Roman states and Tuscany at the present day. They consisted of a strong and rather short mast, placed a little before the centre of the vessel. In the following figure, taken from the tomb of Nævoleia Tyche, at Pompeii, the mast is hooped, which would seem to indicate that it was built of several pieces. The foremast (*artimonium*) rakes over the bow, and the main-yard, which is fully as long as the vessel, is composed of two pieces, doubled in the centre, exactly as the

[1] Böckh supposes this a mistake, and that it is a square sail, with the middle drawn up (p. 141). I can scarcely suppose that the engraver could have given the details, unless warranted by the original; he has represented 'the ear-rings' or upper corners overlapping each other. After a century's exposure, the original is much faded; it is in the Museo Borbonico at Naples, but at such a height I could not make out the details.

lateen yards of large sails are at present; the main halyard block, which does not differ in any respect from that of the modern Italian craft, is formed by a

large block of wood, not strapped, but at the upper end of it there is a hole, through which the pendant of the halyard is passed.

We have no means of knowing with accuracy the internal arrangements, or the manner in which the decks were laid with respect to breaks or hatchways. In the ship of Theseus we observe a break in the decks at the poop. Lucian mentions cabins near the stern in the Alexandrian ship, which he describes in his dialogue of the ship. In the following figure, taken from the 'Antichità di Ercolano' (tom. ii. pl. xiv.), we see the roof of one of these cabins (*οἰκήσεις*).

This is an interesting fragment, because the artist, although evidently quite ignorant of the details, must have had an accurate prototype to copy from. The subject is Theseus abandoning Ariadne.[1] In order to give it the air of rude antiquity the mast is formed by the trunk of a tree inverted ; a rope, thrown carelessly over the yard, is seen to pass between it and the sail ; the wind blows the rope in one direction, whilst it fills the sail in another ; another rope passes between the sail and the bolt-rope, and the feather

ornament at the stern is absurdly exaggerated. In spite of all these blunders, this is perhaps the most instructive representation of an ancient ship which has been preserved ; and, when we remember that it was painted within sight of the port to which the Alexandrian wheat-ships resorted, and probably at the time when St. Paul's ship was in existence, we are warranted in supposing that many of the details

[1] I was unable to discover the original when at Naples.

agree with the class of ships to which she belonged. In the account of the voyage, I have referred to this painting for evidence to prove that the ships of the ancients were fitted for anchoring by the stern, as well as to show the manner in which it was done. The rudders, in such a case, were necessarily lifted out of the water, or unshipped; in either case, the rudder-port, or rudder-case, served the purpose of a hawse-hole. In the ship of St. Paul we know that the rudders were secured.

In a vignette to the splendid copy of Virgil printed at Rome in 1761, we have the figure of a ship anchored by the stern, taken from an ancient marble. In this case the rudders are unshipped; the cable is passed through the rudder-case, and is seen within board, coiled round a windlass.

We have ample evidence, therefore, to prove that the ships were fitted for this manner of anchoring. I have already stated the reasons why it was put in practice in the case of St. Paul's ship.[1] The success with which it was done, under circumstances of no ordinary difficulty, affords convincing proof of the

[1] The anchoring by the stern has always been a stumbling-block to the sailor only acquainted with ships of the present day. I have heard it called 'lubberly;' and an old Scotch sailor who had made many voyages with me on the west coast of Scotland declared that 'there was just ae thing in the Scriptures he could na quite gae alang wi'—St. Paul's anchoring by the stern; nae doubt the Apostle was an inspired man, *but he should hae keepit her head til't.*' John Auld's sole difficulty in the Scriptures would, I think, have been removed, could the friend to whom he confided it have explained to him, that the ship was alike at both ends, had only paddle rudders which could be triced up, had hawse-holes at the stern, was not running, but laid-to, when she anchored, and finally, that the object was to cut the cables, and beach the ship at daylight.

superiority of the ancients in this important branch of seamanship. The anchors differed but little from those of the present day, except that they do not appear to have had palms, or triangular plates of iron (flukes), attached to the extremities of the arms. It is by no means certain that this addition increases the holding powers of anchors. The Dutch anchors, which have no palms, but merely the extremities of the arms flattened, are known to hold remarkably well.[1] The following extract from a recent newspaper[2] is interesting both in an antiquarian and geological view, and shows that Ovid was quite correct in referring to anchors for proofs of geological changes :—

'A few days ago, as some parties were employed in trenching a piece of moss on a hill in the vicinity of Kishorn, Lochcarron, some miles from the sea, they found the stock and flukes of a rudely-constructed anchor situated between the moss and a substratum of clay. The part which appeared to have been imbedded in the clay was wholly eaten away, and only distinguished by a rusty outline ; that which lay in the moss only remains. The stock is furnished with an inside and outside ring, and must have been used according to some method now unknown. The flukes are sharp at the ends, somewhat like the blade of a penknife, and the very nature of the metal seems changed into a substance more resembling lead than iron.'

In the above description the *stock* is evidently mistaken for the *shank* : the two rings are very often seen

[1] Rodgers' patent, which have very small palms, or rather none, but the extremities of the arms flattened and barbed, have also great powers of holding, as I can testify from experiments I witnessed near Portsmouth.

[2] *Glasgow Courier*, 8th Aug. 1846.

in ancient anchors; in fact, the description corresponds exactly with the anchors of the Romans. Modern writers *de re nauticâ* tell us that the anchors of the ancients were without stocks:[1] this is one of those traditional blunders which have been handed down from Scheffer. The ancients did not excel in perspective, and very often omitted the stock, which is at right angles with the arms; but there are several ancient coins which represent it, such as the annexed

of Antoninus Pius,[2] which will show how perfectly it resembles the modern anchors.

The next point which requires elucidation in our present inquiry is the mode of undergirding the ships. Here also we have to clear away a considerable mass of error, resting in a great measure on the remarks of a scholiast evidently ignorant of the subject, as to

[1] Berghaus, vol. ii. p. 432. Böckh: 'Uebrigens fehlt allen Ankern der Alten bekanntlich der Stock, oder das an dem Schafte befindliche Querholz (p. 166). Scheffer: 'Nullis in transversum lignis, sicut hodie consuevit, vulgo apud veteres inveniri instructas, sive pictorum incuriâ, sive quod magis credo quoniam in usu non fuerant.' Beechey: 'The transverse piece or anchor-stock is found wanting in all of them' (xxii).

[2] From the British Museum.

the meaning of a word in Aristophanes. In the 'Knights,' an informer accuses a person of stealing the 'zomeumata' (*ζωμεύματα*) of the Peloponnesian galleys,[1] an intentional misnomer for hypozomata (*ὑποζώματα*); 'and the question is, What were the hypozomata?' The explanation given by the scholiast is that they were the timbers (*τὰ ξύλα*) of ships. Scheffer, Le Roy, and Bloomfield contend that they were of wood. According to Scheffer, the hypozomata were the wooden bends (*ζωστῆρες*), or belts, which encircle the ship externally. Le Roy supposes they were the decks;[2] and Bloomfield, wooden stays to be applied internally.[3] It is not now necessary to discuss these explanations, because we learn from the Attic Tables, an authority quite conclusive in this case, that the hypozomata did not form part of the wooden gear (*σκεύη ξύλινα*). What, then, were they? In the first place they were external, as the name implies, 'under-zones.' Plato, in his legend of the Vision of Er, compares the most distant starry zone to the hypozomata of galleys, binding the whole together.[4] It is probable that ships were occasionally undergirded with wooden planks; but this could only

[1] Τουτονὶ τὸν ἄνδρ' ἐγὼ 'νδείκνυμι, καὶ φήμ' ἐξάγειν
ταῖσι Πελοποννησίων τριήρεσι ζωμεύματα. ('Ιππεῖς, v. 278.)

[2] Le Roy translates the hypozomata of the ship of Ptolemy Philopater, 'Il avoit douze ponts ou étages!' (*Hist. de l'Acad. des Inscriptions*, tom. xxxviii. p. 589.)

[3] Note upon Acts xxvii. 17. Taylor also, the translator of Plato, renders them the 'transverse beams of ships' (vol. i. p. 471).

[4] *De Republic.* lib. x. sec. 13. Καὶ ἰδεῖν αὐτόθι κατὰ μέσον τὸ φῶς ἐκ τοῦ οὐρανοῦ τὰ ἄκρα αὐτοῦ τῶν δεσμῶν τεταμένα· εἶναι γὰρ τοῦτο τὸ φῶς ξύνδεσμον τοῦ οὐρανοῦ, οἷον τὰ ὑποζώματα τῶν τριήρων, οὕτω πᾶσαν ξυνέχον τὴν περιφοράν.

be done in harbour. In the Louvre there is a statue of a marine goddess standing upon a galley, upon the sides of which planks are seen placed vertically. Polybius talks of ships being 'undergirded'[1] before putting to sea, evidently meaning that they were to be repaired in a temporary manner; but this can have no reference to the 'helps,' which were carried with the ships for the purpose of being applied at sea when required, which were necessarily flexible. Isidore of Seville mentions 'the mitra' as a *cable* by which the ship is bound round the middle.[2] Hesychius says also that they were 'cables binding ships round the middle.'[3]

The next question to be considered is, How were they applied? One would have thought this easily answered,—that the hypozomata should be bound round the middle of the ship, at right angles to the length, and not parallel to it. As, however, Böckh endeavours to prove that they were applied lengthways,[4] and as this view is adopted by others (see Smith's *Dictionary of Greek and Roman Antiquities,*' p. 880), it is necessary to examine their arguments. Böckh, in the first place, quotes a passage in Vitruvius, who describes certain ropes as being attached

[1] Ναῦς συμβουλεύσας τοῖς Ῥοδίοις ὑποζωννύειν. (*Leg.* 64.) This mode of strengthening old ships is still in use. The *Rainha*, an old Portuguese line-of-battle ship, was very successfully fitted with external braces and girders, and sent to sea during the late civil wars.

[2] 'Mitra, funis quo navis media vincitur.' (*Orig.* lib. xix. c. iv.)

[3] Ζωμεύματα, ὑποζώματα σχοινία κατὰ μέσην τὴν ναῦν δεσμευόμενα. Scheffer refers to 'Boysii Roma Subterranea' for a figure of the application of the hypozomata. I searched through the work twice, but could not discover it; Böckh makes the same remark (p. 135).

[4] *Urkunden*, p. 134.

to the beam of a battering ram in the same manner as 'a ship is kept from head to stern.' 'Quemadmodum navis a puppi ad proram continetur.' After searching for the passage, which is erroneously cited,[1] I found that the important word 'malus,' mast, was omitted, and that the meaning was, that the ropes were attached to the beam in the same way as the standing rigging was attached to the mast, which is intelligible. The next quotation is from Isidore, and is more to the purpose, because it does appear that ropes were occasionally applied in a longitudinal as well as in a transverse direction, to prevent ships from straining. 'The tormentum is a cable in *long* ships, which is extended from stem to stern, in order to bind them together.'[2]

Isidore mentions two kinds of cables for the purpose,—the mitra, to bind them round the middle, and the tormentum; this, he says, is so called because it is twisted. There is nothing which implies that it was passed round the ship externally; and it is not clear how a ship could be bound together in the mode supposed: the 'naves longæ,' from the weight of the rostra and towers at the extremities, and from their

[1] Erroneously cited, in both the works referred to, as x. 15, 6, in place of x. 21. This is one of the annoyances to which a person determined to examine authorities for himself is subjected; but a proof of the necessity of the task. The passage is as follows: 'A capite autem ad imam calcem tigni contenti fuerunt funes quatuor, crassitudini digitorum octo, ita religati quemadmodum *malus* navis a puppi ad proram continetur.' The word 'malus' is omitted in the edition of Schneider, but is retained in the later carefully edited edition of Poleni, Utini, 1829.

[2] 'Tormentum, funis in navibus longis, qui a prora ad puppim extenditur, quo magis constringantur; tormentum autem a tortu dicta.' (*Orig.* xix. 4.)

great length, must have been extremely apt to 'hog,' or fall down at each end; but as the stem and stern-posts rose above the rest of the vessel, a simple way of preventing this would be to pass a rope round them, and heave a strain upon it by twisting the parts together, as was done in the military engines called tormenta; and Isidore's etymology of the name 'tormenta, a tortu dicta,' seems to confirm this. Böckh also notices the hypozomata of the great ship of Ptolemy Philopator. I agree with him that the word ἐλάμβανε (took) shows that they were not fixed to the ship; but I do not see anything in the account of Athenæus to prove that they were meant to be applied lengthways, and still less that this was the only mode.

The last proof which he adduces in favour of this hypothesis, is taken from a bronze relief in the public museum at Berlin. It is figured in the *Thesaurus Brandenburgicus* of Beger (vol. iii. p. 406), and in Montfaucon.[1] I have not seen the original bronze, but the figures do not warrant the inference. The rope mouldings are evidently ornamental, and three out of the four do not go round the vessel, but are interrupted by the stem-post. The 'Victoria and Albert' royal yacht has also a rope moulding exactly where the antique has it; it would scarcely be a fair inference to suppose that it was meant to hold a crazy vessel from falling to pieces. I cannot therefore see any reason for supposing that ships were undergirded lengthways, a mode which must have been as impracticable as it would have been unavailing for the purpose

[1] *Antiquité Expliquée*, tom. iv. pt. ii. p. 214, pl. cxxxiv.

of strengthening the ship. It would appear from the Attic Tables that the hypozomata formed a regular part of the gear of every ship, and that they were laid up in the magazines.

In the account of St. Paul's Voyage, I have adduced examples to show that the practice of undergirding ships is still occasionally resorted to.

I have only a few remarks to offer on the capabilities of the ancient ships in working to windward. Paul Hoste has observed that no person could infer *à priori* that a vessel impelled by the wind could sail to a place which, in respect to that from which it started, was directly to windward. This may be true; but, on the other hand, no person who tried to impel a vessel by sails could avoid making the discovery; for on the most unfavourable supposition, that of a sail set at right angles to the keel, it would be discovered that even though the wind did not blow directly upon it, so long as the sail was full the vessel would go ahead, and of course, if the yard could be braced, that she could go nearer to the wind than at right angles to it, or within eight points. We have no information as to the exact angle with the wind at which an ancient ship could sail. It must, however, have been less than eight points, but more than six, the usual allowance for a modern merchant-ship in moderate weather. I have, therefore, in my calculations taken seven as the mean between these extremes; and I cannot suppose it would be much greater or less.

Notwithstanding the imperfect manner in which the ships were rigged, they appear to have made excellent passages. Pliny has enumerated several which would be considered respectable in modern times. Thus he tells us that the prefects Galerius and Babilius made quick passages from the Straits of Messina to Alexandria; the former arrived on the seventh, the latter on the sixth day; that in the following summer Valerius Marianus made the passage from Puteoli, on the ninth day, 'lenissimo flatu.' He also mentions passages from the Straits of Hercules to Ostia in seven days; from the nearest port of Spain, in four; from the province of Narbonne, in three; and from Africa, in two.[1] Upon these passages Admiral Beechey offers the following remarks:—

> 'It does not appear that there is any mistake in the numbers here mentioned by Pliny; for the instances are all of them consistent with each other, one only being below 140 M.P. per day, and another 143: two examples afford 160; two 175 and 185. The lowest of these rates of sailing may be reckoned at between six and seven M.P. per hour, and the highest at something less than eight; giving a mean of seven M.P. per hour, which would be reckoned a good one for ships of the present day.' (Appendix to *Travels in Africa*, p. xxxviii.)

The most rapid run which I have met with is mentioned by Arrian, in his Periplus of the Euxine (p. 5), who stated that 'they got under weigh about daybreak,' *ἄραντες μὲν ὑπὸ τὴν ἕω*; and that by midday they had come more than 500 stadia, *καὶ ἤλθομεν πρὸ τῆς μεσημβρίας σταδίους πλείονας ἢ πεντακοσίους*, that is, more than fifty geographical miles, which is at least eight miles an hour.

Major Rennell, in his *Observations on the Geo-*

[1] *Hist. Nat.*, Procem. ad lib. xix.

graphy of Herodotus (p. 678), supposes that the average rate of a day's sail was only thirty-seven miles. Vessels navigating unknown coasts, such as those of Africa when Herodotus wrote, and putting into port at night, may not have made more in a day ; and it would be no objection to the credibility of a narrative were this stated to be the case ; but it is absolutely impossible that ships four times as long as they were broad, with a large square sail, could make so little progress with a fair wind ; and the foregoing examples prove that they did not. When St. Luke states that the ship sailed from Rhegium on one day and arrived at Puteoli on the following, he tells us that the wind was south (xxviii. 13). Now, as the course is nearly due north, the vessel was running right before the wind, which to a single-masted vessel is the most favourable point of sailing. The distance is about 182 miles. If we suppose she sailed at the rate of seven miles an hour—the mean of the foregoing examples—the time consumed would be about twenty-six hours, which agrees perfectly with St. Luke's account.

The passage, therefore, from Rhegium to Puteoli, which terminated on the day following that upon which they left it, although a quick one, was by no means unprecedented.

We are apt to consider the ancients as timid and unskilful sailors, afraid to venture out of sight of land, or to make long voyages in winter. I can see no evidence that this was the case. The cause of their not making voyages after the end of summer arose, in a great measure, from the comparative obscurity of the sky during the winter, and not from the gales which prevail at that season. With no means of directing their course, except by observing the heavenly bodies, they were necessarily prevented from putting to sea when they could not depend upon their being visible.

In what manner they calculated the distance, as well as the direction of their course, is uncertain. Vitruvius describes what may be termed a perpetual log; that is, a mode of estimating the distance passed over by the revolutions of a wheel (x. 14). From the manner in which he speaks of it, it appears rather to be a scheme which might be adopted, or the tradition of one which had been in use, than the description of an instrument actually in use. The wheels were, or were supposed to be, fixed to the sides of the ships. It appears to be one of those plans that look well in theory, but which the disturbing causes, arising from the inclination of the vessel or the violence of the sea, would render of little value.

The internal arrangement of the rowers in the war galleys of the ancients is a problem of great difficulty, as to the true solution of which much difference of opinion exists. No work expressly describing the arrangement is extant, and it is one not well fitted for graphic representation. The incidental notices of ancient writers, and the representations on coins, marbles, bronzes, and pictures, however, in a great degree limit the problem, and, as appears to me, when combined with the essential condition of practicability, lead us to the true solution.

I shall, in the first place, notice the solutions which have been proposed by other writers.

M. Jal, the latest writer on the subject, cuts the

knot, by disbelieving the possibility of three ranks being placed one above the other. Speaking of the figures on Trajan's column, he says:—

'La colonne représente des navires à trois rangs de rames superposés et d'autres à deux rangs. Pour les birèmes, bien qu'elles soient mal rendues, pas de difficulté ; j'admets les birèmes ; le texte des Tactiques de l'empereur Léon est trop clair, trop positif pour me laisser un doute. Quant aux trirèmes, c'est différent. La longueur de la rame supérieure aurait dû être telle qu'il n'y a ni bois assez long pour la faire, ni bras assez forts pour la mouvoir.' (*Archæol. Nav.* i. 34.)

M. Jal, in this passage, apparently proceeds upon the assumption that the calculations of Lescallier, the author of 'Vocabulaire des Termes de Marine,' are correct. That author supposes that the lower oars were 44 feet long, and that each rank of oars was separated by a deck, like the tiers of guns in a line-of-battle ship, both of which suppositions are in direct opposition to the evidence which has come down to us. According to his calculation, the oars of the second rank must have been 77 feet in length, of the third 110 feet, &c. Such oars could not be pulled by one man ; but it is clear, from the description of the bireme given by the Emperor Leo, which M. Jal admits as an authority, that there was only one rower to each oar. According to the emperor, there were two ranks, one above and one below, seated upon benches, of which there were twenty-five above, and as many below,—fifty in all. Upon each bench were seated two rowers—*one* upon the right side, and *one* upon the left, so that in all, both rowers and soldiers above and below there were a hundred men.[1] With regard to the triremes, there is no point better established than this, that their oars were pulled by one man each; and the late discovery of the Attic Tables proves that the longest oars in this class of vessels did not exceed in length those of an ordinary row boat of the present day. (I. 9, 14, &c).

De Baif and others suppose that the ranks were not placed directly one above and overlapping the other, but that the thranites, or highest rank, were placed at the stern; that the zygites were placed in the middle of the ship, lower than the thranites; and the thalamites at the bow, and lower than the zygites.

The only authority which is cited for this arrangement is a passage in the ancient scholia on the 'Ranæ' of Aristophanes, which is to the following effect:—

'Thalamax, one who rows in the lower part of the trireme. The thalamaces receive low pay, on account of their using short oars compared with the other three ranks of oars, because they are nearer the water. There were three ranks of rowers; the lowest rank were called thalamites, the middle zygites, and the upper thranites. The thranite, then, is

---

[1] Ἔχων μὲν τὰς λεγομένας ἐλασίας δύο, τήν τε κάτω καὶ τὴν ἄνω, ἑκάστη δὲ ἐχέτω ζυγούς, τὸ ἐλάχιστον πέντε καὶ εἴκοσι, ἐν οἷς οἱ κωπηλάται καθεσθήσονται, ὡς εἶναι ζυγοὺς τοὺς ἅπαντας, κάτω μὲν εἴκοσι καὶ πέντε, ἄνω δὲ ὁμοίως εἴκοσι καὶ πέντε, ὁμοῦ πεντήκοντα, καθ' ἕνα δὲ αὐτῶν δύο καθεζέσθωσαν οἱ κωπηλατοῦντες εἷς μὲν δεξιᾷ, εἷς δὲ ἀριστερᾷ, ὡς εἶναι τοὺς ἅπαντας κωπηλάτας ὁμοῦ καὶ τοὺς αὐτοὺς καὶ στρατιώτας τούς τε ἄνω καὶ τοὺς κάτω ἄνδρας ἑκατόν. (*Tactica*, Meursii Opera, t. vi. 829.) It has been doubted whether this description applies to the war galleys of the period when Leo wrote (ninth century), but it is evident that it did, for they were fitted with a syphon (σίφωνα κατὰ τὴν πρῴραν) for darting Greek fire.

placed towards the stern, the zygite in the middle, and the thalamite towards the bow.'[1]

This passage has always been understood, both by those who with De Baif suppose that the three classes of rowers were placed as last mentioned, and by those who suppose that they were placed directly one above the other, to mean that the thranites as a body were placed at the stern of the ship, the zygites as a body in the middle of the ship, and the thalamites as a body next the bow; and those who suppose that the ranks were placed directly one above the other accuse the scholiast of having committed a blunder. But were such the meaning of the scholiast, the last part of the passage would be alike inconsistent with the first, and with the jest, such as it is, which it is meant to illustrate. The words thranite, zygite, and thalamite, in the last part of the passage are in the singular; and the true meaning of the passage appears to me to be that each thranite was placed nearer the stern than, and therefore in front of and above, a zygite; and each thalamite nearer the bow than, and therefore behind and below, a zygite and a thranite. This mode of arrangement is actually figured on a coin of Adrian, of which I have given an engraving on a subsequent page, and by this construction the passage from the scholiast becomes sensible, and an authority for an arrangement different from that in support of which it has been cited.

[1] Θαλάμακι· τῷ κωπημλατοῦντι ἐν τῷ κάτω μέρει τῆς τριήρους. Οἱ δὲ θαλάμακες ὀλίγον ἐλάμβανον μισθόν, διὰ τὸ κολοβαῖς χρῆσθαι κώπαις παρὰ τὰς ἄλλας τρεῖς τάξεις τῶν ἐρετῶν, ὅτι μᾶλλον εἰσιν ἐγγὺς τοῦ ὕδατος· ἦσαν δὲ τρεῖς τάξεις τῶν ἐρετῶν· καὶ ἡ μὲν κάτω, θαλαμῖται, ἡ δὲ μέση ζυγῖται, ἡ δὲ ἄνω θρανῖται. Θρανίτης οὖν, ὁ πρὸς τὴν πρύμναν, ζυγίτης ὁ μέσος, θαλάμιος ὁ πρὸς τὴν πρῷραν. (*Schol. ad Ranas*, v. 1074.)

General Melville supposes that the sides of the galleys formed an angle of 45° with the water.[1] Such an overhang would admit of several ranks of rowers, without adding much to the height of the vessels; but it would be destructive of their stability, and is unsupported by evidence.

The most general explanation given is that the oar-ports were arranged diagonally in echelons along the sides of the vessel, thus:—

Isaac Vossius[2] and others estimate the rate of the ship from the number of oars in each echelon. According to him, a ship with oar-ports arranged as above would be a trireme. Mr. Howell[3] adopts the same arrangement, but estimates the vessel's rate from the number of echelons. According to him, the above figure represents a portion of the oar-ports of a quinquereme. The oar-ports of a trireme he supposes to have been arranged in the following manner:—

But this mode of arrangement is unsupported by any ancient authority, and would not admit of the number of oars which we know triremes carried; some of

[1] Pownall on the *Study of Antiquities*, p. 119, and Appendix, 235.

[2] *De Triremium Constructione.*

[3] *Essay on the War Galleys of the Ancients.* Edin. 1826.

them, as we learn from the Attic Tables, having 170. (Böckh, *Urkunden*, p. 119.)

The arrangement of the oar-ports, according to Vossius, does not differ materially from what I conceive to have been the true arrangement, except as to their mutual distances. His internal arrangement of the rowers makes it necessary to suppose that the distance between two oar-ports of the same rank was seven feet, even allowing scanty room for the rowers. This distance between the oar-ports would not admit the requisite number of oars. A trireme carrying 170 oars must, on this arrangement, have been considerably more than 200 feet long, a length which is quite out of the question.

It will be convenient, before I offer any conjectures of my own, to state what are the well-established facts respecting the mode by which the ancient galleys were impelled by oars. They are—

1st. The oars were ranged in horizontal tiers; those in each tier being so near each other as just to admit of the rowers pulling without interfering with those immediately before and behind them. This appears to me to be evident from every representation which has come down to us, and is confirmed by a passage in Vitruvius, who calls the interscalmium, or space on the ship's side between the oar-ports, *διπηχαίκη*, or two cubits' length (navibus interscalmio quod *διπηχαίκη* dicitur, i. 2). Now two cubits, or three feet, is the smallest space which will allow rowers in the same rank to pull with facility.

2nd. That the ranks were arranged one directly above the other, the vertical distance of two adjoining ranks not being more than one-half of the distance of the two adjoining oar-ports of the same rank. On this point all the representations agree.

3rd. The oars, at least in the triremes and all below that rate, were pulled by one man; this is proved by the extracts of the Emperor Leo's work already quoted; by the account given by Thucydides of the night march of the Peloponnesians, in which each man carried his oar; and by the dimensions of the spare oars, given in the inventories of the Attic navy, none of which are more than 9½ cubits, or 14 feet 3 inches. (Böckh, *Urkunden*, p. 123.)

4th. The fighting-men, epibatæ, pulled, when not engaged in combat, on platforms or gangways laid along the sides of the vessels.

Having premised these established facts, I shall now proceed to explain what I conceive to have been the arrangement of the rowers in the trireme, showing the considerations by which I have been guided, and comparing the result with the notices in ancient writers, and with ancient representations which have come down to us.

The row-boats to which we are accustomed have only one rank of rowers. Such boats are not adapted for the ancient mode of fighting at close quarters. The oars would impede the free motion of the soldiers on the decks. To allow of this, a platform or gangway must be laid above the oars and along each side of the vessel. This may be a complete deck, in which case it must be higher than the heads of the rowers; or it may only extend a short distance from the side, not covering the rowers, in which case the height need only be such as to allow free motion to the handles of the oars; or it may partly or wholly project over the side of the vessel, in which case it need be a very little higher than the row-locks or oar-ports. That the war galleys of the ancients must have had such gangways we might have inferred from the necessity of the case; but it also distinctly appears from ancient coins, pictures, and medals.[1]

From these it appears that the gangways generally projected to some distance over the side of the vessel. In combat this gangway or platform must have been cleared of oars; but this was the exceptional case. When not actually engaged in combat, the gangways were disposable for the purpose of rowing; and if oars were placed so as to dip into the water in the intervals between the oars of the men below, they would not interfere with those; and here again we might have inferred, independently of ancient authorities, what however is amply confirmed by them, that when the ships were not engaged in combat, and particularly when speed was of vital consequence, as in pursuit or flight, there was a second tier of oars pulled from the gangways. Thus, then, we arrive at the conclusion, almost independently of ancient authorities, that war-galleys must have been fitted to row with at least two tiers of oars; the upper tier, or thranites, being em-

[1] Montfaucon has given a representation of a naval combat (vol. iv. pl. 142), copied from a marble at Seville, in which soldiers are seen fighting from the gangways. Winckelmann, in his *Antichità Inedite* (vol. ii. fig. 207), has figured a trireme in action, the soldiers engaged in combat, with two ranks of oars pulling below. In Smith's *Dictionary of Greek and Roman Antiquities*, one of the galleys from Montfaucon and the galley from Winckelmann are figured (p. 877). In Piranesi's great work on ancient vases, marbles, &c. (vol. i.), will be found a large and accurate representation of the galley first figured by Winckelmann; it is now in the Vatican. In the coins of Adrian, figured pp. 228 and 229, the upper ranks are seen pulling from the gangways.

ployed in rowing when not engaged in combat; the lower row, or zygites, rowing at all times.

In the case we have supposed, each thranite is placed above, and nearer the side of the vessel than the corresponding zygite. It will, however, be easily seen that two tiers of oars may approach still nearer to each other, when the rowers in the lower tier are nearer the side of the vessel than those in the upper tier. They may then be placed so that the handle of an oar of the upper tier may work as it were in the lap of a rower of the lower tier; and as the oars are moved in the same direction at the same time, a comparatively small vertical and horizontal distance of the row-locks will keep the handle of the oar of the rower of the upper tier from striking the arm or face of the rower of the lower tier who is behind his oar, or the back of the rower of the lower tier who is before it. Thus, then, a third tier of rowers, the thalamites, may be added at a very small distance below the zygites; and if the zygites are supposed to sit on benches placed on the deck, and the thalamites on the deck itself, the height of the vessel would not be increased by the introduction of the thalamites.

The thalamites will be placed immediately under the thranites, but covered by the platform or gangway, on which the thranites sit. These ranks do not therefore interfere with each other within the vessel; and if the oar-ports are so placed that the oars of one rank dip into the water in the intervals between the oars of the other, they will not interfere externally.

Of the practicability of this arrangement I satisfied myself by actual trial. I cut two oar-ports to represent the row-locks of the zygites, at a distance of three feet six inches from centre to centre, which is the distance allowed in launches of a man-of-war, which are pulled 'double-banked,' or with two rowers on each bench, as in the ancient galleys ; and I found that by cutting an oar-port 14 inches below those of the upper tier, and at about one-third of their horizontal distance, reckoning from bow to stern, a rower seated on the deck, and rowing in the lower oar-port, was not interfered with by the rowers seated on benches nearer the centre of the vessel, and rowing in the upper oar-ports. It was unnecessary to make a similar experiment with regard to the thranites. Sitting on the gangway they could not interfere internally with the zygites or thalamites ; and in order that they should not interfere externally, it would only be necessary that the horizontal distance of the oar-port of a thranite from the oar-port of a zygite next before him should be one-third of the distance between two consecutive oar-ports of the zygites.

Such, then, I suppose to have been the arrangement of the rowers in a trireme, which I will shortly recapitulate. The thalamite I suppose to have sat on the deck, not far from the side of the vessel, and to have rowed with a short oar in an oar-port little higher than the deck, and probably little more than two feet above the water ; and the distance between two successive oar-ports of the same tier I suppose to have been about three feet six inches. About 14 inches nearer the bow, and about 14 inches higher than the oar-port of a thalamite, was the oar-port of a zygite, who sat on a bench or stool placed on the deck, on the inner side of a thalamite, about 14 inches behind his seat, and whose oar worked in the angle made by the head and arms of the thalamite. Immediately over the heads of the thalamites a platform extended from the side of the vessel, probably not extending so far inwards as the zygites, but reaching to the shoulders; and this platform projected a short distance over the side of the vessel. On this platform the thranites sat and rowed. Their oarports were arranged along the outer edge of the platform, each oar-port being about 14 inches nearer the bow than the nearest oar-port of a zygite, and 14 inches nearer the stern than the nearest oar-port of a thalamite, and being about three feet higher from the water than the oar-ports of the thalamites, and one foot nine inches higher than the oar-ports of the zygites. The highest oar-port was, therefore, probably not more than five feet above the water,—a height not too great for the use of the oars mentioned in the Attic Tables, viz. nine or nine and a half cubits, or about 14 feet.[1]

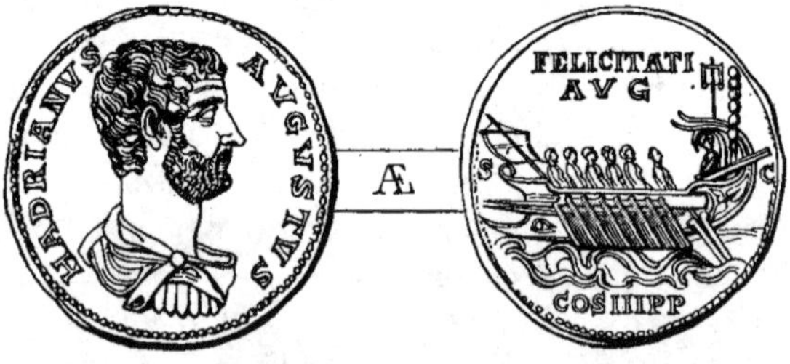

[1] Mitford cites the bouanga of the Philippine Islands, described by Pagès (*Voyages*, i. 169), as a case in point of an existing trireme; but as the bouanga has an outrigger upon which rowers are seated, it may be called a double vessel. The main body of the vessel is a bireme, with a tier of oars pulled from a projecting bamboo gallery. The corcore of the Moluccas is, however, a regular bireme, not depending on an outrigger for stability (in which the upper or outer oars are pulled from a projecting gallery). (Freycinet, *Voyage*, ii. 11, pl. 37.)

The general external agreement of the arrangement I have supposed with that of ancient ships will

appear from the annexed engravings of two coins of the Emperor Hadrian. One represents a bireme, the other a trireme.

We have no similar means of testing what I have supposed to be the internal arrangement; and I shall, therefore, examine some of the passages in ancient authors which most directly bear on this point. And to assist my readers in this examination, I annex a diagram (see p. 230), drawn to a scale, of the transverse section of a trireme; the oars on one side dipping into the water, the oars on the other side lifted out of it.

It will be observed that I have represented the oars of the different tiers as dipping into the water at the same distance from the side of the vessel, and the middle oar, that pulled by the zygite, to be the longest. This appears to have been the case from several passages in ancient authors. Galen says, speaking of the human hand, that, although the fingers are of unequal length, yet when the hand is shut their extremities come together, 'just as in triremes the ends of the oars extend to an equal distance, although they are not all of equal length, but in that case also the middle ones are longest.'[1]

It is only necessary to look at the diagram to see that the comparison is by no means a far-fetched one. Aristotle, also, observes that 'the middle finger, like

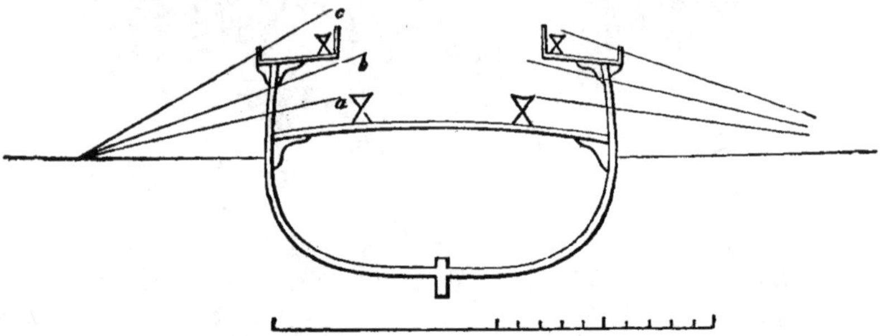

a, oar of thalamite seated on deck. *b*, oar of zygite seated on stool on deck. *c*, oar of thranite seated on stool on gangway.

the middle oar, is the longest.'[2] The longest oars, in the above diagram, are of the length indicated in the Attic Tables.

I am aware that Professor Böckh, who is high authority in matters of Grecian antiquity, differs from

[1] Καθάπερ, οἶμαι, κἀν ταῖς τριήρεσι τὰ πέρατα τῶν κωπῶν εἰς ἴσον ἐξικνεῖται, καί τοι γ' οὐκ ἴσων ἁπασῶν οὐσῶν, καὶ γὰρ οὖν κἀκεῖ τὰς μέσας μεγίστας ἀπεργάζονται. (Galen, *De Usu Partium Corporis Humani*, lib. i. cap. 24.) [The context of this passage from Galen is not given quite correctly. The point illustrated is that in grasping a large round object, the fingers reach the circumference of a circle.]

[2] Καὶ ὁ μέσος μακρός, ὥσπερ κώπη μεσόνεως. (*De Partibus Animalium*, iv. 10 [27].) [The word here used by Aristotle (μεσόνεως, a probable emendation for the MS. reading μέσον νέως) appears fixed to mean amidships by a passage in his *Mech.* ch. iv., where the use is quite clear.]

the explanation I have given of the passages from Aristotle and Galen, and supposes that the 'middle oars,' which these authors said were the longest, were in the middle of the vessel with respect to length, and not with respect to height, and supports this construction of the passages by an entry in one of the Attic Tables (ii. 56; Urkunde, p. 288), from which it appears that out of forty-eight damaged thranitic oars, ten might serve as zygitic, implying that the thranitic oars were at least as long as the zygitic. It may, indeed, be true that the oars in the centre of the vessel were longer than those near the bow and stern, and we may, perhaps, thus explain the passage in the Attic Tables; for it might well be that the longer of the thranitic oars might serve for the shorter of the zygitic; but the difference of adjoining oars of the same rank must have been imperceptible, and could scarcely have suggested the comparison of Galen.

Eustathius tells us that the thalamites rowed under the thranites.[1] Julius Pollux tells us that the part of the ship where the thalamites rowed was called the thalamus, *i.e.* sleeping-place.[2] A glance at the foregoing diagram will explain the propriety of the appellation; it is the only part of the deck sheltered from the weather. He also tells us that the middle of the ship was called zyga, or the beams, where zygites sit; and that the seat round the gangways or platform

[1] Ὅθεν μεταφορικῶς καὶ θαλαμῖται καὶ θαλάμακες ἐρέται οἱ ὑπὸ τοὺς θρανίτας. (*Comm. ad Homeri Il.* 640, 10: vol. i. p. 107.)

[2] Καλοῖτο δ' ἂν καὶ θάλαμος, οὗ οἱ θαλάμιοι ἐρέττουσι· τὰ δὲ μέσα τῆς νεώς, ζυγά, οὗ οἱ ζύγιοι κάθηνται· τὸ δὲ περὶ τὸ κατάστρωμα, θράνος, οὗ οἱ θρανῖται. (Julius Pollux, lib. i. 87.)

(*καταστρωμα* [1]) was called thranos, where the thranites sat.

I shall now consider whether this mode of arrangement could be extended beyond three tiers of oars. The ancients, we know, had quinqueremes, or galleys with five banks of oars. Of these we have no graphical representations, and are left still more to conjecture than in the case of triremes. The quinquereme must, of course, have been larger than the trireme. A vessel twice the size of another, if the proportions are the same, is one-fourth larger in every dimension. If the height of the gangway of the one is 5 feet above the water, the gangway of the other will be 6 feet 3 inches. If the deck remains at the same height as before above the water, the additional height of the gangway will allow space for an additional tier of oars under the gangways, the oar-ports of which must be placed in the same position relatively to the oar-ports of the zygites, as the latter are relatively to the oar-ports of the thalamites. This third rank of rowers must be placed nearer the middle of the vessel than the zygites, either standing on the deck or sitting on seats more elevated than those of the zygites. But the oars of this third rank of rowers would interfere externally with the oars of the thranites if these remained as before. This may be remedied by increasing the length of the oars of the thranites, or by making the gangways project further from the side of the vessel, so that the oars of the rowers on the gangways may always dip into the sea outside of the oars

[1] '**Καταστρωμα**' tabulatum quo navis superiore ex parte striata est, quodque nautas discurrentes aut milites propugnantes sustinet.' (Scapula.)

of those who row below the gangways.[1] This being done, it will be evident that one, or even two, additional ranks of rowers may be placed on the gangways, without interfering with the other rowers; and we thus obtain a quinquereme or sexireme. This arrangement of the oars of a quinquereme is shown in the annexed figure, which is drawn to a scale.

The longest oar in the case here represented is 20 feet, a length quite within the power of one man.[2]

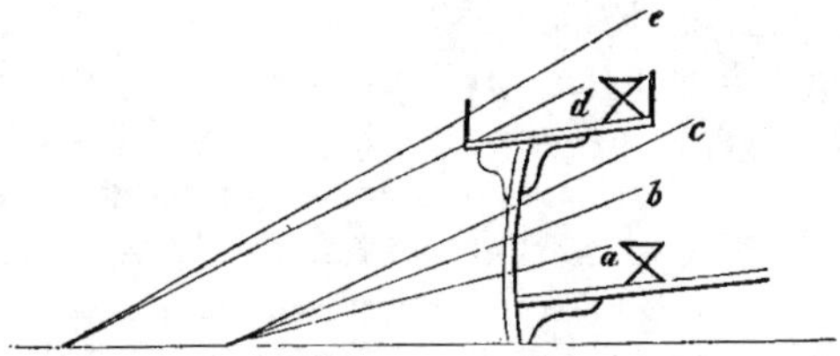

I do not consider it necessary to inquire how far this mode of adding to the number of ranks can be carried. Meibomius,[3] and after him Witsen,[4] have arranged the alternate ranks nearer and further from the side, as I have done; but, instead of placing the upper rower, when there are three ranks, either upon a

[1] Lucan notices the greater distance from the ship's side at which the oars struck the water in a sexireme:—

> 'Celsior at cunctis Bruti prætoria puppis
> Verberibus senis agitur, molemque profundo
> Invehit, et summis longe petit æquora remis.'
>
> (*Phars.* iii. 533.)

[2] The sweeps used in decked boats are sometimes 22 feet long, and are pulled by one man.

[3] Meibomii *de Fabrica Triremium*, Amst. 1671, p. 1.

[4] *Aeloude en Hedendaegsche Scheepsbouw en Bestier.* Door N. Witsen. Fol. Amst. 1671. Appendix, p. 4.

projecting gangway or nearest the middle of the ship, they place him next the side: hence, according to their representation, he is obliged to grasp his oar at one-twelfth of its length from the fulcrum; but no oar could be rowed in this manner.

I shall now offer a few remarks on the galley of Ptolemy Philopator, which, according to Plutarch[1] and Athenæus,[2] had forty ranks of oars, and, according to Pliny,[3] fifty. The dimensions given by the two former authors are the same; and as the account of Athenæus is the most particular, I shall offer some remarks upon it. It is said to have been 280 cubits, or 420 feet, in length; and 38 cubits, or 57 feet, in breadth. I see no impossibility in the size. The breadth is less than that of some of our line-of-battle ships. If we suppose that the length of the keel bore the same proportion to the extreme length as in the 'Sovereign of the Seas' already mentioned, her measurement would be about 4,000 tons, or about one-third more than our first-rates.[4] There is certainly nothing improbable in the supposition that a despotic prince could construct such a vessel. Plutarch says, that it was little better than an immovable building, more calculated for show than use. It was so constructed that it could be moved with either end first, having rudders and rostra at each end.[5] The oars of

[1] *Vita Demetrii.* [2] Lib. v. c. 37. [3] *Hist. Nat.* lib. vii. c. 56.

[4] The *Persia* steamer measures 3,600 tons.

[5] The rostra are described as having seven beaks, one principal one in the centre, and three on each side, gradually shorter (ἔμβολα εἶχεν ἑπτά, τούτων ἓν μὲν ἡγούμενον, τὰ δ' ὑποστέλλοντα). The two prows, two sterns, and four rudders of this ship have occasioned much needless perplexity to commentators and nautical antiquaries. M. Jal, who never believes what he does not understand, and is, it must be allowed,

the highest ranks were 38 cubits, of 57 feet, in length. These are certainly not very extraordinary dimensions —not longer than the sweeps formerly used in our sloops of war, or in the Maltese galleys. They are, however, obviously too large to be pulled by one man. If we deduct from the length of the oar what must have been in the inside of the vessel, which cannot be less than one-fourth, and allow at least ten feet to be dipped in the water, such an oar could not be pulled with advantage, were the oar-ports more than 25 feet above the water. Now, it is obviously impossible to

exceedingly sceptical in treating of ancient ships, does not believe in the double prow, because the shocks of the sea in the re-entering angle would strain the ship and impede her sailing ; nor in the seven beaks ; nor in the length of the oars, 57 feet, when the height of the ship was 72. It does not appear to me that any of these points present difficulties. Athenæus does not say that the two prows were at the same end. The ship was evidently built so that she could move with either end first. M. Jal's own explanation of Tacitus is quite applicable to Athenæus :—'Ce vaisseau, qui a une proue à chacune de ses extrémités (*utrimque*), pour être toujours prêt à donner ou à recevoir l'abordage' (i. 122). Such a vessel must have had four rudders, two at each end. Dion Cassius describes similar vessels fitted with rudders at each end, ἑκατέρωθεν καὶ ἐκ τῆς πρύμνης καὶ ἐκ τῆς πρῴρας πηδαλίοις ἤσκητο, and states as the reason that they were so, that they did not require to be turned, ὅπως αὐτοὶ μὴ ἀναστρεφόμενοι, κ.τ.λ. (ii. 1252).

With regard to the rostra, that of every ship had a principal beak, and at least two shorter ones, one on each side :—

'Totumque dehiscit,
Convulsum remis rostrisque tridentibus, æquor.'
(*Æn.* v. 142.)

That a ship of this size and power should have three on each side, can excite no surprise. As to the height mentioned by Athenæus, it is to the top of the acrostoleum, or bow or stern ornament, which rose much above the other parts of the ship. M. Jal thinks it would take an hour to get such a ship round—a very sufficient reason for having her fitted so as not to require turning.

arrange forty tiers of oars above each other in this space, nor can we see what object would be gained by such an arrangement. I do not pretend to explain the meaning of the forty ranks here ; but it does not follow that, because we cannot explain this particular case, we are to doubt the fact so clearly established by ancient authorities respecting the arrangements of the galleys with fewer tiers of oars. It appears, from Athenæus, that the very large galleys had several gangways, one above the other : thus the great galley of Hiero, king of Syracuse, had three gangways (*τριπάροδος*), the lowest, the middle, and the upper one.[1] I have shown that it is quite possible to arrange three ranks upon each deck or gangway. This ship, therefore, might have had three tiers of oars from each of her gangways, and three from the deck below them, or twelve in all.

I conceive it quite possible that six tiers might be pulled by oars, with one man at each ; and certainly there is no difficulty in supposing that triremes could be pulled by such oars.

Dio Cassius states that some of the ships of Antony, at the battle of Actium, had ten ranks ; and Polybius (lib. xvi.) that there were ships of that size at the naval battle at Chios. But ships with so many ranks are always noticed as being of extraordinary magnitude. I therefore conceive that their oars may have been arranged, and their rates reckoned, on the same principles as those of the triremes and quinqueremes. But in ships of forty ranks of oars, the rate must have been reckoned on some other principle as yet unknown.

[1] Athen. lib. v. cap. 41.

EDITIONS OF AUTHORS REFERRED TO IN THE DISSERTATION ON THE SHIPS OF THE ANCIENTS.[1]

Appiani Opera. Tollii. 8vo. Amst. 1670.

Arriani Expeditio Alexandri. Raphelii. 8vo. Amst. 1757.

Arriani Periplus Euxini ap. Geog. Min. 8vo. Oxon, 1707.

——————— Maris Erythræi, Ibid.

——— Epictetus. 8vo. Leips. 1799.

Arrian writes like a seaman, and even in his 'Epictetus' uses sea phrases.

Athenæi Deipnosophistæ. 8vo. Arg. 1801.

Aubin, Dictionnaire de la Marine. 4to. Amst. 1702.

See page 198.

Bayfius, De Re Navali. 4to. Par. 1536.

———, ib. ap. Gronovii Thes. Græc. xi. 567.

This author supposes, but with doubt, that the three ranks of oars were on the same deck. He says: 'Nec tamen verebor ingenue fateri mihi adhuc non liquere an hæc nostra conjectura vera sit.' See 'Dissertation on the Ships of the Ancients,' for his remarks on Artemon, page 195.

Bechi, Istoria dell' Origine e Progressi della Nautica Antica. 8vo. Firenze, 1785.

Beechey (Capt. F. W.), R.N., Expedition to the North Coast of Tripoli. 4to. Lond. 1828.

In the Appendix there is an article on ancient ships, avowedly taken from Potter: it contains, however, some good remarks on the rate of sailing of ancient ships. (See page 216.)

---

[1] This list contains the titles of some works consulted, although not quoted in the text.

Begeri Thesaurus Brandenburgicus. Fol. Col. 1696.

See page 214.

Berghaus, Geschichte der Schiffartskunde bey der vornehmsten Völkern des Alterthums. 8vo. Leips. 1792.

See remarks on this work, note to page 184.

Böckh (Aug.), Urkunden über das Seewesen des Attischen Staates. 8vo. Ber. 1840.

In excavating the foundation of a building in the Piræus in 1834, a number of inscriptions were discovered, which proved to be inventories of the appurtenances (σκευὴ ξυλίνη and σκευὴ κρεμαστή) of each ship of the Attic navy, which were laid up in store-houses, specifying those which were serviceable and those which were not. We have thus, in the most authentic form, a great mass of information respecting the ships of the ancients.

Breydenbach (Erhard), Peregrinatio in Terram Sanctam. Fol. Mogunt. 1486.

The earliest printed voyage which is illustrated with prints. The figures of shipping are correct in the details. The most important will be found in the article 'Ship-building' in the 'Encyclopædia Britannica,' 4th edit.

Bushnell (Edmund), the Compleat Shipwright. 4to. Lond. 1554.

Calcagnius, De Re Nautica, ap. Thes. Græc. Gronovii, xi. 758.

Carli (Il Conte), Delle Triremi, Quinqueremi, ec. : Opp. t. ix.

Count Carli takes nearly the same view as Bayfius respecting the arrangement of the rowers.

Charnock (John), History of Marine Architecture. 4to. Lond. 1801.

Gives the lines of the Navicella at Rome.

Complaynt of Scotland. 16mo. 1542; reprinted and edited by Leyden. 8vo. Edin. 1802.

Contains a curious description of a ship weighing anchor and setting sail.

Crescentio (Bartolomeo), Nautica Mediterranea, nella quale si mostra la Fabbrica delle Galee, Galleazze, e Galeone. 4to. Rom. 1607.

A correct description and representation of the ships of the period.

Creuze (A.), On Ship-Building. 8vo. Edin.

From the 'Encyclopædia Britannica.'

Description of an Ancient Galley. United Ser. Mag., May 1831.

This is evidently the Palestrine galley, figured and described by Winckelmann, Ant. ined. ii. pl. 207. The author supposes the rowers stood side by side on external gangways, and pulled with the oar vertical.

Deslandes, Essai sur la Marine des Anciens. 8vo. Par. 1768.

Desroches, Dictionnaire des Termes de Marine. 4to. Par. 1687.

Doletus (Steph.), De Re Navali, Gronovii Thes. Græc. xi. 628.

Eustathii, Archiepiscopi Thessalonicensis Commentarii ad Homeri Iliadem. 4to. Lips. 1827–1830.

Falconer (William), Marine Dictionary, by Burney. 4to. Lond. 1815.

——— Shipwreck. 8vo. Lond. 1810.

Fabretti, De Columna Trajana Syntagma. Fol. Rome, 1683. Cap. V. De remorum ordinibus in veterum triremibus et aliis multiremibus navigiis.

Excellent illustrations from an ancient marble in the church of S. Lorenzo fuori le Mura, which have been copied by Montfaucon and subsequent writers.

Galeni (Claudii) Opera Omnia. 8vo. Lips. 1822.

Gyraldi (Lylii), De Re Nautica. 12mo. Bas. 1540.

——————— Idem. Opera, fol. Amst. 1696, p. 601.

Explains ancient terms, but offers no conjecture respecting the arrangement of the rowers.

Hasæus, De Navibus Alexandrinis, Crit. Sacra, tom. xii. p. 717.

Howel (John), Essay on the War Galleys of the Ancients. 8vo. Edin. 1826.

See page 222.

Jal (A.), Archéologie Navale. 8vo. Par. 1840.

The chief value of this work is derived from the original documents inserted in it. M. Jal, as he informs us, was educated at a naval school; he therefore understands his subject. (See page 198, &c.)

Isidori Hispalensis Opera. Fol. Par. 1601.

Leo Imperator, Tactica ap. Meursii Opera, fol. Flor. 1745, tom. vi. p. 828.

Lescallier, Vocabulaire des Termes de Marine. 4to. Par. 1777.

Manwayring (Sir Henry), The Seaman's Dictionary. 4to. Lond. 1644.

Meibomius, De Fabrica Triremium. 4to. Amst. 1671.

The internal arrangement of this author has been adopted by Witsen, and by Potter in the illustrations of his Grecian Antiquities. He has shown that by placing the rowers of the different tiers alternately nearer and further from the ship's side, the vertical distance between them need not exceed eighteen inches. He places the upper rank next the side; but it would be impossible to pull oars as he has represented them, from the necessary disproportion between the length of oar outside and inside of the vessels. (See page 233.)

Melville (General), On the Rowers in Ancient Gallies, in the Appendix to 'Pownall on the Study of Antiquities.' 8vo. Lond. 1782.

See remarks on p. 222.

Monson (Sir William), Naval Tracts, in Churchill's Collection of Voyages. Vol. iii.

Montfaucon (Bernard de), L'Antiquité expliquée. Fol. Par. 1719, tom. iv. pt. 1.

Compiled from Scheffer, Fabretti, and Potter. He, however, gives an original engraving of the Seville marble, representing a naval combat, pl. 228.

Morisoto, Orbis Maritimus. Fol. Div. 1643.

Neumann's Marine Dictionary. 12mo. Lond. 1800.

Nortumbrio (Dudley, Duca di), Arcano del Mare. Firenze, 1661.

Good figures of ships of the period.

Opelius, De Fabrica Triremium, ap. Græv. Thes. tom. xii.

Palmerius, Exercitationes in Auctores Græcos. 8vo. Lugd. Bat. 1669.

Contains good remarks on the arrangement of the rowers.

Pantero Pantera, L'Armata navale. 4to. Rome, 1614.

Contains a vocabulary of Italian nautical terms of the period. The word Artimone does not occur in it. The author's remarks on the trireme are not very intelligible; he says it was 'così chiamata delle tre remi con che si vogava ad ogni banco.'

Pitture Antiche di Ercolano. Fol. Nap. 1763.

Plinii Historia Naturalis. 8vo. Lond. 1829.

Pollux (Julius), Onomasticon ex recensione Bekkeri. 8vo. Ber. 1846.

Pollux (Julius), Lederlini et Hemsterhuisii. Fol. Amst. 1706.

Rennell (Major), On the Geography of Herodotus. 4to. Lond. 1800.

Contains remarks on the rate of sailing of ancient ships, p. 678. (See page 216.)

Le Roy (D.), Mémoires sur la Marine des Anciens, Hist. de l'Acad. des Sciences, t. xxxviii. p. 542.

——— La Marine des Anciens Peuples expliquée. 8vo. Par. 1777.

——— Les Navires des Anciens considerés par rapport à leurs Voiles. 8vo. Par. 1783.

——— Nouveaux Recherches sur les Navires des Anciens, Mém. de l'Institut, an vii. p. 478.

See remarks on this author in note to p. 184.

Saverien, Dizionario di Marina. 4to. Ven. 1769.

See page 197.

Savile (Sir Henry), Translation of Tacitus. Fol. Lond. 1604.

Appended to it is 'A View of certain Military Matters for the better understanding of the ancient Roman Stories,' which contains an account of the different classes of ships.

Schefferus, De Militia Navali Veterum. 4to. Upsal, 1654.

——— De Varietate Navium, Gronovii Thes. xi. 770.

See remarks on this author, p. 194. His work 'De Varietate Navium' is confined to the rowing galleys.

Sovereign of the Seas (Account of). Lond. 1673.

For the title of this curious work, see p. 189, note.

Stewechius, Commentarius ad Vegetii Libros de Re Militari. 8vo. Ves, 1670.

The author supposes, with Bayfius and other authors, that the rowers were on the same level, in groups of seven each. His descriptions are not very intelligible, and his figures in illustration unsupported by any authority.

Strutt (Joseph), View of the Manners and Customs of the English, &c., till the time of Henry VIII. 4to. Lond. 1774–6.

Gives good figures of mediæval ships from the drawings which illustrate MSS. The paddle rudders appear as late as the reign of Stephen.

Vegetius, De Re Militari, ap. Veteres de Re Militari Scriptores. 8vo. Vesal. 1670.

Treats of naval warfare. The largest galleys in his time had five ranks; but his descriptions afford no clue to the mode in which the rowers were arranged.

Virgilii Opera, Lat. Ital. Fol. Rome, 1761. Illustrated with vignettes from the antique.

See page 208.

Vitruvius. Poleni, 4to, Utini, 1829.

Vossius (Isaac), Observationes Variæ, de Triremium Constructione, &c. 4to. Lond. 1693.

——————— Idem, Grævii Thes. tom. xii.

See page 222.

Us et Coutumes de la Mer. 4to. Rouen, 1672.

See page 115.

Willet (Ralph), On British Naval Architecture, Archæologia, xi. 154.

Winckelmann, Monumenti Antichi Inediti. Fol. Rom. 1783.

Witsen (Nicolaes), Aeloude en Hedendaegsche Scheepsbouw, &c. Fol. Amst. 1671.

That is, 'Ancient and Modern Ship-building.' This work gives a good account of the state of naval architecture, and the mode in which ships were rigged, when the work was written. The author, however, cannot have had any practical knowledge of his subject, otherwise he would not have given such absurd restorations of ancient ships as he has done. Amongst others, he has given a restoration of the great galley of Ptolemy Philopator. It is said by Athenæus to have been 280 cubits (420 feet) long. Taking this as a scale, Witsen's representation is that of a ship 100 feet high above the water, with a palace on her deck nearly 100 feet more, or 200 feet in all. All his other restorations (for he has given several) are equally absurd. In the Appendix he gives the figures of Meibomius, published at Amsterdam the same year as Witsen. Baron Zach, in his correspondence, speaks of this work as follows :—'M. Le Roy, qui a beaucoup travaillé et écrit sur la marine, et sur l'architecture navale des anciens, n'a point connu l'ouvrage de Witsen, apparemment parce qu'il est écrit en Hollandois, langue connue encore moins que l'Allemande, mais surtout parce que ce livre est devenu si excessivement rare qu'on ne le trouve pas même en Hollande à aucun prix ; il y en a cependant un exemplaire à la Bibliothèque du Roi à Paris. Tout ce qui regarde la marine des anciens y est traité avec une exactitude et une érudition égale.' (Zach, ix. 97.) There are copies of this work in the British Museum and in the Library of the Royal Society.

DISSERTATION IV.

ON THE GEOLOGICAL CHANGES IN ST. PAUL'S BAY.

In attempting to identify places on the seacoast with the descriptions or notices in ancient authors, we must always take into account the geological changes which may or must have taken place in the interval.[1] Such changes must be owing to one or other of the following causes :—

First. Violent disturbances, such as would affect the configuration of the land.

Second. Movements of elevation or depression.

Third. The wasting action of the sea.

Fourth. The siltage of the disintegrated matter.

With regard to the first of these causes, there is no reason to suppose that any change has been produced by these since the island has been inhabited by man. Nor is there any reason to suppose that any movement of elevation has taken place within the same

[1] Major Rennell is, if I mistake not, the first author who pointed out the necessity of this in his paper 'On the Place where Julius Cæsar landed in Britain.' (*Archæologia*, p. 499.)

Captain Copeland, R.N., who states that he is not a geologist, speaking of the seacoast of Megara, says, 'The localities described by Thucydides do not agree in any one particular with the present features of the coast. (Arnold's *Thucydides*, ii. 396.) My friend Captain Spratt, R.N., who is a geologist, has proved that if we allow for the necessary changes, the notices of Thucydides agree perfectly with the localities. (See *Journal of Geographical Society*, viii. 205.)

period. There has, however, been a slight movement of depression within the human period, but it belongs to a remote antiquity, anterior in all probability to the time of the shipwreck. That such a movement has taken place is proved by the tracks of wheels, not connected with existing roads, which are deeply impressed on the upper surface of the rocks, and are seen at different points of the island to pass under the sea.[1]

There is, however, a geological proof that the extent of this change of level has been very small, and not sufficient to have produced any perceptible change in the relative positions of the soundings, and of the headlands and shores of the bay.

The proof is this: In the narrow channel which separates the sea, on the outside of Selmoon Island, from St. Paul's Bay (a place where two seas meet), there is to be seen under water a vertical escarpment, running across from the island to the mainland (see dotted line on chart, p. 129), which is evidently an ancient sea-cliff, and which must have been scooped out by the action of the sea, during the period of stationary level which preceded the present. From the transparency of the water it can easily be observed. I estimate the change of level which this appearance indicates at ten feet. In Captain Smyth's chart the difference in the soundings on each side of the escarpment is two fathoms, which agrees very well with my estimate. If we assume that the depression has taken place since the shipwreck, it would make only a slight change in the absolute position of the sound-

[1] See a paper by the author on 'Recent Depressions in the Land.' (*Journal of the Geological Society*, Aug. 1847, p. 235.)

ings, and of the two headlands of the bay, but none at all in their relative positions. The point of Koura, before the last depression, must have extended farther to the north, but so must the line of twenty fathoms. The point of Salmonetta, or Selmoon Island, must have extended farther to the east; but the line of fifteen fathoms must have been just so much farther to the east; hence the reasoning in both cases would be the same. It is only necessary to look at the dotted line parallel to the coast, which marks the depth of three fathoms, to show that a much greater change of level than what has actually taken place would make but a trifling alteration in the contour of the shores of the bay. If, then, the depression did take place since the shipwreck, the conclusions to be drawn from the comparison of the locality with the narrative would be the same.

The only effect which the wasting action of the sea could have, would be that of rendering it impossible to ascertain the exact point of appulse of the ship when she was run ashore; but this I have not attempted to do. In every other respect, an allowance for the changes arising from this cause strengthens the conclusions we draw from the present state of the coast.

The shore from Salmonetta Island to Mestara Valley is now girt with mural cliffs, where a ship could not be stranded with safety; but there is a creek in this line of cliff, now without a beach, which we know, from the form of the land, must at one time have had a beach which has been worn away, in the course of ages, by the wasting action of the sea. The degradation of the land actually taking place at this point is proceeding with more than usual rapidity, owing to the inclination of the beds, and the tendency which large fragments of the rock have to fall over when undermined by the sea.[1] I therefore think it not improbable that the beach existed at the time of the shipwreck. If so, this creek, which, as may be seen on the chart, is immediately to the south of the place which Captain Smyth has marked as the traditional place of the wreck, agrees perfectly with the spot where a ship from the eastward anchored in the entrance of the bay would be driven in a gale from the E.N.E. (Euro-aquilo), and is close to a place where two seas meet.

The rate of siltage at the bottom of the sea must, from the structure and size of the island, be extremely slow. The rocks disintegrate into minute particles, which are of course carried by the action of the waves and the currents to a great distance before they are finally deposited on the bottom of the sea. There is but little alluvium washed down by streams from any part of the island; and at St. Paul's Bay there is scarcely any. The surface of the island, which is very flat, is composed of a series of beds of tertiary rock, which overlies a thick stratum of clay. The superincumbent rock is much fissured. The rain which falls on the surface, passes through the fissures, is absorbed by the clay, and finally reappears in

[1] Abela, who wrote in 1642, states, on the authority of an ancient manuscript, that the ruins of the residence of Publius, the chief man of the island, stood here. He says: 'Villam hospitalem S. Publii, vicinam rupibus dithalassis, quibus (Act. 27) navis Pauli quassata maris tempestate stetit impacta donec solveretur a fluctibus, fuisse in clivo ad orientem ac septentriones adversam,' &c. (p. 230.)

springs. No stream flows into St. Paul's Bay, except one which issues from a translucent spring, which the natives term 'Ayn tal Razzul,' or 'The Apostle's Fountain,' a name which proves the great antiquity of the tradition ; for the signification of the Phœnician word Razzul (Apostle) is unknown to the Maltese.[1]

During the excavation of the dry docks at Valetta, my friend Mr. John Anderson, of the engineer department, paid particular attention to the phenomena, from which the amount of siltage during the human period could be deduced. According to his report, in that branch of the harbour of Valetta, works of art are not found more than six or eight feet below the present bottom of the sea. But the deposit there must be much more rapid than in any part of St. Paul's Bay.

The dock is situated in a deep inlet, at the mouth of an extensive valley, and its shores have been from the earliest times the site of a town. In such a situation, the rate of siltage must have been much quicker than in the comparatively shallow inlet of St. Paul's Bay, where none of those causes of rapid

[1] 'Fons Paulinianus ex arenti solo in mare profluit cui nomen Ayn tal Razzul . . . ignota nunc indigenis significatione nominis ; at Tyris et Phœnicibus fontem Apostoli sonat.' (Quoted from an ancient MS. by Bres, a Maltese : 'Malta Antica Illustrata,' p. 395.)

On a stone near this fountain there are inscribed, or rather were, for I was unable to discover them, the following lines, which I give from Bryant (p. 67) :—

'Hac sub rupe cava, quam cernis ad æquoris undas,
  Exiguus trepidat fons salientis aquæ.
Religione sacra latices venerare, viator ;
  Naufragus has dederit cum tibi Paulus aquas.'

deposition operate. The events of the shipwreck, moreover, did not take place in the bay, but in the open sea, at its mouth, where the action of the waves and currents would tend to prevent deposition. From these considerations, I am satisfied that no change caused by siltage in the depth of that part of the sea, which a ship driven hither from Crete must have passed over, could have been perceptible in so rough a measurement as that of which the unit is a fathom.

The rocky point of Koura must anciently have extended further to the north than it does at present; hence a ship driving into St. Paul's Bay, eighteen centuries ago, must have been nearer the breakers than one at the present day, under the same circumstances, would be. Hence the possibility of passing them unobserved was less then than it is at present; and consequently the agreement between the locality and the narrative even more perfect.

APPENDIX.

No. I.

Extract from the Journal of the Yacht 'St. Ursula,' Hugh Tennent, Esq., of Wellpark, Glasgow, dated Calolimounias, January 16, 1856; by the Rev. George Brown.

THE 'St. Ursula' left Malta for Alexandria, on Thursday, January 10, 1856, and being favoured with fair winds and fine weather, by Sunday afternoon she sighted the west end of the island of Candia, whose snowy mountains stretched for many miles along the horizon. By ten P.M. we were abreast of the island, and it was resolved by Mr. Tennent to take the opportunity presented of visiting, if possible, the two places mentioned in the narrative of the voyage of St. Paul, in the 27th chapter of the Acts. These places are the Fair Havens and Phenice; the one being the harbour which the Apostle's ship left on the eve of a storm in which she was wrecked, and the other the harbour where she was to have spent the winter, but which the gale in question prevented her from reaching. The latter, being furthest to the westward, claimed attention first.

The position of Phenice, as we learned from Mr. Smith's Essay on Paul's Voyage, has been a point considerably disputed among commentators. He says, p. 48,[1] 'Phenice no longer retains its name. Ptolemy mentions both a city

[1] See p. 87.

and a port of Phenice, or rather Phœnix. Lutro, Sphakia, and Franko Cástello, places on the south coast of Crete, have each been supposed to be Port Phenice. For our present purpose of ascertaining the ship's course it is not very material which of these is meant. I am, however, satisfied that it is the harbour of Lutro.' Mr Smith supports his decision by very satisfactory evidence, in a dissertation of several pages; but as he had not visited the spot, and as he says he could find no hydrographical description of the harbour in question, in any sailing directions, ancient or modern, we resolved to touch at Lutro, examine the place, and find out, if possible, its ancient name from the inhabitants.

At daybreak on Monday we ran along the south coast of the island, before a freshening western breeze. The coast for many miles is magnificent. Lofty precipices overhang the sea, and between them the slopes of *dèbris* are so steep as almost to preclude vegetation. Immediately behind rise the White Mountains (Λευκὰ Ὄρη), their Alpine sides dotted with trees, and their brows and summits covered with snow. Lutro is put down in the charts as about thirty-two miles east of Cape St. John, and as almost due north of the island of Gozzo: and those accordingly were our directions for reaching it. Owing, however, to a slight error in the chart which we followed, and to the circumstance that the port in question makes no appearance from the sea, we ran past it for a point further to the eastward. (9 A.M., wind suddenly fell; succeded by puffs and light airs, from south and south-east: becalmed till midday.) After lying for some time off a village, we resolved to land, and examine a bay two miles beyond it. Mr. Tennent, Mr. Paul, and myself, with four seamen, got into the jolly-boat, and pulled towards the bay, leaving the vessel becalmed. Before, however, we could reach the bay, we saw a heavy squall from the north blowing out of it; and, to avoid a wetting, pulled right ashore for a creek with a gravelly beach halfway between the village and the bay. There we landed, and hauled up our boat; the 'St. Ursula,' meanwhile, shortening sail as fast as possible.

All agreed that it would be a risk to attempt to reach her till the squall should blow over, for it was now spreading rapidly over the sea, and opposite to every glen was raising clouds and vortices of spray. The place where we landed was surrounded by steep conglomerate rocks; and one or two of the natives appeared, peeping at us over them. At last we brought them to a parley, but found that they could speak nothing but Greek, and that, of course, in dialect and accent very different from the Greek we had learned at the schools. They let us know, however, that the village hard by was Sphakia; that we had passed Lutro by several miles; and that there was a Turkish governor in the neighbourhood. We then gave a boy a shilling to go for the governor: but thinking such a proceeding disrespectful, one of the men and myself followed the boy. Mr. Tennent and Mr. Paul sat down under shelter of a rock, and two of the men remained close to the boat (in which were two muskets). The Greeks then all disappeared; but Dan and I had not gone very far when we met a large party of them, some with knives in their girdles, and others with yataghans. It occurred to us that it was imprudent to separate from the rest, in so unknown and remote a place; and so we slowly retraced our steps, joined Mr. Tennent and Mr. Paul, and returned to the boat. The Greeks hallooed to us, and came skipping over the rocks like goats. One of the men, whose acquaintance with the inhabitants had rendered him suspicious, urged us not to trust them, but to attempt to regain the vessel, and pulled the boat's head round; but the prospect to leeward seemed hopeless. The vessel was two miles off, or at least a mile and a half, labouring heavily under a three-reefed mainsail and fore-stay-sail. Sometimes her hull disappeared behind the seas; and sometimes we lost sight of more than her hull, in the whirlwinds of spoondrift. We felt extremely anxious, of course, about her management; still, our boat was small, and had seven persons (more than her complement) on board; and in a sea broken by the current, it seemed next to impossible that she should live. We were about a hundred yards or so from the shore of the creek by this time; and now that we were convinced we must hug the land, it was no easy matter to regain it. It cost us three-quarters of an hour hard pulling, and a good wetting, to reach a creek to the west of the one we had left.

This creek was a semicircle, almost surrounded by precipices sixty or seventy feet in height; and these were hollowed out into caves of considerable depth. At one point it was possible to land on some pointed rocks, but nowhere could the boat be hauled up. Soon the Greeks appeared in great numbers, nestling on the ledges of rock, like gulls and scarts on the Craig of Ailsa, and holding on with their hands to keep themselves from being blown over. The creek looked like a pot of potatoes beginning to boil,—the squalls falling from above upon its centre, and radiating all round in hissing foam. Occasionally it was calm; but sometimes the oars were blown out of the rowlocks. Sometimes men appeared with gayer dresses than the rest, and armed with silver-mounted firelocks. Poor Dan and Tom felt certain they were going to fire upon us; though we assured them that if the men's intentions were hostile, they would conceal rather than display their arms. At last a very handsome young man, with richly mounted pistols, came down towards the point, accompanied by a person who hailed us in Italian, asking who we were and what we wanted. We told him we had a clean bill of health from Malta, and a passport visé'd by the consul of the Sublime Porte. As we could hardly hear each other speak for the wind, I leaped ashore, and went up to the young man (who proved to be a Turkish commandant), to show him the passport. He would not touch it, or me, and told me, through the interpreter, that there was no health officer nearer than Lutro, and that nobody else could examine our papers. He said, however, that we might land, and report ourselves to the Turkish governor at Sphakia, or else row round to that village. Now Sphakia was at the bottom of the bay to the west, and it was questionable whether we could face the tempest which raged on the other side of the point. The men were clear for passing the night in the creek; but we told them that, cold and wet as we were, and hungry besides, we would, for our part, put up at the governor's, or at anybody else's who would take us in. I stepped on board again to deliberate, and the commandant proceeded to strike a light. Tom became terrified that it was for his matchlock; but when, to our great amusement, the gentleman simply lighted his pipe, Tom felt wonderfully reassured, and, finding his own creature cravings awakened by what he saw, exclaimed, 'Well, he don't look such a bad feller after all: I think I'll just step ashore and ask him for a light.' A man then came down with a bottle of rum, put it on the edge of the rock, and desired us to put the money into a hole. We did so. They stirred about the money well with a stick in the puddle, and at last took it. We were shivering with cold, and found the rum a most seasonable cordial. But how silly we must have looked, paddling about in the creek overlooked by fifty or sixty men, many of them armed! Our deliberations were cut short by the appearance of a caique, or fishing-boat which came round the point, manned by stout rowers, and steered by an aged Greek with a long white beard. The old man of the sea hailed us in Italian, and said that the governor had sent him round to give us a tow. Our men, however, felt revived by the rum, and declared themselves able for the pull without assistance; so, telling the Greek to lead the way, we bent to our oars, and then came the tug of war.

Mr. Tennent steered right in the wake of the caique,

through the blinding spray and spoondrift, and amidst the cheers of the crowd on the rocks. We struggled gradually onwards, now driven back for a moment by a squall, and then making progress in the succeeding lull. In less than an hour we gained the beach of Sphakia; a gun was fired, I suppose in honour of our arrival, and most of the inhabitants seemed gathered about the governor, who stood on a breastwork, with his pipe, his sabre, and his beads. The 'St Ursula' in the meanwhile had been obliged to lower her mainsail, in order to get the fourth reef down, and had made three tacks; but being sadly baffled by varying squalls, had been driven further and further from shore and was now standing far to the westward.

We asked the governor, through the interpreter, if he would give us rooms, or man a large caique to send us off to the vessel. He said the caique would never get back again, and so he would give us a house, if we promised to touch nobody; for, till the health officer came, we must remain in quarantine. I was amused at his way of keeping order. When the crowd became too curious, and a man approached too near us, he lifted a little stone and pelted the intruder.

The old Greek was appointed our guardian, and led us to our lazaretto. It was a house overhanging the seashore, consisting of one apartment, which somewhat resembled the lower story of the little Cumbrae Castle. There was no furniture, and the floor was made of clay. Two unglazed windows were closed with wooden shutters, and a wide chimney in one corner showed the possibility of a fire. A man soon came round to say that he had orders from the governor to get us whatever we wanted. We replied, everything he could possibly think of: a fire, beds, chairs, coffee, bread and butter, milk and eggs, and some beef-steaks. He said beds were out of the question, for we were 'sporci' (unclean), being in quarantine. It made one indignant to hear him say that to our faces; as if we would not suffer much more than the beds by coming to close quarters. Then, as for eggs, the Sphakia hens don't lay in winter; and beef was quite unknown. However, things began to drop in: a barrel with a chauffer of charcoal in it, as big as a washing-tub; a good supply of firewood for the chimney; a bag of bread as hard and dry as Bath brick; several coffee pots; a paralytic table, with cups; and seven chairs. Three eggs and three fishes were also procured. It was now sunset, 5.30 P.M., and after having given thanks, we made a tolerable meal. In fact, between cooking and eating, and drying ourselves at a blazing fire, we spent nearly two hours. The inhabitants were very inquisitive about us; and although, owing to the Turkish manners of the place, the more curious sex could not make their appearance, yet the men showed curiosity enough to serve for all.

Mr. Tennent, who was dressed in a Yacht Club suit with gilt buttons, and had a gold band about his cap, was an object of great respect. I overheard one Greek say to another, while looking at Mr. Tennent, Στρατηγὸς μεγάλος (a great commander); Μάλιστα (undoubtedly), was the reply. Our Greek guardian, when we had supped, asked leave to partake of our provisions. I said to him, 'Remember they are compromised.' 'Ohè, in verità,' said he, 'a poor man must not lose such a supper for quarantine laws:' and a hearty meal he made. He then suggested a glass of wine, for, said he, I am seventy years old! We ordered it for him, and Mr. Tennent desired him to drink to the Inglesi, Francesi, Turci, and Greci. He gave a roguish laugh, and exclaimed, 'Viva i Muscoviti!' and drank it off.

The Sphakian mountains are inhabited by Greeks, who having suffered dreadfully in the war of independence (1821–30), and having groaned ever since under the Turkish yoke, naturally look to Russia as their ally. The town of Sphakia seemed to contain between one and two hundred houses; but at least half of them are in ruins. Many of the inhabitants of the mountains winter there. There seems to be little communication between the southern and northern parts of the island, especially in winter, when the passes must be encumbered with snow.

At eight o'clock, the half-dozen Greeks who had intruded into our apartment suddenly disappeared, and the governor was announced. He came, attended by two Turkish soldiers, and made us a graceful salaam at the door, placing his right hand on his left breast and bending slowly forwards. He then sat down between us and the door : and as the latter would not remain shut, he made a soldier sit down on the threshold, and put his back to it. He introduced himself as Zair Bey, governor of the province of Sphakia ; and we had a long interview through means of the old Greek. Joannes Nicephorus (for such was our interpreter's name) had but a small stock of Italian ; but when people are anxious to understand each other, a few words go a great way. The scene was picturesque enough : the flickering light of our fire now blinked on one group and now on another, revealing capriciously their varied forms and features. Our draggled appearance, as we crouched over the fire, was a fine foil to the graceful picture presented by the Turk, who smoking his long tchibouque and wrapped in his elegant mantle seemed the very image of repose. And then the sailors, who had all come to anchor under the lee of the charcoal stove in the best berths they could find, were quite as strong a contrast to the pale effeminate Roumelian guards. Nicephorus was the Nestor of the party ; the faint rays of our cruse, falling on his weathered face and silvery beard, made him look truly venerable. After an hour's conference the governor took his leave, promising to see us in the morning.

Not forgetful of our object, we asked Nicephorus (the old Greek already mentioned) what was the ancient name of Lutro? He replied without hesitation, 'Phœniki,' but that the old city exists no longer. This, of course, proved at once the correctness of Mr. Smith's conclusion. We were told further that the anchorage is excellent, and that our schooner could enter the harbour without difficulty. We next inquired the ancient name of the island of Gozzo, and he said at once, Chlavda, or Chlavda Nesi (Χλαῦδα or Κλαῦδα Νῆσι), a reply equally satisfactory. He told us also that there is a tradition in these parts that Ἅγιος Παῦλος Ἀπόστολος (Saint Paul the Apostle) had visited the Caloli-mounias (the Fair Havens), and had baptised many people there.

Instead of beds, we had the floor strewn with withered bushes of thyme, for neither straw nor hay was to be had. Before retiring to rest we cleared the room once more of the Turks and Greeks who had dropped in, by telling them we were going to worship. Nicephorus and one other man remained, and seemed pleased at our proceeding. We sang the twenty-third Psalm which sounded very sweet to my ears ; and then, thanking our Father in Heaven for our protection from the storm, we committed ourselves and our friends aboard the vessel to his gracious care. I had a parcel of modern Greek tracts, which Mrs. Paul had given me ; and as I sat spelling out one of them by the fire, an intelligent young Greek begged it from me saying he could read. I gave him the packet ; he hid it in his bosom, thanked me, and disappeared with his treasure.

The Euroclydon blew a gale all night, which made the sailors observe that no wonder St. Paul was blown off the coast in such weather. Towards daylight it moderated, and at six we saw the yacht's white sails appearing on the south-western horizon. She was evidently making for Sphakia, where they had concluded we had passed the night. The shopkeeper, who had served us the evening before, brought up some coffee and fresh bread for our breakfast ; and we were setting the table when a new misfortune took place. One of the men put two or three bunches of dried thyme on the fire at once, as our wood was exhausted. It blazed up the chimney and set fire to the roof. When I saw the flames glowing in the ceiling, I thought the whole would fall a prey to them in a few minutes, for just above the rafters there was a wattling of sticks. The roof, however, was flat, and covered with lime, which prevented a draught. One of our men soon climbed to the top of the house, and let down a sash, to which we fixed our solitary pitcher of water. By pouring it down and around the chimney the fire in the rafters was extinguished though the wattling still spread the flames. The Greeks assembled at some distance, but would not bring us any more pitchers, and indeed seemed rather entertained at the misfortune—I suppose, because the house belonged to the governor, who was a Turk, or at least to the government. Our pitcher, however, was often replenished from the sea ; and Tom, filling a basin repeatedly, dashed bucketsful of water upon the ceiling from below. This he did with such skill, that in half an hour the fire was quite put out. The governor, with true Turkish indifference, came sailing round the corner at his usual pace, and stood calmly smoking his long pipe without saying a word.

After breakfast and prayers, we saw the 'St. Ursula' off Lutro, three miles to the westward. She had been boarded by the health officer there, in his caique, who had received a message from our friend the Bey, ordering him to let them know that we were well. The captain did not rightly understand him, but stood on for Sphakia. The governor, when we proposed to go on board, seemed uneasy, but at length allowed us, on our promise to send him a certificate that we had been sheltered and protected. He said he was responsible for our treatment to Vely Pasha, the chief man of the island. When the vessel came near, we pulled off, and found all well, though the men, of course, were fatigued with their labours. They said no boat could have boarded them in such a sea as they had the previous day : so, had we gone off, our only chance would have been to run for Gozzo (Clauda), fully fifteen miles to leeward.

Soon after we reached the vessel it fell calm ; and we were all day trying to work up to Lutro. At last, about two o'clock, we took the boat once more (Mr. Tennent not being disposed to give up his point), and rowed to the harbour. The captain's instructions were to follow us with the vessel. After an hour's pull along the shore we reached the port and took the soundings ; we found the shores steep and perfectly clean. There are fifteen fathoms in the middle of the harbour, diminishing gradually to two close to the village. The lead brought up stiff white clay. As the beach is extremely narrow, and the hills immediately behind steep and rocky, the harbour cannot have altered its form materially since the days of the apostle. Mr. Smith, following an old French chart, supposes that the island lies opposite to the harbour mouth, affording two entrances, one to the N.E. (Βλέποντα κατὰ Λίβα), the other to the S.W. (Βλέποντα κατὰ Χῶρον). We found, however, that the island is merely a continuation of the rocky point which defends the harbour on the south, and that there is only 3 to 6 feet of water between it and the land. Again, the land cannot have risen materially since the Christian era, for we found an ancient tomb or columbarium, with its entrance close to the water's edge (not 8 feet above it), in the inside of the point ; and if the land has sunk since ancient times, then the island and point must have formed one. The health officer told me that, though the harbour is open to the east, yet the easterly gales never blow home, being *lifted* by the high land behind, and that even in storms the sea rolls in gently ('piano piano'). He says *it is the only secure harbour in all winds on the south-coast of Crete ;* and that during the wars between the Venetians and the Turks (the latter

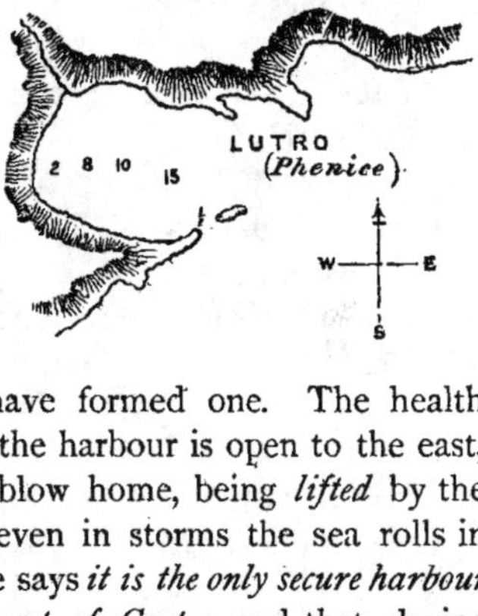

took the island in 1688, I think) as many as twenty or twenty-five war galleys had found shelter in its waters. He further showed us an inscription on a large slab which he says was found among some ruins on the point, and took us up the hill to see the traces of the site of the ancient Phœniki. The outline of its ramparts is clearly discernible, and some cisterns hollowed in the rock; but the ploughshare has been driven over its site, and it displays 'the line of confusion and the stones of emptiness.' I hastened back to decipher the inscription; but it was growing dark; and before our boat left the shore, all I had made out was the following :—

JOVI OPTIMO MAXIMO
IMPERATORE CÆSARE NERVA
ALEXANDRIÆ GUBERNATOR.[1]

(Nerva, who succeeded Domitian about the end of the first century, was of Cretan extraction.) Looking east from the harbour of Lutro, the grand pyramid Mount Ida is in full view forty miles off. We then got on board, the vessel being now at hand, and set sail for the Fair Havens. They lie forty miles to the eastward, just beyond Cape Matala. The wind blowing pretty fresh, we were opposite to them at daybreak, and easily recognised the spot from the drawing in Mr. Smith's work.

Wednesday, January 16.—No soundings being given in any of our charts, Mr. Tennent, the captain and myself, with two men, pulled in among the islands, in the boat to survey the harbour. We found good anchorage inside with eight or ten fathoms. The charts are very incorrect. An island marked 'Anchorage Island,'[2] and lying to the eastward, has a bad reef of rocks behind and around it, and an island called by the natives Trapho; while the true anchorage island lies due south of the bay. We brought in the vessel,

[1] For a more accurate copy of this inscription, see p. 269.
[2] Megalo Nisi. Admiralty Chart.

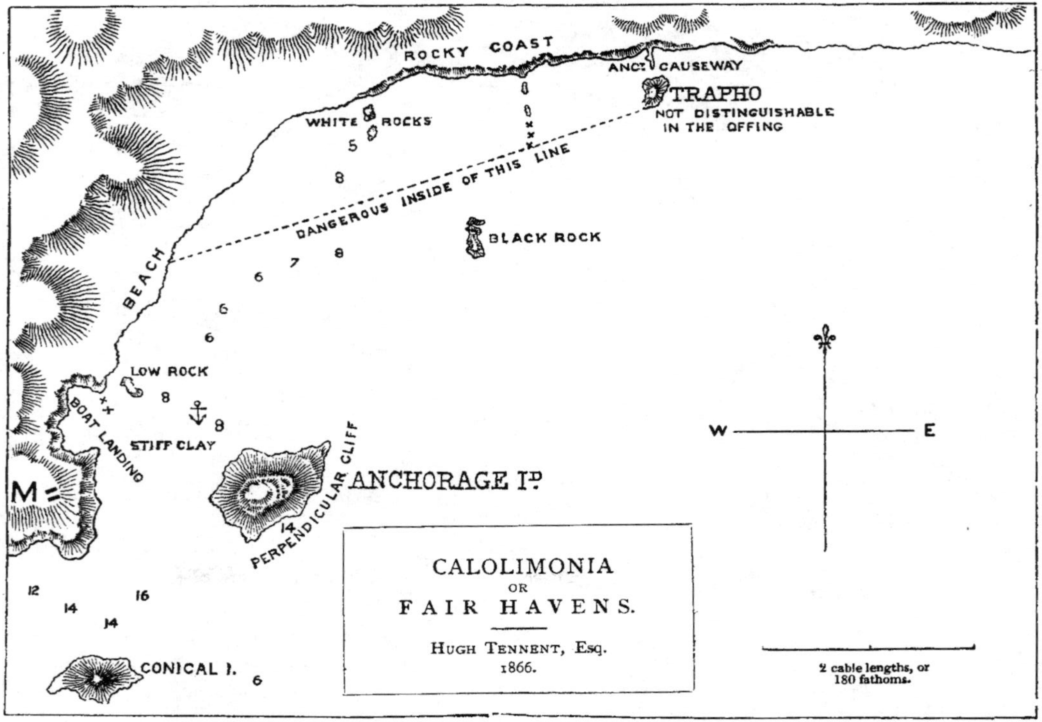

CALOLIMONIA
OR
FAIR HAVENS.

HUGH TENNENT, Esq.
1866.

and came to at the spot indicated by an anchor in the chart. The captain subsequently made a survey of the place with the bearings, which we shall preserve.

Early in the afternoon some natives appeared on the beach, and hailed us. We landed, but found that they were Greeks, and could speak only their native tongue. One said he was Guardiano of the place, and pointed out to us his house two miles off. The country round the harbour is a sad wilderness, the land high and rocky, with here and there stunted trees and thorny shrubs. The Guardiano took us to see the ruins of a monastery (marked M.), which he called "Αγιος Παῦλος (St. Paul), and which, he said with great indignation, had been destroyed by the Turks. Two or three broken columns of white marble lie among the rubbish, and on one of them are the remains of an inscription, but all that is legible is a κ, two omicrons, and a Π which has lost a leg. Fit puzzle for an antiquary.

The Greek spoke much of a monastery in the mountains, Μοναστήριος ἀπεσάνες (?) "Αγιος 'Αντώνιος, which, he said, was great and beautiful: had twenty fathers and many *μετόχια*, or dependencies; and that it was only three hours distant. Now it occurred to me that surely there somebody could speak Italian or French, and that we might get interesting information about that part of Crete from the Fathers, and perhaps procure some old manuscripts or records. Mr. Tennent felt quite inclined to go. The Guardiano, whose name is Joannes, promised to bring his mule the next day, and to be our guide; and, in short, the expedition was agreed upon. I suspect we were 'out of order' in going up the country, as our bill of health had not been visé'd or approved. The health officer at Lutro would not examine it, as we did not come to anchor; and besides, he kept us at arm's length, and said something about performing quarantine. But then, on the other hand, the Guardiano asked no questions, and the nearest Bey lived three hours off, quite in another direction from the monastery: so the Campbells' proverb, 'It's a far cry to Loch Awe,' was our comfort.

On Thursday morning Mr. Tennent and I left the vessel at ten o'clock, and landed opposite Trapho, taking two men with us in their white blouses and blue collars, the club uniform. The men had each a musket, and we had six-barrelled revolvers; so we looked very respectable indeed. I believe that in Candia the Greeks have been kept quite down by the Turks since 1830; but we hear that in these countries it is always the custom for travellers to carry arms. There was something peculiarly interesting in exploring this part of Candia. It is not described in 'Murray,' and it has seldom been visited by our countrymen: the monastery perhaps never. A range of mountains called the mountains of Messara, runs parallel with the coast. They are from two to three thousand feet high, except one of them, Mount Kophīnos, which lies to the east, and must be five thousand. Beyond this chain on the north lies the great plain of Messara, and from its northern side again springs the magnificent Mount Ida (Ψιλόριτι) Psiloriti. Well, under the guidance of Joannes, we walked along near the coast for two miles, by a steep and difficult path, among ravines, till we reached the Platē Pyrāmata, a valley with a dry river-course, and high steep hills on either side. The loneliness of the country struck me exceedingly. Nobody was to be seen in the three miles we travelled up the vale; and yet its level bed, level like the vale of Lucerna,[1] might bear good crops; and its sides, if cultivated with care, might overflow with wine and oil. An olive-tree here and there showed us what might be produced. It was the first time I had seen the blighting effects of the Turkish yoke; and as I wandered on I fell into a long train of musings on the subject. 'Lord, what shall the end of

[1] In Piedmont.

these things be?' Why should the countries where the Gospel was first preached be a prey to the spoiler? Here is Crete, where Titus was busy in 62 or 64, ordaining elders in all its hundred cities; and now a wilderness!

After walking to the end of the level part (northwards), we came upon two peasants, and soon after, turning to the right, saw, high above us, the little village of Adheschāri. The day was hot, and we sat down to rest and bait in sight, at least, of human habitations. After much climbing, we approached the pass that leads to the plains on the north, and on gaining it found a plateau to the right, on which the monastery was situated. It is like a great farmyard, with low buildings round it, flat-roofed. The church stands attached to one side. As we approached I could have fancied it was the time of the Crusades, so quaint and old-fashioned did everything seem. Stiff pre-Raphaelite-like trees stood here and there; the houses, probably once disturbed by an earthquake, had the uneasy look of a drawing that is all out of perspective, and the whole scene would have made a copy to illuminate a manuscript. We entered the outer gate, and found three aged Fathers sitting with long staves in their hands on a stone settle, stroking their beards and looking before them. They slowly rose and did obeisance to us, and we took off our hats to them. Then they led us into the court, which might be 160 feet square, and knocked at the door of the ἡγούμενος, or abbot, whose name was Julius. He came out, and led us into his apartment, but we found, to our great disappointment, that no one in the place could speak anything but Romaic Greek. It was but a few words that I could understand or speak, and of course anything like conversation was impossible. The Abbot was a most pleasing person, middle-aged, with a mild and intellectual, or at least thoughtful face. I requested a sight of the library; but he said, with a sigh, that all the books and manuscripts had been burnt by the Turks. However, a Father brought me an old Lucretius (1640), and made one of the boys read a passage, which he did with a Greek accent, disregarding all the quantities of the syllables. They showed us a Gospel of John, printed in Venice in 1811, and richly bound. It was in the ancient Greek, but when I read a verse or two aloud they smiled at my utter disregard of accents, etc. All their books seem to come from Venice, which is natural, as the island of Candia belonged to Venice down to the end of the seventeenth century. There are ten διδάσκαλοι, or youths, under training in the monastery. The Fathers teach them, cultivate the land, look after the flocks and herds, perform the daily services in the church, and occasional services in the μετόχια, or out-stations. The boys were playful and healthy, and the Fathers had not the sinister or dronish look with which one is disgusted in the monks of Italy. The abbot wore a Greek dress and turban, but had a monastic habit to put on over it. We had been four hours and a half on our journey, owing to the badness of the track and the heat, and it was now three o'clock. As they pressed us to stay all night, we agreed to do so rather than be obliged to go over the difficult ground by moonlight. The tablecloth was then spread, and bread, cheese, wine, honey, and coffee were set before us. Our men looked very *blate* when bidden take their dinner with an abbot.

After dinner we climbed a hill in the neighbourhood, a few hundred feet above the pass; it commanded a grand and extensive view of the interior of the island. The plains of Messara lay at our feet to the north; and Mount Ida, the birthplace of Jupiter, rose beyond the plain, towering to a great height. Kōphīnos, a very remarkable hill, like an exaggerated Scuir of Eigg, was the prominent feature to the east. We must have been 2,000 feet, at least, above the sea. In the southern and western horizons the sea was the boundary, and Clauda (Gozzo) and its islet were distinctly visible. This view well repaid our toil.

Two coarse swaggering Turkish soldiers, and a subaltern officer, had arrived at the monastery, and, though evidently unwelcome guests, were taking up their quarters for the night with the air of lords of the soil. I read them our passport (not a word of which they understood), and their commander bowed most graciously. The Hegoumenos seemed to dislike their company extremely, and came and sat beside Mr. Tennent and me at the kitchen fire. Supper, however, was set for the Turks and our party in his own apartment, though he did not appear. Halil Aga, the officer, sat next Tennente Effendi (for so they called him), on the sofa ; only the Aga sat cross-legged and Mr. Tennent as a European. After supper we went to the kitchen, and one or two of the Fathers and several of their pupils gathered around us. The boys seemed to be on excellent terms with their teacher. One of them made me understand that the latter was the *ποιμήν* (shepherd), and that they were *τὰ πρόβατα* (the sheep). Finer boys I never saw : we were both delighted with their intelligence and good manners. I drew out a packet of Greek tracts (not of a controversial nature) from my pocket, and they read one aloud in turn with great spirit and animation. I then divided the packet among them and the Fathers, who all seemed pleased with the little gift. A little fresh literature in those parts must be a great acquisition, but who knows whether true love to Christ may not burn in such a retreat? Perhaps something our tracts contained may have refreshed some thirsty soul.

We slept, with our men, in an upper chamber. At evening worship we prayed that peace might rest on the house. At daybreak we rose, and found many peasants, men and women, assembling in the church for morning prayers. The service, alas ! was unmeaning enough. They wanted us to wait and breakfast ; but, being anxious to enjoy the cool of the morning, we started at 6.30, and had a charming walk down the glen. Between eight and nine o'clock we took some biscuit and beer, sitting under the shadow of a great rock, and after a hot march from our resting-place reached the vessel at half-past ten.

Friday, 18th.—Nothing now remained to be done but to ascertain the exact position of Lasea, a city which Luke says was nigh to the Fair Havens. Mr. Smith notes that it is mentioned by no other writer, and that its ruins have not been observed. I asked our friend the Guardiano, ποῦ ἐστι Λασέα (Λασαία); (Where is Lasea, or Lasaea?) He said at once, that it was two hours' walk to the eastward, close to Cape Leonda, but that it is now a desert place. Mr. Tennent was eager to examine it; so, getting under weigh, we ran along the coast before a S.W. wind. Cape Leonda is called by the Greeks Λέων, evidently from its resemblance to a lion couchant, which nobody could fail to observe either from the west or the east. Its face is to the sea, forming a promontory 350 or 400 feet high. Just after we passed it, Miss Tennent's quick eye discovered two white pillars standing on an eminence near the shore. Down went the helm, and putting the vessel round we stood in close, wore, and hove to. Mr. H. Tennent and I landed immediately, just inside the Cape, to the eastward, and found the beach lined with masses of masonry. These were formed of small stones, cemented together with mortar so firmly that even where the sea had undermined them huge fragments lay on the sand. This sea wall extended a quarter of a mile along the beach, from one rocky face to another, and was evidently intended for the defence of the city. Above we found the ruins of two temples. The steps which led up to the one remain, though in a shattered state; and the two white marble columns noticed by Miss Tennent belonged to the other. Many shafts, and a few capitals of Grecian pillars, all of marble, lie scattered about, and a gully worn by a torrent lays bare the substructions down to the rock. To the east a conical rocky hill is girdled by the foundations of a wall; and on a platform

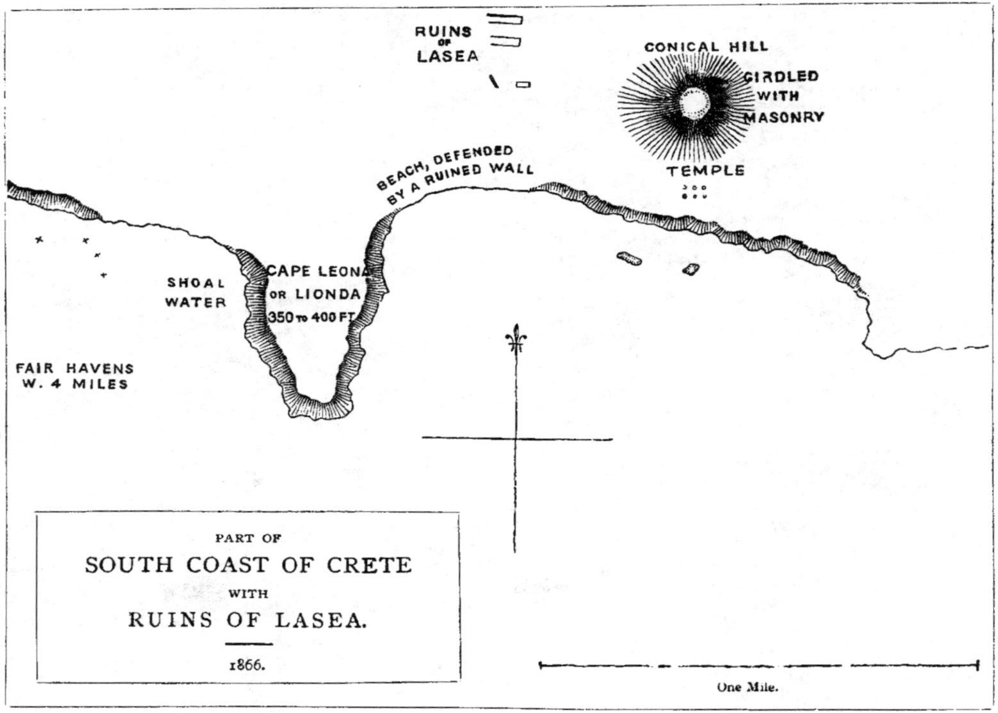
RUINS OF LASEA
CONICAL HILL
GIRDLED WITH MASONRY
TEMPLE
BEACH, DEFENDED BY A RUINED WALL
CAPE LEONA OR LIONDA 350 TO 400 FT.
SHOAL WATER
FAIR HAVENS W. 4 MILES
PART OF
SOUTH COAST OF CRETE
WITH
RUINS OF LASEA.
1866.
One Mile.

between this hill and the sea the pillars of another edifice lie level with the ground. Some peasants came down to see us from the hills above, and I asked them the name of the place. They said at once, 'Lasea,' so there could be no doubt. Cape Leonda lies five miles east to the Fair Havens, but there are no roads whatever in that part of Candia. We took away some specimens of marble, and boarded our vessel; at 4 P.M. sailed for Alexandria.

Alexandria, January 22.—We have plans of Lutro and Fair Havens *in retentis*, which I dare say will interest Mr. Smith. The gale we had at Candia has been severely felt here, three vessels having been wrecked.

No. II.

AFTER visiting Egypt, the yacht returned to Crete, encountered the Euroclydon a second time, on February 19, and took shelter in Lutro (Port Phenice), which Mr. Brown describes as smooth as a mill-pond. The master of the yacht remarks: 'The east winds never blow home in the port of Lutro. We were twice caught with the Tramontana, or north wind, which blows off in fearful squalls, but on arriving close under the high land, a good half-mile to the east of the port, it fell calm, and continued so to the harbour.' At this visit Mr. Brown took an accurate copy of the inscription mentioned in page 262. It is as follows:—

JOVI . SOLI . OPTIMO . MAXIMO.
SERAPIDI . ET . OMNIBVS. DIIS . ET.
IMPERATORI . CAESARI . NERVAE.
TRAJANO . AVG . GERMANICO . DACICO.
EPICTETVS . LIBERTUS. TABVLARIVS
CVRAM . AGENTE . OPERIS . DIONYSIO.
SOSTRATI . FILIO . ALEXANDRINO . GVBERNATORE
NAVIS . PARASEMO . ISOPHARIA CL . THEONIS

This interesting and important inscription may be translated thus :—

'Epictetus, the freedman and Recorder (Notary) to Jupiter O. M., to Serapis and all the Gods, and to the Emp. Cæsar, Nerva, Trajan, Augustus, Germanicus, Dacicus. The work was superintended by Dionysius of Alexandria, the son of Sostratus, and master of the ship whose sign is Isopharia—of the fleet of Theon.'

It proves, in the first place, the prolonged stay of a ship of Alexandria at Port Phenice; otherwise the master of the Isopharia could not have had time to superintend 'the work' whatever it was,—clearly pointing to a case of wintering in this harbour ; and, in the next place, it proves the accuracy with which St. Luke employs the nautical terminology of Alexandrian seamen in his designations of the master τῷ κυβερνήτῃ (xxvii. 11), Gubernatore (Inscr.), and of the ship παρασήμῳ (xxviii. 11), parasemo (Inscr.). The Tabularius was an officer of importance in the fleets of the ancients, as appears from the inscription given in the Lexicon Antiquitatum Romanarum Pitisci, i. 458.

CINCIO . L . F . SABINIANO . TABULARIO . CLASS . RAVENN.

We can now understand the reasons for the anxiety of the master and owner of St. Paul's ship to move to what appears to have been one of the winter stations between Alexandria and Italy. On the other hand, we can now see that the advice given by St. Paul to remain at Fair Havens was in every point of view sound and judicious : we must remember that the situation of a ship unprovided with a compass was, when blown out to sea at a season when neither sun nor stars could be seen, all but desperate. Now the experience of Messrs. Urquhart, Spratt and Tennent shows the great probability of such a casualty in crossing the Gulf of Messara, from Fair Havens to Phenice. The reasons for removing from Fair Havens are by no means so strong as I formerly supposed : a certain degree of shelter is afforded by Anchorage Island, to which hawsers could be carried, whilst the stiff clay of the bottom rendered the chance of being driven either on shore or the island very small to a ship well provided with anchors and cables.

The subject was, as may be supposed, discussed by the 'master and owner' of the schooner whose sign is St. Ursula, whilst anchored at Fair Havens, and the conclusion arrived at was, that a ship might winter there without much danger.

No. III.

ON EURO-AQUILO.

(*From* DR. BENTLEY'S *Remarks on a late Discourse on Free thinking*, *p.* 97.)

'STEPHENS followed what he found in the *King of France's* copies, Acts xxvii. 14, ἄνεμος τυφωνικὸς, ὁ καλούμενος ΕΥΡΟΚΛΥΔΩΝ, and he is followed by your translators, "There arose against it a tempestuous wind, called *Euroclydon*;" . . . if that printer had had the use of your *Alexandrian* MS., which exhibits here Εὐρακύλων, it is very likely he would have given it the preference in his text; and then the Doctor, upon his own principle, must have stickled for this.

'The wind *Euroclydon* was never heard of but here; it is compounded of Εὖρος and κλύδων, the *wind* and the *waves*; and it seems plain *a priori*, from the disparity of those two ideas, that they could not be joined in one compound; nor is there any other example of the like composition.

'But Εὐρακύλων, or, as the Vulgate *Latin* here has it, *Euro-aquilo* (approved by *Grotius* and others) is so apposite to the context, and to all the circumstances of the place, that it may fairly challenge admittance as the word of *St. Luke.*

''Tis true, according to *Vitruvius*, *Seneca*, and *Pliny*, who make *Eurus* to blow from the winter solstice, and *Aquilo* between the summer solstice and the north point, there can be no such wind nor word as *Euro-aquilo*, because the *Solanus*, or *Apheliotes* from the cardinal point of East, comes between them. But *Eurus* is here taken, as *Gellius*, ii. 22. and the Latin poets use it, for the middle equinoctial East, the same as *Solanus*; and then in the table of the twelve winds, according to the ancients, between the two cardinal winds *Septentrio* and *Eurus*, there are two at stated distances, *Aquilo* and Καικίας. The *Latins* had no known name for Καικίας, "Quem ab oriente solstitiali excitatum Græci Καικίαν vocant, apud nos sine nomine est," says Seneca, *Nat. Quæst.* v. 16.

'Καικίας, therefore, blowing between *Aquilo* and *Eurus*, the Roman seamen (for want of a specific word) might express the same wind by the compound name *Euro-aquilo*, in the same analogy as the *Greeks* call Εὐρόνοτος, the middle wind between *Eurus* and *Notus*, and, as you say now, *North-east* and *South-east.* Since, therefore, we have now found that *Euro-aquilo* was the *Roman* mariner's word for the Greek Καικίας, there will soon appear a just reason why *St. Luke* calls it ἄνεμος τυφωνικός, a tempestuous wind, *Vorticosus*, a whirling wind, for that is the peculiar character of Καικίας in those climates; as appears from several authors, and from that known proverbial verse—

Ἕλκων ἐφ' αὑτὸν ὡς ὁ Καικίας νέφη.

So that with submission, I think our *Luther's* and the *Danish* version have done more right than your *English* to the sacred text, by translating it *Nord-ost*, *North-east*; though according to the present compass, divided into thirty-two, *Euro-aquilo* answers nearest to *Ost-nord-ost, East-north-east*; which is the very wind that would directly drive the ship from Crete to the African *Syrtis*, according to the pilot's fears in the 17th verse.

No. IV.

NOTE ON THE READING 'EURO-AQUILO.'

(*From* GRANVILLE PENN'S '*Annotations to the Book of the New Covenant*' (*Testament*).)

'OF the two readings, Ευρακυλων and Ευροκλυδων, the former has the testimony of the highest antiquity. Bishop Marsh, with Shaw, and all his other learned predecessors, thought it peculiar to the *Alex.* MS. (Michaelis, *Introd.* vol. ii. p. 110, 620); but it is the reading of the far more ancient *Vatican* MS., and is witnessed also by *Jerome*, and the *first* or Latin translation. The difficulties experienced by commentators in endeavouring to settle the reading of this word have been owing to a pre-assumption that it is to be interpreted from *the Greek*; and if anyone should attempt to explain σπεκουλατωρ, φραγελλοω, or κηνσος, by *the Greek*, he would find himself in a similar dilemma. Dr. Shaw, objecting to the reading *Euraquilo* in his *Travels*, etc. (p. 360, fol.), observes, "As the ship was of Alexandria, sailing to Italy, we *may suppose* the mariners to have been *Grecian*; and too well acquainted with the received and vernacular terms of their occupation to admit of this *Græco-Latin* or *barbarous* appellation, as they may think it." But it would be full as reasonable to suppose that the mariners might have been *Egyptian*, or even *Italian*, as the ship was freighted for Italy, to supply that country with corn. Dr. Bloomfield enforces Shaw's objection, by observing that *Eur-aquilo* would be *heterogeneously compounded of Greek and Latin.* Now this objection would extend equally to prove that *no wind* was denominated by the Latins "*Euro-auster,*" for Aulus Gellius (lib. ii. c. 22) expressly declares *Auster* to be a *Latin* term ; and yet we know that the S.E. wind was actually so denominated by the Latins. Besides, every reader of Virgil and Horace knows that the name *Eurus* had become so thoroughly naturalised in Rome, as no longer to be regarded as a foreign name. The latter of those learned critics observes, "Ακυλων could not well represent *Aquilo* ;" yet, if he had referred to the relative orthographies *Aquila* and Ακυλας, in Acts xviii. 2, Rom. xvi. 3, etc., and had recollected the relative dialectic terminations *o* and *ων* of the two languages (*Plato*, Πλατων), he would have perceived that *Aquilo* must have been represented in Greek orthography by Ακυλων. We cannot reason positively and accurately of winds from the employment of their names by the poets, because they used them with licence, according to the demands of their metre. In Aulus Gellius we have a minute enumeration of them, with their names and quarters, as represented on the following page.

'Pliny places *Aquilo* "inter septentrionem et exortum solstitialem" (*N. H.* ii. 47) ; *Euro-aquilo* will be still more eastward, or *East-north-east.* The *Eth.* version paraphrases *ventus Aquilonarius*, a N.E. *wind.* Ευροκλυδων of the *jun.* Greek texts, as also Ευρυκλυδων Ευτρακηλων *Copt.*, Ευρακλυδων *Syra post.*, Ευρακυκλων *Arm.*, Ευρακηλων *Sahid.*, will all, therefore, have been successive transcriptural *errata.* Dr. Bloomfield thinks it "clear, that both external and internal evidence unite in requiring the common reading, Ευροκλυδων, to be retained, and that it was sometimes used as an adjective, as appears from the adjective ερικλυδων, which is used by a later Greek writer *ap. Steph. Thes.*" We are much obliged to the learned annotator for drawing our attention to this solitary word, which might otherwise have remained for ever unnoticed. This word is employed in a metrical chronicle of one of the Byzantine historians, Constantine Manasses, who lived in the middle of the twelfth century.

> Ὁ Καισαρ γαρ εφυσησε, βορβας ὡς βαρυβοας,
> ὡς ερικλυδων αγριος, ὡς δυσπνους απαρκτιας. (p. 104.)

Which lines are thus interpreted by Leunclavius :—*Cæsar autem adflabat, tanquam graviter spirans Aquilo, vel sævus ille* tempestatesque ciens *Subsolanus.*

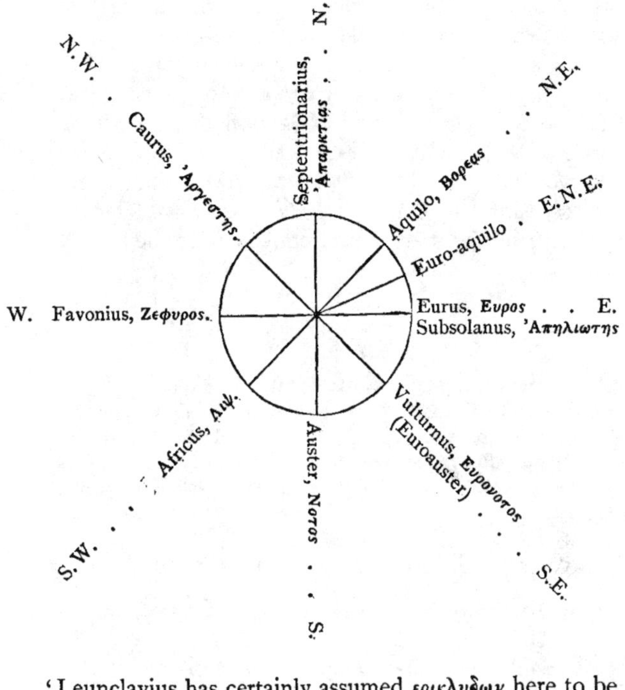

'Leunclavius has certainly assumed ερικλυδων here to be an *adjective*, but a little closer inspection will reveal to us that the poet used it, not as an adjective, but as a *substantive*, as the proper name of one of three north and east winds, which he specifies, and, in fact, the very wind mentioned by St. Luke: which, in the *junior* or Constantinopolitan copies of the Scriptures best known to the poet, had been changed to ευροκλυδων, and in the printed copy of this poem to ερικλυδων.

"For Cæsar raged like the deep-roaring Boreas;
Like the fierce Ericlydon; and like the hard-blowing Aparctias."

'But we have specially to consider that St. Luke heard the name of the wind on board an Alexandrian ship, that the two oldest documents which record the name are Alexandrian, and that both record the name Ευρακυλων, *Euraquilo*; and further, that the technical language of the conquering nation was extensively adopted in the countries enclosing the Mediterranean, particularly in those maritime cities that were in most frequent and active intercourse with Rome, as was eminently *Alexandria*. The whole context is wanting in the *Cod. Ephr.* from c. xxvi. 20 to xxvii. 16, and in the *Cod. Bezæ* from c. xxii. to the end of the book.'

No. V.

[The following note was printed by Mr. Smith as an appendix to the first and second editions. It was omitted in the third, probably under the belief that the question of Malta and Meleda had been finally settled. But as the question has been raised once more by Mr. T. Falconer, it has been thought expedient to restore the extract from Bochart.]

REMARKS ON THE MELITA OF ACTS XXVIII.

(*From* BOCHART'S '*Chanaan*,' lib. i. cap. xxvi.)

'SED altera hic sese offert majoris momenti quæstio ad utram appulerit Paulus. Sunt enim quibus videtur de Illyrica egisse Lucas. In his Constantinus Porphyrogenneta a quo ponitur in censu insularum Illyrici littoris: Νῆσος ἑτέρα μεγάλη τὰ Μέλετα, ἤτοι τὸ Μαλοζεᾶται, ἣν ἐν ταῖς Πράξεσι τῶν Ἀποστόλων ὁ ἅγιος Λουκᾶς μέμνηται, Μελίτην ταύτην προσαγορεύων. *Alia magna insula quæ Meleta ceu Malozeatæ vocatur cujus in Actis Apostolorum meminit Sanctus Lucas, Melitam eam nominans.*

'Cui sententiæ fovere volunt:—1. Quod in Adria jactatur Paulus antequam in Meliten appellat (Actor. 27. 27), unde colligunt agi de insula sinus Adriatici. 2. Quod barbaros habuit incolas (Actor. 28; 2, 4), cum Africanam Meliten Græci pridem incolerent. 3. Quod in insula Melite nullius oppidi meminit Lucas, cum Africana urbem habuerit insulæ cognominem, quæ superstes hodieque est.

'Sed hæ objectiunculæ tanti non sunt, ut quemquam dimovere debeant a vulgari sententia quam firmissimæ rationes adstruunt. Primo, enim (Actor. 27; 13, 14), circa Cretam quum navigaret Paulus, excitatur ἄνεμος τυφωνικὸς ὁ καλούμενος Εὐροκλύδων,—*ventus turbulentus* qui vocatur *Euroclydon*, vel ut legit Vulgatus Interpres, Εὐρο-ακύλων, *Euro-aquilo*; quam lectionem si sequaris, res est confecta; neque enim *Euro-aquilo* potuit e Creta navem in Illyricum impellere. Praestitisset id *Euronotus*, non sub-contrarius *Euro-aquilo*, ut docet situs locorum. Sed quoquo modo legas, ventum illum Euroclydonem in Austrum inclinasse potius quam in Septentrionem inde palam est, quod illo flante nautæ metuunt ne in Africæ Syrtim incidant. (Actor. 27. 17.) Nihil tale formidaturi si ventus navem in Illyricum impulisset, quæ ora est Syrti et Africæ obversa.

'2. Actor. 27. 41.: Περιπεσόντες εἰς τόπον διθάλασσον ἐπώκειλαν τὴν ναῦν, *cum incidissent in locum bimarem illiserunt navem.* In locum bimarem, id est in isthmum. Horat. *Od.* 7. lib. i.:—

> Aut Ephesum bimarisve Corinthi
> Mœnia.

Ovid. Eleg. 12, lib. i. *Trist.*:—

> Aut postquam bimarem cursu superavimus Isthmum.

Hic Isthmus ad insulæ ortum æstivum hodieque ostenditur, et vocatur ab incolis, *La Cala di S. Paolo* S. Pauli, adpulsus.

'3. Actor. 28. 7: *Circa locum illum erant* χωρία τῷ πρώτῳ τοῦ νήσου ὀνόματι Ποπλίῳ, *prædia primo insulæ nomine Publio.* Eum intelligo quem insulæ Romani præfecerant. Nam hujus insulæ præfectos ita nominari solitos et ex hoc loco colligere est, et ex veteri epitaphio quod in marmore Græcis literis se Melitæ vidisse refert Quintinus: Λ. ΚΑ. ΥΙΟΣ. ΚΥΡ. ΙΠΠΕΥΣ. ΡΩΜΑΙΩΝ. ΠΡΩΤΟΣ. ΜΕΛΙΤΑΙΩΝ. *L. Ca. filius Cyr. eques Romanorum,* PRIMUS *Melitensium.* Nempe idem antea nominis fuerat præfectis Carthaginiensibus, qui Punica phrasi dicebantur *primi.* . . .

'4. Tres menses continuos in illa insula hæsit Paulus cum centurione et aliis (Act. 28. 11), qui numerus hominum fuit cclxxvi (Act. 27. 37). Quod vix quisquam crediderit de Illyrica Melite; quia cum nonnisi quatuor passuum millibus a continenti distet, et Epidaurum in conspectu habeat, portum celeberrimum et hospitibus commodissimum, centurio Romanus maluisset eo trajicere, quam totam hyemem in misera insula degere, in qua tam multos advenas sine gravibus incommodis diversari fuisset nefas.

'5. Jam quod iidem dicuntur Puteolos vecti fuisse in Alexandrina nave quæ in eadem insula hyemaverat (Act. 28. 11), quis de Illyrica Melita intellexerit? Cum ab Ægypto Puteolos contendentibus, Africana Melite pene invitis sese offerat. At quisquis Alexandria Puteolos iturus Illyricam Melitem petit merito dici queat, sin minus toto cœlo, saltem toto salo, aberrasse.

'6. Hoc potissimum quod Lucas e Melite profectos addit primo Syracusas deinde Rhegium appulisse (Act. 28. 12, 13); quæ via, quam est recta si profectio fuit ex Africana Melita, tam flexuosa fuerit et præpostera, si ex Illyrica discesserunt, e qua potius per Rhegium Syracusas iter est quam per Syracusas Rhegium, quia Rhegium est vicinius.

'7. Jam si authoritate certatur, Constantino Porphyrogenneta longe antiquior est Arator Sub-Diaconus, qui sic habet, lib. ii. *Historiæ Apostolicæ* :—

Sicanio lateri remis vicina Melite.

'Nec difficile est solvere quicquid contra objiciunt. Nam in Adria quidem jactari dicitur navis appulsura Melitam (Act. 27. 27); non tamen in Adriatico sinu, quo multo latius patet Adria, seu quod Idem est Adriaticum Mare. Sinus enim Adriaticus cum Illyrico desinit. At Mare Adriaticum idem est cum Ionio: Hesychius—'Ιόνιον πέλαγος ὁ νῦν 'Αδρίας, *Ionium Mare quod nunc Adria.* Juvenalis, vetus scholiastes—*Diu navigatura de Tyrrheno mari ad Adriacum;* Adriacum pro Ionio dixit. Ita enim Juvenalis :—

Tyrrhenos igitur fluctus, lateque sonantem
Pertulit Ionium.

'Hinc Ptolomæus Siciliam ab ortu, Epirum et Achaiam a meridie, et Peloponnesum adeoque Cretam ab occasu definit Adriatico pelago. Et in Ovidio non semel Adriam ab Ægæo dividit Isthmus Corinthiacus. Sic lib. iv. *Fastorum* :—

Adriacumque patens late bimaremque Corinthum.

Et in lib. i. *Trist.* eleg. 12 :—

Aut hæc me gelido tremerem cum mense Decembri
  Scribentem mediis Adria vidit aquis,
Aut postquam bimarem cursu superavimus Isthmum,
  Alteraque est nostræ sumpta carina fugæ.

'Proinde Philostratus, lib. ii. *Imaginum*, in Palæmone, eum isthmum scribit, Αἰγαίου καὶ 'Αδρίου μέσον κεῖσθαι, *medium esse inter mare Ægæum et Adriaticum.* Et in *Apollonio* suo, lib. iv. cap. 8, Neronem idem tradit de hoc isthmo scindendo cogitasse ut Adriaticum Ægæo mari misceret. Eodem facit quod Alpheus apud Suidam in 'Αλφειός et rursus in 'Αρέθουσα, e Peloponneso in Siciliæ Arethusam influere legitur δυόμενος διὰ τῆς 'Αδριάδος θαλάσσης, *pelagus subiens per mare Adriaticum.* Hinc de Alpheo Pausanias in *Arcadicis* Ἔμελλε δὲ ἄρα μηδὲ Ἀδρίας ἐπισχήσειν αὐτὸν τοῦ πρόσω, *neque illius cursum Adria cohibitura erat.* Cætera ibi vide.

'Quid quod Adriaticum mare ad Africam usque extensum est, si Ethicum sequimur et Orosium, apud quos Tripolitana provincia, ubi Arzuges et Leptis Magna, habet a septentrione mare Adriaticum, et a meridie Creta finitur *mari Lybico, quod et Adriaticum vocant.*

'Nec aliter sensit Hieronymus in *Vita Hilarionis*, ubi medium Adriam pertranseunt ab Ægypti Paraetonio ad Siciliæ Pachynum appulsuri. Sed ad rem id maxime est quod in Procopii *Vandalicis*, lib. i., insulæ Gaulus et Melita Ἀδριατικὸν καὶ Τυρσηνικὸν πέλαγος διορίζουσιν, *Adriaticum et Tuscum pelagus disterminant.* Scite, igitur, sacer scriptor et ex geographicorum usu e Creta Melitam delatos, vi ventorum ingruentium jactari dicit in Adria. Porro in eadem insula barbarorum nomine Pœnos ab illo designari docuimus quorum reliquiæ in agros hæserant. Oppidi denique non meminit, quia nihil erat necesse. Ita, Actor. 21. 1, Paulus appulisse narratur in insulas Coum et Rhodum absque mentione urbium quas tamen utraque habuit insulæ cognomines.'

No. VI.

ON 'ADRIA.'

BY THE EDITOR.

It seems necessary to add something to Mr. Smith's remarks on the vexed question of the limits of 'Adria' (Acts xxvii. 27). He has hardly done full justice to the arguments of those who maintain that the channel of Otranto formed in St. Luke's time, as now, the southern boundary of the Adriatic.

The question is one of great importance, as the tense of St. Luke's expression (διαφερομένων ἡμῶν ἐν τῷ Ἀδρίᾳ), whatever may be the exact meaning of the word, implies that they were in Adria when they were approaching Melita, and not merely at some time during the previous fourteen days' voyage. Thus, if we could establish that the name was limited in St. Luke's time as Bryant and Falconer maintain, it would be impossible to suppose that an accurate writer like St. Luke had applied it to a tract of sea at least 300 miles further south. This view is urged with great vehemence and an embarrassing wealth of quotations by Mr. Thomas Falconer.[1]

It is impossible for me to examine in detail his quotations, which have, for the most part, little bearing on the point at issue; but I will state as succinctly as possible the conclusions at which I have arrived on this question, and the most important evidence by which they are supported. In this task I have derived help from Mr. Falconer's collection of quotations, but more from a most interesting and lucid essay contained in Letronne's 'Recherches Géographiques et Critiques sur le livre De Mensura Orbis Terrae par Dicuil,' Paris 1814 (pp. 170–223).

The name of Adrias, or Adrias Kolpos, derived from the town called Adria at the mouth of the Po, was at first applied to the northern part of the Adriatic, but was gradually extended to the south. For several centuries before the Christian era, Adria was definitely bounded by the narrow neck of sea between Hydruntum and the Acroceraunian mountains, which evidently forms a natural division. The systematic geographers, Strabo, Pomponius Mela, and Pliny, all limit it here. As this point is important, I will give some of the clearest passages in full. Strabo (who was born about the year 66 B.C.) tells us (v. 1 3) that Adrias is like in shape and size to Italy south of the Apennines, with

[1] See preface, p. xii.

the 'heel' and 'toe' cut off. ἔστι δ' ὅμοιον τὸ σχῆμα τοῦ Ἀδρίου καὶ τὸ μέγεθος τῇ Ἰταλίᾳ τῇ ἀφοριζομένῃ τοῖς τε Ἀπεννίνοις ὄρεσι καὶ τῇ θαλάττῃ ἑκατέρᾳ, μέχρι τῆς Ἰαπυγίας καὶ τοῦ Ἰσθμοῦ τοῦ κατὰ τὸν Ταραντῖνον καὶ τὸν Ποσειδωνιάτην κόλπον. τό τε γὰρ πλάτος τὸ μέγιστον ἀμφοῖν ἐστι περὶ χιλίους καὶ τριακοσίους σταδίους· τὸ δὲ μῆκος ἔλαττον οὐ πολὺ τῶν ἑξακισχιλίων.

In Strabo vii. 5. 8, 9, we read: Ὠρικὸν καὶ τὸ ἐπίνειον αὐτοῦ ὁ Πάνορμος καὶ τὰ Κεραύνια ὄρη, ἡ ἀρχὴ τοῦ στόματος τοῦ Ἰονίου κόλπου καὶ τοῦ Ἀδρίου. τὸ μὲν οὖν στόμα κοινὸν ἀμφοῖν ἐστι, διαφέρει δὲ ὁ Ἰόνιος, διότι τοῦ πρώτου μέρους τῆς θαλάττης ταύτης ὄνομα τοῦτ' ἐστιν, ὁ δ' Ἀδρίας τῆς ἐντὸς μέχρι τοῦ μυχοῦ, νυνὶ δὲ καὶ τῆς συμπάσης.

He intends apparently to distinguish between the inner and outer parts of what is now the Adriatic, and to tell us that this sea was formerly divided into Adrias and the Ionian Gulf; but that in his time the former name had been extended to the whole. But M. Letronne explains the passage differently.

Pomponius Mela and Pliny were strictly contemporaneous with St. Luke. In the writings of both we find the word used in the same limited sense as by Strabo. The former enumerates the places on the east coast of Italy from north to south, ending his list as follows: 'In Calabria Brundusium, Valatium, Lupiae, Hydrus mons, tum Sallentini campi et Sallentina litora, et urbs Graia Callipolis. *Hucusque Hadria*, Hucusque Italiae latus alterum pertinet,' ii. 66, 67. This quotation is so clear that it is unnecessary to give two others no less distinct which are quoted by Mr. Falconer from Mela, i. 3, and ii. 3.

In Pliny ('Nat. Hist.' iii. 16) we have a passage to the same effect: 'Promontorium, quod Acram Iapygiam vocant, quo longissimè in Maria excurrit Italia. Ab eo Basta oppidum et Hydruntum decem ac novem M pass. *ad discrimen Ionii et Adriatici maris,* qua in Graeciam brevissimus transitus.'

So far our authorities have been strongly in favour of a limitation of the word Adria which would be fatal to the claims of Malta. But we have sufficient evidence of a curious change of usage which began before the Christian era and gradually developed itself during the succeeding centuries. We often, especially in poets, find the terms *Ionian* and *Adriatic* used as loosely synonymous; for instance, Lucan, v. 613, says: 'Sonat Ionio vagus Adria ponto,' and 'Illyris Ionias vergens Epidamnus in undas. Huc fuga nautarum, cum totas Adria vires Movit.' Moreover, the passage quoted above from Strabo bears distinct testimony to a change in the meaning of the word. The quotations from Horace and Ovid given on p. 173 show clearly (*pace* Mr. Falconer) that these poets gave a much more extensive signification to the term in question than did Strabo and Mela. The same inference seems to follow from a passage of Livy, who argues for the ancient importance of the Tuscan race in these words, 'Mari supero inferoque quibus Italia *insulæ modo cingitur*, quantum potuerint nomina sunt argumento; quod alterum Tuscum communi vocabulo gentis, alterum *Hadriaticum* mare, ab Hadriâ Tuscorum colonia vocavere Italicæ gentes' (v. 33). But within a century at latest from the time when the Acts were written, we find one who is no vague writer, but a thoroughly scientific geographer, repeatedly employing the name in its new and extensive application.

In Ptolemy, the Ionian Sea—which washes the coasts of Calabria and Apulia, and which bounds on the west Macedonia and Epirus as far as the Acroceraunian mountains—intervenes between the Adriatic *Gulf* (Ἀδρίας κόλπος) and the great Adriatic *Sea* (Ἀδριατικὸν πέλαγος) which bounds Sicily to the east, washes Magna Graecia, bounds Epirus to the West from the Acroceraunian mountains to the river Achelous, Achaia to the south 'along the shore of the Corinthian Gulf from the river Achelous' as far as the Isthmus of Corinth, bounds the Peloponnesus to the west and south, and Crete to the west.

Pausanius no less clearly uses the term Adrias of the sea between the Peloponnesus and Sicily (vide l.c., p. 166, note), and also speaks of waves driven out of Adria into the straits between Messina and Rhegium. Now a glance at the map will show that such waves must have come from a southerly direction. (For the dates of Ptolemy and Pausanias, see pp. 166, 167.)

Later writers gradually extend the name Ionian northwards till it has absorbed the whole of the gulf, whilst the Adriatic expands to the south till it reaches Tripoli; and in the ninth century we even find it washing the coasts of Egypt.

It will be noticed that I have quoted no authorities near to St. Luke's time who distinctly extend the term Adria quite so far south as we desire, that is to say to the part of the sea east of Malta. But I think Ptolemy comes sufficiently near to our purpose. It is not impossible that if he had had occasion to define that region he would have called it Adria, for Mr. Falconer's repeated assertion that he places Malta in the African sea is erroneous, and he does distinctly call the sea about sixty miles to the north Adria. This we must note, that if there is a change of usage going on, there is sure to be a popular as well as a more conservative and scientific use. That which Ptolemy calls Adria, and very likely more, had no doubt been called so by poets, sailors, and travellers long before. It is quite unnecessary that we should expect from St. Luke, in his purely casual expression, anything else than conformity with common language. The burden of proof rests not with those who say he *may* have been speaking in a sense of which we have no positive evidence till some centuries after his time, but with those who say he *can* not have so spoken and by this one argument (for every other turns out on examination worthless) hope to destroy a whole chain of varied reasoning.

INDEX.